COTTAGE HOSPITAL DOCTOR

COTTAGE HOSPITAL DOCTOR

The Medical Life of Dr. Noel Murphy 1945-1954

Written by
Noel Murphy C.M.

Edited by
Marc Thackery

St. John's, Newfoundland and Labrador
2003

Le Conseil des Arts | The Canada Council
du Canada | for the Arts

We acknowledge the support of The Canada Council for the Arts for our publishing program.

We acknowledge the financial support of the Government of Canada through the Book Publishing Industry Development Program (BPIDP) for our publishing program.

Front Cover Photo: Doctor Noel Murphy
Back Cover Photo: Western Brook (Pond)
∞ Printed on acid-free paper

Published by
CREATIVE PUBLISHERS
an imprint of CREATIVE BOOK PUBLISHING
a division of Creative Printers and Publishers Limited
an Print Atlantic associated company
P.O. Box 8660, St. John's, Newfoundland and Labrador A1B 3T7

First Edition
Typeset in 11.5 point Goudy Old Style

Printed in Canada by:
PRINT ATLANTIC

National Library of Canada Cataloguing in Publication

Murphy, Noel F., 1915-
        Cottage hospital doctor : the medical life of Dr. Noel Murphy, 1945-1954 / written by Noel Murphy ; edited by Marc Thackery.

ISBN 1-894294-72-6

        1. Murphy, Noel F., 1915- 2. Physicians--Newfoundland and Labrador--Norris Point Region--Biography. 3. Physicians--Newfoundland and Labrador--Biography. 4. Bonne Bay Cottage Hospital--History. 5. Norris Point Region (N.L.)--Biography.
I. Title.

R464.M78A3 2003   610'.92   C2003-904384-3

DEDICATION

This book is dedicated to my wife, Edna Grace Murphy, who made my work on the Great Northern Peninsula possible. As well, I want to pay respects to the people who staffed the Hospital–the Nurses, Aides, general staff members, and, particularly, Martin Bugden, the hospital janitor, who kept the hospital mechanically operational, to the District Nurses who served the area of St. Barbe District with great dedication, and to the residents who provided support and encouragement over the years.

It was a daunting task to undertake the responsibility of doctor single-handed. It was an unique experience, and I deeply appreciate all the help I was given over my almost ten year tenure.

I would also like to express my special thanks to Mary (Foley) Lannon who typed the original script from my taped material, and to Professor Thachery, or Sir Wilfred College, who very kindly edited the material, to make it readable, and had it re-typed. Without their help this would never have happened.

The area served by the Bonne Bay Cottage Hospital extended from Chimney Cove to Reef's Harbour.

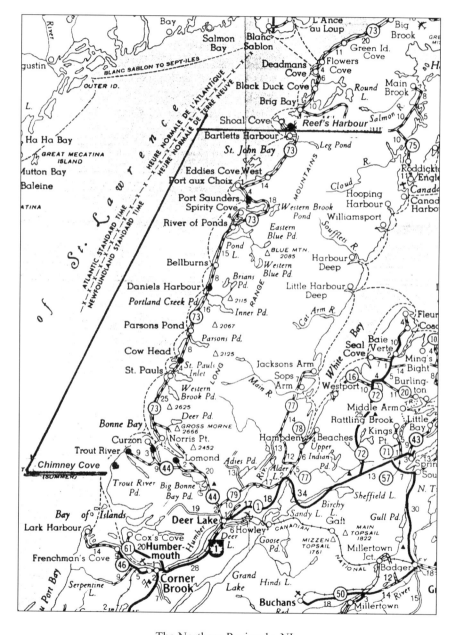

The Northern Peninsula, NL

TABLE OF CONTENTS

PROLOGUE

I met Edna Grace Kicks, the girl who would become my wife, when we were both students at East London College (later Queen Mary College), London University, in the Fall of 1934. East London College was about a mile down the Mile End Road from the London Hospital and the Medical School at Whitechapel, where Sir Wilfred Grenfell graduated in the 1880s, as did my own father, Dr. John Murphy, in 1915. Edna was studying for a degree in Chemistry. I was doing Pre-Med, prior to entering the Medical School. When Edna finished at Queen Mary College she went into teaching while I had moved to the Medical School, but we maintained contact.

On September 1, 1939, a state of emergency was declared in Britain. I was summoned to the Dean's office where I was told that I was being sent to the Southend General Hospital, in the mouth of the Thames, with a number of other senior medical students, to man the hospital as Britain prepared for war. Except for two brief periods–one when I was sent to Bethnal Green Hospital in October 1939 to set up a blood transfusion service, and later when I was sent to the Rochford Municipal Hospital to do my Obstetrical training–I was kept at Southend until I graduated. Initially, I was appointed House Officer at Rochford, followed by Junior House Surgeon, and later Senior House Surgeon at Southend until I joined the Royal Air Force in 1943.

Just before Christmas 1939, I proposed to Edna. We were married on January 20, 1940. Our daughter, Edwina, arrived in December 1940. Until the end of the war they followed me and kept close whenever it was possible wherever I was stationed.

When I joined the Royal Air Force I was appointed Medical Officer with the 125 (Newfoundland) Squadron–Newfoundland's only Air Force Unit in the RAF. Just before Christmas 1944, I received a letter from the Newfoundland Government telling me that they were very short of doctors and asking me if I would consider coming home to take over a Cottage Hospital in Bonne Bay. The end of the war in Europe was getting close, and my next posting might well be to the Far East. I had not been home since 1936. I discussed the Newfoundland offer with Edna, and we both felt it would be the right move, so I accepted the appointment. I left the RAF at the end of March. We travelled to Glasglow to spend a few days with Edna's parents, and to Liverpool to board the S.S. *Cavina*, a banana boat, which would take us to Halifax.

The journey took nineteen days in a convoy of 122 ships. We obviously went far south (we could tell by the balmy weather) and then far north (we could tell by the temperature drop and the fog!). We learned of the death of President Roosevelt during the voyage.

After a quick trip from Halifax to Toronto to see my mother and sister, Patricia, we set off for Newfoundland. We took the train from Toronto to Sydney, Nova Scotia, and then the ferry to Port aux Basques and the train to St. John's. From there, we would make our way to Corner Brook and then on to Norris Point, where we were to spend the next nine years.

Chapter 1

FIRST DAYS

I had been asked to go to St. John's before I left for Bonne Bay, and so we arrived from Britain in St. John's just two days after V. E. Day (Victory in Europe Day). I was delighted because I was coming home and would have a chance to see my family and my friends, and my wife would have a chance to see St. John's, about which I had been telling her for so many years. Our five year old daughter, Edwina, was at an age when she was beginning to enjoy the travelling and the new places and new people. She took the journey in her stride.

We had ten days in St. John's during which time I reported to the Department of Health and Welfare and met for the first time the Deputy to the Commission, Dr. Leonard Miller. He gave me a warm welcome and, after briefing me on what to expect and what was expected of me, suggested that he would like me to meet the Commissioner Sir John Puddester. I had been warned to be on my guard because, as it was put to me, "this is a man you will never see eye to eye with." I didn't really know what to expect and as I followed Dr. Miller to Sir John's door and entered I was certainly not prepared for what evolved.

Sir John was sitting at his desk writing. Dr. Miller and I approached, and Dr. Miller said, "Sir John Puddester, I would like you to meet Dr. Noel Murphy, who is going out to take charge of the Bonne Bay Cottage Hospital." Sir John Puddester rose and turned towards me and put his hand out and, as I looked at him, it was difficult not to burst out laughing. Sir John had the most severe squint I've ever encountered. It was obvious that no one would ever see eye to eye with him. As I stood there trying not to laugh, I realised how my leg had been pulled. Nonetheless, I found Sir John most friendly and anxious to be helpful. After a short talk with him, Dr. Miller and I withdrew.

One of the main problems I discovered was that I was going to an isolated hospital where difficulties of transportation made it important to be as self-contained as possible. One of the pieces of equipment at the hospital was an x-ray machine, and I, like all my fellow practitioners, had had no training whatever in the operation of an x-ray machine or the developing of the x-ray plates, but only in the reading of the finished product. Dr. Miller advised me that arrangements had been made to give me some instructions on the type of machine that I would be using, and I suggested that perhaps it would be wise if my wife Edna came with me to take the instructions because it sounded very much as if I would need as much help as possible.

At the Bonne Bay Cottage Hospital, I would be responsible for the medical care of patients, their diagnosis and treatment, surgical care up to the limit of my capabilities, obstetrical care, the outpatients department, and the x-ray department. I was also to be responsible for making house calls over a large part of the district, although the actual practice was confined to Bonne Bay itself and Rocky Harbour extending as far as Sally's Cove. It was quite apparent from discussing the general picture with Dr. Miller that a doctor working single-handed and trying to operate a small hospital at the same time would have his hands full and would need whatever extra help was available. And so I managed to convince my wife that she should come along with me and take the instructions on the operation of the x-ray machine.

The type of x-ray machine which had been installed in many of the Cottage Hospitals, including Bonne Bay, was a General Electric D 3, and there was such a machine in St. John's in use at St. Claire's Hospital. It was therefore to this machine that we were taken for a one hour course of instruction. During this time we were shown the machine and told how to operate it. I think we took one or two pictures to prove that it could be done. We were then given a manual of operating instructions and sent on our way.

At that moment I was convinced that I knew how to operate this x-ray machine, but a week later when I was on my own and facing the same model machine for the first time I couldn't remember very much about the operation of the machine and Edna and I between us had to reread the manual of procedure and literally start from the very beginning.

The briefing sessions in St. John's gave us time to recover from our long journey. I took the opportunity to renew acquaintances and enjoy coming home after nearly ten years. We also examined a plan of the doctor's residence, and using this plan as our guide we had to then choose between the scarce items which were available, the furniture and fittings for our new home in Bonne Bay. It wasn't difficult in some cases, and in fact in the case of the dining room suite it was quite simple. There was only one available in St. John's, and it was a question of take it or leave it. We took it.

Over our ten day stay in St. John's we were busy purchasing all the equipment and furniture for the house, being briefed on my duties, and learning how to operate the x-ray machine. Each day found us weary as we checked our lists to see what we had forgotten and what we still had to do the next day. It was May of 1945, the shipping season had just about started for the year, and we received assurances from all the stores that everything we had ordered would be shipped by the next boat, and we should get it in a few days.

We left St. John's with good wishes from everyone and travelled by train 700 kilometres across the island to Corner Brook. There we were met by Dr. Robert F. Dove, who had been the first Medical Officer with the Bonne Bay Cottage Hospital and had left at the end of the previous summer. The plan was that we would spend a day in Corner Brook where I would have a chance to meet the doctors in the Corner Brook area and be briefed by Dr. Dove.

On arrival in Corner Brook, Bob Dove took us to the Glynmill Inn where we had reservations and we spent a very pleasant day talking with him, meeting the other doctors and generally being filled in on the local situation. While in St. John's we had visited Bob Dove's wife, Margaret, who was in St. Clare's Mercy Hospital, where she had just given birth to their first child, a son, Roderick. Bob was full of pride over the birth of their first child and we were able to tell him about our visit with his wife and new baby.

Arrangements had been made for us to travel the next day to Lomond. Bob was going to drive us in his car and we would be met there by A. Bryant Harding in his boat and taken the rest of the way to Norris Point where the hospital was located. And so the next morning we loaded ourselves and our luggage into the car and drove over the unpaved highway to Deer Lake and thence by a wood's road, for it couldn't be called much else, to Lomond. It was a hard, bumpy trip. Many spots on the road were soft. Largely, the road consisted of two ruts. We spent most of our time trying to avoid getting in them. It took about three hours and we were considerably shaken and weary when we did arrive at Lomond.

I think the entire settlement turned out to see the arrival of the new doctor, for everybody knew that I was on my way. Waiting on the wharf was a welcoming party consisting of Bryant Harding, William Prebble, and John Harding, Bryant's son. We were to proceed on the rest of the journey in Bryant's boat, *The Tuna*. After the introductions, Bill Prebble handed me a package and told me that these were letters that had been forwarded to the hospital or to him or to Bryant for immediate attention when the doctor arrived. He was losing no time in making sure that they were delivered personally. When I had a chance to open them I found that some had been written as much as six months previously and they all carried a similar message which was roughly "Dear Doctor, please come at once as so and so is sick." We boarded *The Tuna* and Bob Dove accompanied us on our way up the Bay. This part of the trip took the best part of an hour. When we arrived at Norris Point another large crowd had gathered to witness the arrival of the new doctor. Bryant invited us into his house, where we met his wife Em, and his mother Nan.

Over tea we were able to talk about local problems and they had a chance to size me up. One of the things that I remember well was a discussion of my family, and it appeared that up to this point they only had the vaguest idea and many rumours as to who and what type of man I was. These ideas ranged from an Irishman to a Disabled Veteran, and I felt it was with a degree of relief that they heard me confirm that I was a Newfoundlander and the son of a St. John's doctor.

Bryant's other son, Milton, was presently a prisoner of war in Germany, having been captured when he was shot down while serving with the R.C.A.F. Bryant was naturally anxious to learn all he could about conditions in Britain, news of any release of prisoners, particularly now that the war in Europe was over. It was difficult to have to tell him that I knew nothing that would give him any hope concerning Milton.

After tea the hospital truck, driven by Martin Bugden, was ready outside Bryant's house. Our luggage had been loaded on it and we made our way to the hospital which lies about a mile in from the Point. During all this time I was still in uniform for we only had with us the luggage that we could carry. The remainder of our luggage, including my civilian clothes, had been sent on and we hadn't the faintest idea when we might see our belongings again.

The Nurse in Charge of the Hospital, Miss Hilda Gallant, R.N., had been there for some time, and was a well-trained and most efficient nurse and administrator. She made us at home and helped to get us settled in by showing us around the place. The Doctor's suite at the top of the hospital consisted of a bedroom, a bathroom and a sitting room with a little corridor, and then a door which blocked this little suite off from the rest of the living quarters of the staff. We had many things to learn including the fact that the diet, which was much better than we had been used to during the war, at the same time was going to be a little different than we had hoped for. Because of war conditions, there was rationing and many items were in short supply or unavailable. Fresh butter, fresh meat, marmalade, and many other items were very scarce and somewhat of a luxury. Fortunately, we enjoyed fish and there was plenty of cod, herring and salmon available to help break the monotony. There was also plenty of salt meat, both pork and beef, and the vegetables consisted largely of cabbage, turnip, and potatoes. The bread was homemade and delicious, and while the menu may not have been too varied, it was certainly very satisfying.

Bob Dove came into the hospital to introduce us and to show me around. He spent an hour showing me the operating room, the x-ray department, and the out-patient department. He then took me on a tour of the doctor's residence. The doctor's residence had been built by Bob Dove as his home and had been his own property until it was taken over by the Department of Health for the resident doctor. He had the plans drawn for the house by Payne of Montreal, who incidentally was also responsible for the plans of the Western Memorial Hospital and the West Coast Sanatorium a few years later. Having completed his job of introducing and showing us around, Bob wished me good luck, assured me that anything he could do to help I had only to ask, bade us farewell, and left for Corner Brook.

I was now on my own, and I felt that it would be unwise to get off on the wrong foot. I discussed the question with Miss Gallant, and it was agreed that I would need two or three days to orient myself, to get everything unpacked, and I would commence work on the Monday. It was then Thursday evening and I would therefore have three days to prepare myself.

On my arrival at the hospital there was one patient, an elderly woman who had been in the hospital for seventy-two days. She had sustained a fracture of the neck of her left femur, and had been brought to the hospital for treatment. There being no doctor in residence, the nurse had tried to get her people to take her on to Corner Brook, but she refused to be moved because rumour had it that the doctor would be arriving any day, and she was determined to stay at the hospital where she was within reach of her relatives and wait for the doctor to come to her. By the time I arrived all hope of bone union was gone, and she had in fact got fibrous union which would result in a sliding joint so that she would always be a cripple.

This first patient was incidentally the subject of our first x-rays to confirm the diagnosis and the present situation of the fracture, and these plates I forwarded to St. John's to Dr. Louis Conroy, who was an Orthopedic Surgeon there. Later he came on a visit to Bonne Bay to see this patient and advised that there was nothing that he or anyone else could do. She was discharged with a fibrous union of the fracture.

The first night I went to bed secure in the knowledge I had three days of preparation ahead of me, but before morning came the first emergency call arrived. It was still dark when there came a violent hammering on our bedroom door. I must admit that I woke up wondering what on earth had happened. The nurse was at the door and explained to me that it was approximately 6 a.m., that the Anglican Minister from Woody Point had come to the hospital and, in spite of her telling him that I was not starting work until Monday, he was begging to talk to me about an emergency. I put on my dressing gown and went downstairs and met the Minister. He told me that his wife was in labour, and that the midwife was experiencing some difficulty. It was their first child and he was very anxious that nothing go wrong. Accordingly, he begged me to come and do what I could.

I realized that it would be impossible to turn my back on a situation like this, no matter how much I wanted to wait for three days to organize myself. I agreed to go. I quickly dressed and the nurse prepared a bag with everything in it which she felt I would need to deal with the situation and we left for the Point. The ferry had brought the Minister across the Bay and was waiting to take us quickly back. We arrived at the house at about dawn.

My first greeting as I entered the door was from the midwife who rushed down the stairs and begged me to tell them it wasn't her fault. She kept on repeating "Tell them it's not my fault, tell them it's not my fault, tell them I did everything I could." I wasn't at all sure what she was talking about, but as soon as I entered the patient's room I was pushed towards the cot in the corner by the midwife and found a dead baby lying in it. I understood now what she meant. The Minister's wife was naturally very upset for she had guessed that the baby had not survived. After checking her to make sure that she was alright I had to admit to them both that it was too late for me to do anything. The midwife was distraught and could not give a clear account of what had happened.

It was a hard experience for my first case. It was over before I arrived. The experience, however, started me along a line of thought which eventually saw the majority of maternity cases brought into the hospital for delivery, for there we had the personnel and equipment to give even better care than could be brought to the homes. The midwife, I am sure, had done all that she could as far as her knowledge would let her, but I was to find out years later that the training that these midwives received was often only nominal. In fact, in the course of six weeks training in St. John's, many a midwife did no more than stand in a corner, watch a few deliveries, and sort the laundry. She would then return to her community thinking that nature would do everything for every patient and that the outcome of each case would be a happy ending.

After this first case, the weekend went quickly as we unpacked what we had and I prepared to start clinics on the Monday morning. We visited the residence each day checking to see if our purchases would fit and we felt that what we had accomplished would start us in the right direction. The floors of the house were not finished. They consisted of rough lumber with paper glued on top. But the house was to be our home and it was pleasantly located with a beautiful view. We looked forward to the arrival of the coastal boat bringing the rest of our luggage and our furniture.

Word had spread around the district by now with my visit to Woody Point and my presence in Norris Point, and Monday morning saw the clinic filled. Some patients had come out of curiosity to see the doctor, while others had been waiting patiently the arrival of a doctor to seek and receive medical treatment for a multitude of conditions. These patients were very friendly and cheerful. They ranged through all age groups, and they came from all parts of Bonne Bay. The ferry did a great business carrying patients to and from the hospital every day.

It soon became apparent that some people wanted to come to the hospital at night time after completing a day's work, while others, often the women, would like to come when their husbands came back from work and could look after the house for them. We set up a schedule of clinics by day and by night which over the years changed when it became apparent that many people were coming at night who in fact could come during the day. I found myself working long hours unnecessarily in the clinic, when my day normally lasted twenty-four hours anyway, seven days a week, and fifty-two weeks a year.

Little did I realise that it would be five years before I was able to get away with my family for my first real holiday. During these years, I was deeply immersed in my work, I kept fully occupied, and I was enjoying it immensely.

I was aware, from the experience of other doctors, that the first weeks would be the most important to establish a relationship between the doctor and the patients, and I was very aware that to establish a reputation for the hospital meant that each case, particularly surgical cases, had to be carefully assessed before being tackled. I didn't realise that my every move was being reported by the staff to the surrounding district with a great deal of enthusiasm, and no doubt much misinterpretation, for apart from the nurse there was little formal medical training for the ward aids and none for the maids. However, it appeared that they took delight in telling their listeners that they were present for various operations or other procedures and making a good story of it.

It became important to plug these leaks for the sake of the patients, and the law was laid down firmly for all employees at the hospital that in no way were they to discuss outside the hospital matters which were pertinent to individual patients. This regulation was resented, but there was nothing new about it. It exists in every hospital and applies to every employee throughout the world. Furthermore it is part of the confidence which every patient can expect when they place themselves in the hands of a hospital and the team which goes with it.

My first few surgical cases went smoothly and after each one, while I had confidence in my ability to perform them, I admittedly gave a sigh of relief that another one was behind me, and each one was helping to bring a feeling of confidence to those who would visit or place themselves in the care of the hospital. However, one of the earliest cases was a baby boy about five weeks old, who was brought to the hospital with persistent vomiting and rapid weight loss. This baby boy was the first child of the family and they were greatly concerned about the welfare of the child and convinced that something serious was wrong. I questioned the mother and found that the child during feeding or shortly thereafter vomited and threw the vomited milk right across the room in a stream. I examined the child and couldn't find very much beyond the fact that the child was losing weight and was far from thriving. I asked the nurse to bring a feeding bottle, and while the child was taking his feeding I was able to watch the abdomen and could see a peristalic wave moving from left to right across the upper abdomen and could feel beneath my fingers a small lump.

I made a diagnosis of a congenital obstruction known as pyloric stenosis which occurs more commonly in the first male child in a family at anywhere from three to six weeks of age. The treatment was surgical and in a big hospital would be quite simple. However, it might be a different matter in a smaller hospital. Fortunately, I had been trained to do this type of work using a local anaesthesia.

The patient was admitted, surgery was slated for the next day, and by infiltrating the upper abdomen, with local anaesthesia and giving the baby a bottle containing his formula and a little bit of brandy I proceeded to enter the abdomen find the obstruction, which is a thickening of the pyloris at the end of the stomach, make an incision along the parietal peritoneum, and split the muscle layer through the thickening down to the outside of the mucus membrane. This procedure relieves the obstruction immediately. The split layer is pushed aside and widened and the abdomen is closed, a dressing applied and the baby is back in its cot very shortly. This was one of the most dramatic and satisfying surgical procedures. The baby's vomiting ceased immediately and he began to gain weight and thrive as he retained his feeding and benefitted accordingly. The news of this dramatic procedure which had such startling results spread around the district and by the time the baby was returned home in about a week or ten days I had the feeling that the hospital's reputation was on the way to satisfying the most demanding patients.

These early days gave me a great deal to think about as I tried to organize my work. The realization came to me that to be effective I would have to be well organized. I had to divide my time between clinics and treating patients in hospital, performing surgery, performing deliveries, paper work, mostly charts, being the x-ray department and the laboratory, and providing service to patients in their homes. There seemed at the beginning to be little chance of doing any school work or preventive medicine although I felt this was important. However, first things come first, and it seemed that the sick took priority and everything else would have to fall into its proper place later.

One of the biggest problems that faced me was the fact that the majority of people, through custom, were staying at home for their deliveries and this necessitated spending a fair amount of time by day or as was most often the case by night out around the district in somebody's home doing the delivery. As the workload grew it became more and more difficult being alone to spend several nights in succession out on cases and at the same time have to face a day in surgery and clinics and house calls and survive. The logical way of surviving was to encourage patients whenever possible to come to the hospital, where diagnostic facilities and equipment were available and my time would be so much better used. Over the months ahead, as we rebuilt the reputation of the hospital and won the confidence of the people, more and more cases came to the hospital and people came to understand that, as the workload grew, there would be less time for me to travel outside. I found myself in fact spending much of my time in the hospital.

One of the busiest times was when the coastal boat arrived and brought with it a load of patients from the coast. Patients came from all parts of the coast. Often, because the boat was coming our way, we got patients from the Grenfell mission area which was adjacent to ours at the top of St. John's Bay. The early occasions when the boat came in took me by surprise, since I didn't really know what to expect. In fact, I don't think any of us expected what in fact began to happen. It was quite common for the coastal boat either the *Clarenville*, which was one of the famous Splinter Fleet, or the *Northern Ranger*, which operated from St. John's to Corner Brook, to arrive at Norris Point sometime during the night.

My first knowledge that the boat had gone through would come to me when I arrived in the hospital in the morning to find a number of patients in bed who hadn't been there the previous night. The first time this happened, I had arrived early and went to see the nurse. I said, "What happened? Last night we had so many patients and this morning we've got so many extra ones, where did they come from, who are they, and how did they get here?" The nurse replied that in fact these patients had arrived at the hospital during the night, the girl on duty (a ward aide) had answered the door bell and one after the other they had assured her that they had been sent by the nurse in their own districts to be admitted. There seemed to be no reason then to wake the nurse, who had done an equally hard day's work the previous day. The patients were simply assigned beds and they promptly crawled in and went to sleep.

My policy was quite clear from this point that no patient would be admitted to the hospital without first being seen so that I knew what it was that I was admitting. Equally, I wanted to know I was capable to deal with them and the hospital was able to provide them service. Many patients who made the trip had little money and didn't want to spend what little money they had on a boarding house. Often the boarding houses that were available were filled up. The patients then used ingenuity to present themselves at the hospital in such a way that the poor girl on duty had really little choice but to admit them. This changed when the policy was made clear, and although there were some good old arguments as to whether a patient should be admitted or not, it was always the patient who argued and not the hospital. This policy did entail a few sleepless nights on the part of the nurse who reinforced the rules with the girl on duty to assure the patients that unless they were emergency cases they would be seen in the clinic the first thing in the morning.

The other attitude that we found disturbing was that some patients would use a visit to the hospital as an excuse to make a trip to Corner Brook. They would catch the coastal boat and instead of going to Norris Point to the hospital and having their medical problems dealt with, they would continue on the boat to Corner Brook and spend a couple of days doing their shopping. Then, since they knew that the boat would sail in the afternoon, arriving at Norris Point at 1 or 2 a.m., they would plan to go through the country by car, taxi, or bus as far as Lomond where they caught the ferry for Norris Point. They would arrive at the hospital at midnight hammering on the door and saying that they had to see the doctor before the boat came because they had been sent for this purpose.

In the early days I would roll out and see patients unaware that in fact they had had two or three days on the town before bothering to come to the hospital. When I discovered what kind of game was being played and how we were getting caught in the trap, the policy was made plain, and from that time on patients were expected to come during regular clinic hours for consultations and diagnostic procedures except in the case of emergencies. Again there were some lively arguments but it was quite impossible to continue to operate under these conditions and common sense prevailed in the hospital.

Needless to say that in both such cases the people understood only too well, and after the first few people were caught trying the same tricks again we had no further trouble.

It's interesting looking back and seeing the gradual development of the system which evolved by trial and error. Clinic times were moved to get the greatest coverage and the most convenient time for patients, at the same time tying in with the hospital work and operations that had to go on. The patients were most understanding and very patient. Most people who came looking for a house visit were reasonable, for it was usual for a man to come into the hospital and explain what kind of case at home necessitated the doctor visiting. However, the man who came looking for a visit and denied all knowledge of what the case involved always bothered me. It seemed very unlikely that a man could have somebody ill in the house and not know roughly what the problem was. These cases, however, were few and far between and often demonstrated the natural reticence of people to talk about somebody else's business or personal affairs. And for this, while sometimes I felt frustrated, at other times I admired them for their refusal to get into a field which they felt didn't concern them.

Another difficulty developed early on which bothered me and which I had to put a stop to quickly. It became the custom for somebody to arrive at perhaps 6:30 or 7:00 a.m. at the hospital to take the doctor on a house call by boat. This necessitated getting to the Point and spending perhaps an hour in a boat to reach the home of the patient. After seeing the patient and giving whatever treatment was necessary, it was apparently thought to be perfectly all right to say to the doctor, "I'm sorry you're going to have to wait until tea time tonight to get home because the man who brought you (be it the husband or son or father or what have you) has now gone into the woods for the day. He has to make a living and he can't afford to miss his day's work." On a number of occasions I had to walk back to the hospital perhaps as much as five or six miles if I was on the North side of the Bay, but if I was on the South side of the Bay then I would have to walk to Woody Point and catch the ferry. No thought had been given to the fact that I had patients to care for and other duties at the hospital which keep me occupied all day and that this thought-lessness was denying other people the service of the doctor.

It was no good getting angry. By this time the men had gone, deliberately no doubt, hoping that the doctor would find his own way back or that somebody else would give him a lift. The solution was simple. As I arrived at the patient's home I would always advise the man who had brought me not to go far away in case I had misjudged his estimate of the case and would need to return immediately to the hospital to get for the patient the necessary treatment. After all I couldn't carry in my bag all the drugs that we had in the hospital and I could only take with me the things that I felt I would need. "Anyhow," I would say, "of course you will be taking me back as soon as I've finished because I have other things to do at the hospital and patients waiting for me there, so you won't go far anyhow will you." With this admonition he always stayed close, but I in turn made sure that we did need something from the hospital, and on returning to the hospital I would give him the necessary drugs for the patient which he would then take back with him. It wasn't long before every-body knew without a shadow of a doubt that if they did fetch the doc-tor to go and see a case they were expected to bring him straight back because other people were involved in the use of the doctor's service too. I never had any trouble, after a few such cases, but I did wear out a fair amount of shoe leather in the early days.

One early case that I will always remember concerned a pregnant woman in Rocky Harbour, which lies about five miles from Norris Point. There was no road as such, but there was a track between the two settlements used mostly during the winter time. In those early days, we had only the hospital truck. The road wasn't fit really for the truck, and you could never be sure it was passable. On many occa-sions when we tried it, Martin and I would take shovels and axes so that we could, when we came to a spot that was washed out, cut a few trees and stuff them in the holes and make our way.

On this particular occasion it was a winter's night, very bad and stormy. There was a lot of snow down, high winds, and a blizzard in progress when the hospital rang to say that a man was at the hospi-tal who wanted me to go out and tend his expecting wife. I got ready, wrapping up well, took my bag, climbed on his sleigh, and we set off.

On that particular night it took about two hours to arrive at the man's house. When we arrived, about 1 a.m., the gale had abated a little bit but it was still a wild night. I was glad to be in out of the weather when I did walk into the home.

The home was simple, consisting of the kitchen which served as the family room as well, with two bedrooms in the back. The stove was in the middle of the kitchen. It was a wood stove, the common type in those days. There may have been a small piece of floor covering, but mostly the floor boards were bare and the wind was coming up between them as I doubt that there was more than the one layer of boards on the beams. A fair crowd seemed to be gathered in the kitchen even though it was so late. I made my way through the kitchen and into the bedroom to look at my patient. My first question concerning her present condition elicited the information that she was fine, was expecting her baby any day, and was not in labour at the moment. However, because it was such a bad night, and because she had heard that the midwife had been called around to the other side of the harbour, they felt it would be wise to summons me and have me stay the night in the house in case something did begin to happen.

I found it difficult to believe that this is why I had been brought so far. After examining the patient and realising that there was no necessity for me to be there, I went out into the kitchen and suggested that since everything was alright they take me home again. The husband informed me that the horse was tired after making the journey into Norris Point and back to fetch me. It had worked all day, would have to work the next day, and would not make the journey again. I suggested that he borrow somebody else's horse or get someone else to take me back because there were other patients to be considered. He assured me that there was no way he could get another horse as they were all busy working in the woods and needed their night's rest. If I would just be patient and wait until morning he would see that I got home. In the meantime he reminded me that his wife might start into labour at any moment and they would all feel happier if I would spend the night with them.

I asked him where I would be spending the night, and he said, "Well boy, you can always bed down on the floor. It's the only place left." And sure enough I looked around and every available spot was taken up with people including a child on the day couch beside which he suggested I sleep.

I had brought a couple of blankets with me. They were somewhat wet after the journey and the heavy snow, but I did as he suggested because there seemed nothing else I could do. I got down on the floor boards and tried to sleep. I rolled my coat up and put it under my head. I covered myself with the blankets, but then I found the wind whistling up underneath was almost strong enough to lift the blankets off me. I sacrificed one of the blankets and put it underneath me and then with the other blanket on top found that I was so cold that I couldn't sleep anyway. The hard floor didn't help and I was not used to sleeping on boards. I may have dozed for a little time at intervals during the night. In fact, I know that I dozed at one point because when the child on the daybed fell off onto the floor next to me, it certainly woke me up with a terrible start. The child, who was now crying, was soothed and calmed and put back to sleep again and everybody returned to their various places. Silence reigned once more in the room except for my continual changing of position as I began to ache, first in one place and then in another.

I welcomed the moment when I felt it safe with dawn approaching to get up. Feeling cold and shivery, I drew up a chair and poked the fire in the stove to get a little warmth. The man of the house at this moment appeared from the bedroom, looked around, stoked up the fire, and took some of the water from the kettle which had been simmering all night and poured it into a basin and proceeded to wash his face and hands. When he had finished he turned to the room and announced "the doctor will now wash." I didn't quite know how to reply, and while I realised that he was offering the hospitality of his home, I didn't fancy using the same water to wash in, although I realised the scarcity of these things and that the whole family used the same basin and the same water.

Somehow I managed to wriggle out of that one and the man of the house in the meantime was combing his hair in front of an old cracked mirror hanging on the wall. When he had finished he turned around, announced to the room "the doctor will now comb his hair," and offered me the comb. I quickly produced my own pocket comb, saying it was quite all right I had a comb, and I promptly combed my hair.

He then suggested that perhaps we would have some breakfast, and I must say that this met with my approval, and I watched as he went about preparing the meal. From the other bedroom had appeared a woman, not his wife, who began to set the table and get out the cutlery and the bread and the margarine, and the children rose and huddled in the corner, washing one by one and speaking only in whispers, presumably because the doctor was there and they were scared they would get a needle. The man disappeared into the pantry and reappeared with a raw leg of lamb and using a short sharp knife, he cut off small pieces of the lamb and threw them into a frying pan on the stove.

The sizzling of the meat in the frying pan soon pervaded the room. The warmth of the roaring stove had now warmed the room. Daylight was beginning to flood the room and, over the first cup of tea, a bit of warmth began to get back into my body although I was stiff and ached in many places.

A plate with two or three pieces of fried lamb was now put in front of me, and with a piece of homemade bread and a strong cup of tea, I tackled it with the knife and fork which provided. However, I found that the fork didn't seem to operate in the correct manner and when I looked at it I found that the tongs of the fork went in four different directions, which did make it a little difficult. However, I enjoyed my meal and shortly afterwards managed to prod the man into getting his horse hooked up to his sleigh. At about nine a.m., after checking my patient again to see that all was well, I said good-bye and we set off for the hospital. We made the return journey a little faster, but it was still about 10:30 a.m. when I arrived at the hospital. I was very tired after a night out on the floor!

The sequel to this story came about a week later when one afternoon I was in the clinic dealing with a fair number of patients, and about halfway through the afternoon, the nurse came in and told me that this man had appeared again and that this time his wife was in labour and would I please come at once.

Well I supposed "once bitten, twice shy," so I decided that before I went I wanted to know a little bit more about the case. I managed to contact the midwife by the telephone, which took a little time, but which was well worth the effort. When the midwife came to the phone she was able to assure me that the delivery was complete, and that they had a lusty baby boy. My services would not be needed.

It was a little later that I went out into the waiting room and told him that I didn't think I would bother to come, which brought him to his feet in a fighting mood. This attitude evaporated rapidly when I told him that I bothered to phone the midwife and was pleased to tell him that it had all ended well. He was father of a lusty baby boy. He was delighted and went cheerfully on his way home, and I heaved a sigh of relief that I wouldn't have to spend another night on the floor.

Chapter 2

BONNE BAY

When I arrived in Bonne Bay, it had been a part of Newfoundland's colonial history for over 200 years. Bonne Bay lies on the West Coast of Newfoundland at about the midpoint of the island from north to south, and also about midway on a circular journey around the Island from the capital city, St. John's. The Bay itself is shaped rather like a clover leaf, the stem being the main entrance to the Bay from the Gulf of St. Lawrence, and the three Arms, the Eastern Arm, the Western Arm and the Main Arm, being the three leaves. It is a deep water Bay with a fine anchorage available in one part or another affording protection against all kinds of weather. It lies about seventy kilometres north-west of the Bay of Islands, and from the largest city on the West Coast, Corner Brook.

The earliest maps show this Bay named as Dead Man's Bay, but the reason for this name appears to have been lost over the years. When Captain James Cook, R.N., carried out his survey of Newfoundland, 1762-67, he mapped this area accurately for the first time. In fact, his charts were so accurate that many of them are currently in use.

Bonne Bay is situated in the centre of what was known as the French Shore, and many of the older residents can recall vividly the experiences they went through in the nineteenth century with French Warships patrolling the coastline and sending ashore parties to destroy the fishing and canning equipment that the settlers were using, for this was forbidden under various Treaties between Britain and France made between 1713 and 1904.

Because of these Treaties and Agreements, settlement in the area and on the entire West Coast of Newfoundland, was slow. Although

English Sovereignty on shore was recognised, the French were guaranteed fishing rights, including the right to land and cure their fish. Any fixed settlements that "interrupted in any manner" the French Fisheries were to be removed. Warships of both countries patrolled the shore, and both countries looked with considerable hostility upon settlers. Yet fishermen settlers gradually increased. They were a mixture of English West Countrymen and French, of which some were European, but more were Acadians from Cape Breton Island.

The Treat of Utrecht (1713) allowed the French to catch and dry fish on Western and Northeast Coasts of Newfoundland from Cape Bonavista to Cape Riche, to erect stages of board and huts necessary for drying fish, and to resort to the Coast only during the fishing season. They were not to winter there, erect permanent buildings or fortify any places, and they admitted British Sovereignty over the Island. Apparently it was extremely difficult to establish just exactly where Cape or Point Riche was, and there appeared to be considerable controversy in the literature at this time. In fact, this Point was established by Captain James Cook.

The Treaty of Paris (1763) ceded to France the Islands of St. Pierre and Miquelon as a shelter for French fishermen, but they were not to be fortified and were to have only a guard of fifty men for police purposes. Twenty years later, the Treaty of Versailles (1783) confirmed for France the occupancy of St. Pierre, but changed the boundaries of the French Shore from Cape Bonavista - Point Riche, now to Cape John - Cape Ray prescribing, however, that the fishery should be carried on as already provided by the Treaty of Utrecht. Declarations were attached to the Treaty by the two Monarchs with respect to this Treaty Coast. The French, however, later read into this Treaty unwarranted provisions. These included the following:

1. That the French right to fish on the Treaty Shores is conclusive and not concurrent.
2. That all permanent British structures there, like French, were illegal.
3. That fish included all marine animals even crustaceans.

4. That Frenchmen could take salmon even in the rivers above salt water.

5. That their drying privileges gave them the strand for half a mile above tide water.

6. That they could force British subjects out of fishing locations they desired for themselves.

7. That they were entitled under the Treaties to set up and work lobster factories there.

8. That they had a prior right to take bait fishes there for their fleet on the Grand Bank.

9. That they could prevent mining or other pursuits there as contrary to the Treaties.

In 1874, the French Government refused to permit the Trans-Insular Railroad to have a terminus on the shore. This action postponed the project for twenty years and woefully retarded the development of the Western Seaboard. The French who had not wished to fish in any particular area saw to it that the Colonists were expelled from their fishing grounds, and British warships were required to undertake this distasteful task at their bidding. The fishing gear was wantonly destroyed by French rivals and in fact no grant of land issued by the Colonial Government was deemed to be effective on the Coast unless it contained the proviso that it was subject to the Treaty Right of France.

It was the lobster fishery, however, which provoked the greatest bitterness. Lobsters were valueless until the process of canning was devised and when this began in 1883, the French cod fishery, whose industry was failing, sought to do the same. The Treaties in fact covered only the cod fishery. The lobster fishery had been thrown in some years later by the French when they realised that it was a valuable industry. At first they took little note and did not object to the settlers canning lobsters; in fact by 1899 they had reversed their policy, and they had fifteen canneries as opposed to forty-nine colonial ones.

However, by this time, the Colonial Government was aware of what was taking place and was vigorously protesting against these French factories. Instead of supporting the Colonial Government in assisting in the removal of the French canneries, the Imperial Government weakly proposed to arbitrate the lobster issue. As a result of the negotiations the two powers recognised each other's canning factories then in existence. They signed an agreement to this effect on March 13, 1890. When it was learned in the Island through the press what had happened, it caused widespread indignation and meetings to protest "the infamous contract" were held all over the Island.

Finally the Colony enacted the famous Bait Law prohibiting the supplying of bait from her waters to French fishermen which may have crippled them completely. France spent four million francs in bolstering up the Newfoundland fisheries. They found Newfoundland adamant in her refusal to relax the Bait Law, and realising what a tremendous cost would be acquired to bolster her fishery, France decided to abandon it without any compensation and make the best of a bad situation. "The French Shore Question" was terminated accordingly in 1904 by the Anglo-Gallic Entente, which chiefly referred to Morocco, France agreeing to withdraw entirely from the Newfoundland seaboard in return for concessions in Morocco in compensation for those of their fishermen who were disposed. This compensation was subsequently fixed by arbitration at £55,000 pounds, a sum the British Treasury paid later, recouping itself to twice this extent by selling these properties to Newfoundlanders who were willing to purchase them.

There are still people living on the West Coast of Newfoundland who remember, as young men and women, the French and British Warships patrolling the Coast, parties being landed from the warships to destroy the equipment that was set up by the settlers for canning of lobster and the general undertakings of the Fishing Industry. There are still descendants of men who jumped ship and lived the rest of their lives in various parts of the West Coast in no small degree of fear, believing that the day might come when search parties from the warships would find them and take them back to what they believed would be a rough form of trial and certain death or life imprisonment.

It is known that the French arrived in the early part of the year, probably around May, and set up their stations on the West Coast and this probably included "rooms" (fishing wharfs and buildings) in

Bonne Bay. The first ones were thought to have been in the Woody Point area. The earliest settlers in Bonne Bay appear to have been English, who arrived around 1820. The first baby is believed to have been born in Bonne Bay in approximately 1836.

In 1818 the United States signed a Treaty with Britain which gave rights to their fishermen on the Western Shore from Bay of Islands North to Port au Choix. From this time on, American ships came in increasing numbers to Western Newfoundland and one of the principal areas of their operation was Bonne Bay.

A good story is told of a family named Humber, which was one of the earliest to settle in Bonne Bay. It appears there were three brothers who had settled and were starting to make a living. They came from England and, having business affairs to settle back there, they decided that one of them would go to England and deal with the business affairs while the other two would remain and carry on working. The chosen Humber then prepared himself, took some supplies, got in a dory and rowed from Bonne Bay to the Straits of Belle Isle, a distance of at least 150 miles. How long it took to row this distance is not recorded. The Straits are approximately ten miles across, and the Labrador Coast can easily be seen from the Newfoundland side, affording a clear view of all shipping through the area. He waited until he saw a suitable vessel going in the right direction, rowed out, hailed the ship, was taken aboard, with his dory, and carried by them to England. His business completed, he then sought a vessel which was sailing for Canada, via the Straits of Belle Isle, took passage and at the appropriate point was put overboard in his dory and rowed home. Such stories show the spirit and determination of the men who settled here at about that time, and I have faith in its truth.

I well remember a story told me by an old lady who said that she married a man who lived some forty miles from her home, and after the wedding they simply got into the dory and rowed home. She admitted that they didn't make the journey in one day and put up about half way along the coast at some settler's home. She also told me that it was not uncommon for them to row down once or twice a year to visit her parents and spend a few days and then row home again. These were not isolated incidents and there are many stories of men and women who experienced great hardships and endured great physical trials as they went about making a living and travelling the coast.

The earliest reports are recorded in various forms. Parish records, diaries of Ministers travelling through their parishes (which in those days were very large), reports made by captains, particularly of naval vessels patrolling the coastline, and accounts of trips made by surveyors and explorers all contain information about life in the area. However, little has been recorded in the form of historical accounts over the years, with the result that there are large gaps in our knowledge of many of the historical events which took place, and the times at which they happened.

Among the earliest important figures who visited Western Newfoundland and probably the Bonne Bay area were Captain James Cook, R.N. (1762-67), his Excellency the Governor of the day, Sir Thomas Cochrane (1829) accompanied by the Rev. William Bullock, Edward Wix (1835), J. B. Jukes, Geological Surveyor (1840), Rev. Ulric Z. Rule, and Rev. Joseph James Curling.

However, by 1900 Bonne Bay had gradually become settled and inhabited by fishermen and their families, and was often visited by French, American, and British ships. Towards the end of the 1800s it was designated by the British Admiralty as one of their main anchorages in Western Newfoundland. The two main anchorages they used on the West Coast were St. George's Bay and Bonne Bay.

In Bonne Bay the British Navy's main anchorage was in the South East Arm, which lies to the East at the far end of the Main Arm, opposite the settlement of Lomond. The Navy markers were still visible within the past ten years. The British Navy also used Neddy's Harbour which lay snugly behind Norris Point, and to this day can be seen the rings securely anchored in the rocks where the ships came alongside to take on supplies of food and fuel. Bryant Harding, whose father was the official agent for the British Navy and from whom he inherited his title, had in his possession, up to his death, photographs of many of the British Warships which came into Bonne Bay and patrolled the Coast.

Chapter 3

NORRIS POINT

In 1945 Norris Point, situated on the Northern Shore of Bonne Bay, had a population of approximately 600 persons. From the Point itself one looks directly across at Woody Point on the Southern side of Bonne Bay. The majority of the homes were situated on the Point itself which had a harbour in the Tickle running between the main entrance to Bonne Bay and the Main and Eastern Arms. The water is very deep and the current fairly fast in the Tickle, but the Point protects the little harbour as it breaks the seas rolling in from the main part of the Bay or, alternatively, coming from the Main Arm. High hills 300 or 400 feet tall loom directly behind the Point itself, dominating the houses scattered below it. A narrow isthmus joins the Point with the main section of land and in so doing forms Neddy's Harbour at the top end of the Main Arm.

The Cottage Hospital was built beyond the Point. In fact, it nestled under the hill which might well be considered the beginning of the Long Range Mountains on the Northern part of the arm. The hills swung around the Eastern Arm and joined the range by Gros Morne, running thence northward to Cape Norman.

Norris Point sustained two general stores, several smaller stores, a fish plant, a general merchant, three churches, the hospital, a telegraph and post office, two schools and a parlour. There was a ferry operating on the Bay, going from Woody Point to Norris Point and on to Lomond on a twice daily basis. The ferry took care of the transportation needs prior to the building of the road which linked Lomond with Woody Point, and was built around 1949. Norris Point itself had a road, if it can be called such, which connected the Point and the hospital. From the hospital there was a track which meandered over the hills to Rocky Harbour about five miles away, but which was hardly suitable for motor driven vehicles and was normally used only by horse and sleigh in the winter. All other transportation around the bay was by boat during summer and by horse and sleigh or dog team during winter.

The majority of people belonged to the Church of England. A smaller group belonged to the United Church and there were also about twenty-five Roman Catholics. No minister was stationed at Norris Point but ministers of all three denominations visited when necessary. The Anglican minister who was stationed at Woody Point visited most weeks and held services, and the United Church minister, who was not as often available, did attend whenever it was possible. The Roman Catholic Priest, who came in the early days from Deer Lake and later from Corner Brook, had a district that went as far north as Parson's Pond and made three or four visits each year.

The Anglican Church was a wooden frame building which had been built many years previously and stood under the great hill dominating Norris Point. Opposite the church was the cemetery with stones dating back almost a century. The United Church building, situated on the isthmus connecting the Point to the mainland, had been built quite recently. A lot of work had gone into the building of this church and just before it was finished a great storm struck and literally lifted the entire church from its foundation and blew it to pieces and scattered it over the bay. It was a great disappointment for the parishioners who had worked hard and sacrificed much to put their beautiful church there. They promptly re-built it and it was better than ever. The Roman Catholic School served also as a Chapel and, while it was mainly one room in which all grades were taught, there was a sliding partition at one end which at the time of the Priest's visit was pulled aside to display an altar and transformed the room into a church. Under the Newfoundland school system, the Churches provided education for all children. However, there was always some difficulty in providing a teacher for the Catholic School because the teacher had to face between fifteen and eighteen pupils from all grades and this was not easy. Several times over the years we saw a young girl who had just finished grade eleven being appointed to the school, suffering a great deal from homesickness, and struggling to maintain order in a class with some students who were her own age. There were times when it must have been disheartening and depressing for a young teacher starting out with little and sometimes almost no training. Very often these young teachers received their complete training at a six-week Summer School following grade eleven. They were then sent to an isolated district in the north to face the difficult task of being the authority and expert in all grades and with all ages of pupils.

Shortly after our arrival, the United Church students moved in with the Amalgamated students. Soon a new school was built which had eight classrooms and was the biggest one on the Coast. The principal of the school had a university degree, which perhaps was the first one among the teachers ever, and with eight teachers the educational standard and ability to provide subject teaching improved to the point of providing each student with a vastly improved education.

We had been very concerned about the educational facilities for our girls and had no hesitation in putting them in the Amalgamated School where they would get the benefit of the vastly superior educational standards and teacher. Edna was very anxious to help and one of the first things that she did was organize and run a sports day, perhaps the first ever in the area. It was agreed by all to be a great success. Later she tackled the formation of the Girl Guides and got a very successful troop going which lasted for many years. This gave her an additional interest for which I was delighted. Eventually, Edna became a Commissioner of the Guides in the Corner Brook area.

In my turn I tried to do some community service, and in my last year I started a Scout Troop. However, I found it difficult because I had many medical duties to attend to and little time to give to the boys. Nonetheless, they were tremendously enthusiastic and anxious to learn and only too understanding when I was not able to be with them. I am sure that even though it was an embryonic unit it may have been responsible for sparking a greater interest in that type of thing. In later years the Army Cadets were introduced in the area.

One of the most important buildings at Norris Point was the L.O.A., the Loyal Orange Association Lodge, and it was in this building that most of the dances or so called "times" were held. These dances were held on certain occasions and were open to the public.

They consisted largely of square dancing and would go on as long as people were willing to dance and as long as the fiddler could play. Everyone in the community attended and they were greatly enjoyed by all.

Edna and I used to get a special invitation to most of the "times" but we would rarely do more than drop in to show our appreciation. We only stayed for a short while because we had the feeling that perhaps our presence would dampen the fun and enjoyment of those present.

One of the most important events, I think, that took place in Norris Point during our stay was the celebration of the Queen's Coronation in June of 1952. The day had been declared a public holiday by the Government of Canada and we decided that perhaps we should celebrate it in some fitting way. It was agreed therefore that there would be a great parade and accordingly all the organizations and groups were invited to take part. All the school children and anybody who could be inveigled into taking part were pushed into it.

The hospital was decorated with flags and the main wharf and the Point were decorated with boughs and flags, a great sign, and an archway. People were invited to fly any flags they could find to make the whole district bright and gay. I was invited, not only to assist in putting the parade together, but also to take the salute when the parade reached the wharf. For this occasion I donned my Air Force uniform which I felt lent a little something to the parade and certainly the taking of the salute.

The parade lined up in the hospital grounds under my direction and having made sure it was in order and they knew what to do, I jumped in my jeep and headed for the Point to prepare myself to take the salute when it arrived. I suppose it took half an hour before the parade bravely marched down the road and appeared at the Point. The people marched onto the wharf saluting the Base as it went by. It was a proud moment for everyone and we all felt strongly that we were participating in the Coronation Day Ceremonies. The parade gathered then for some brief speeches when we were all reminded of our loyalty to the Queen and the Crown. We then broke up to meet again after a sports day event, to hold a fireworks display, and a "time" to conclude the festivities.

That night before the "time" began the fireworks were set off and made a wonderful display greatly appreciated by all, particularly the youngsters and the very old who had never seen such things before. When the display was over, everybody settled in to a dinner and a dance which rounded out a full and memorable day. I firmly believe that most of those people who took part will remember it as an outstanding day, the sort of day that doesn't happen without a great deal of work and without the willing participation of all hands. Our two girls, Edwina and Gerine, felt very strongly that they too should be doing something and from one of her magazines Edwina got the idea that she and Gerine should form a Playmate Club which they proceeded to do. The Club had about twenty members all of their own age and not only did they have fun but they set to work to find a purpose for their existence. They soon found the necessary direction when they looked at the hospital and realised that there were things that were needed there. They set their objective as the donation to the hospital of a rocking horse for the use of sick children who were hospitalized.

Through a series of activities they raised the funds and it was a great day indeed when the entire club gathered at the hospital to present to the Nurse in Charge a brand new and beautiful rocking horse. The horse gave a great deal of pleasure, not only to the members of the Playmate Club who gave it and the hospital staff who received it, but to the many young patients who used the rocking horse over the years.

The Playmate Club, of course, had other activities. They had an annual picnic at the beach, which was a day of great excitement for them. Usually they made their way up the Eastern Arm and had a picnic with paddling and swimming and games on the beach with a big bonfire to warm them and to make tea.

They often gathered in their headquarters, which was the basement of our house. We had transformed it into a playroom, and rain or shine they had somewhere to work and play. They put on concerts and plays and not only entertained themselves but their parents as well. Often, after putting on an entertainment, they would serve cookies and a cup of tea which I am sure made a difference not only to themselves but to their mothers who were the invited guests. Edna and I viewed this activity as a most useful one and were very proud that the girls were leaders in the Club.

One of the things which I remember them doing during the summer was playing games such as rounders, which Edna taught them how to play. Rounders is a game very similar to baseball but much easier and simpler to play. A piece of ground outside the hospital was flat enough for this purpose. Often I would come out of the hospital and find a game in progress, usually with Edna in the midst of it running harder than any of them and enjoying herself along with the girls.

In winter time Edna often took them fishing through the ice, and they would take off with the St. Bernard and a sleigh and head for Neddy's Harbour Pond. Here they would cut holes through the ice and build themselves wind breaks out of branches which they cut and hauled onto the ice. Wrapped in blankets, they would sit down behind their wind break and fish for trout. Surprisingly, they were successful very often and I enjoyed trout brought home by these hardy anglers for tea on many occasions.

Sometimes the Club would go skating on the ice in Neddy's Harbour, which was usually a beautiful sheet with the water frozen smooth and quite level. The snow which fell on it was usually blown away because the wind was vicious as it came across the isthmus and would clean the sheet of ice in no time. The girls all enjoyed skating and Edna tried to join them but was never much good on skates though she always made the effort. We had to stop her trying when she fell on her head one day and concussed herself badly. I think this mishap cured her of her desire to skate but at the same time I know she regretted not being able to take part in this activity with all the children.

Chapter 4

MEDICAL HISTORY

Medical services, as such, were non-existent in the early days in the Bonne Bay area. The nearest doctor would have been found forty miles away by boat in the Bay of Islands, and it would be a considerable undertaking which might take several days to send a message to Bay of Islands and bring the doctor, but it was done on occasion. The other sources of medical attention were the very infrequent visits of naval vessels, which might carry a medical man on board, but the length of time that such a vessel would be in port might be very short.

However, there settled in Bonne Bay, in the Woody Point Area, around 1863, George Prebble, who had a reputation for being able to take care of the sick or injured. The story which is told says that George Prebble was born in the United States but came to Newfoundland on a trading vessel buying fish and bringing supplies to sell to the local settlers in exchange for the fish. It was understood that he had been advised to go to sea for the sake of his health, and that his first job was to represent the company to see that the deals made by the traders were fair and in the interest of the company which he represented.

While in harbour somewhere on the Coast, in company with a number of other vessels, an accident happened wherein a man suffered a severe injury when his gun exploded. It was customary for women to be carried sometimes on vessels and they looked after the duties of cooking and other duties as women normally perform around the house. On a neighbouring ship was such a person, Elizabeth Andrews, and together with George Prebble they tended to the injuries of the patient. With the primitive medicines available and their tender care, they saved his life. George Prebble married

Elizabeth Andrews and built their home in Bonne Bay. His interest in medicine continued, and while he had had no formal medical training, he acquired medical books, studied them carefully, and his practice increased.

Around 1870 the newly formed Newfoundland Medical Society began to look at those people in the colony who, without any formal training, were practising medicine, checked their work, and decided that some of them should be recognised as proficient and allowed to continue practicing. By a special Act of the legislature in 1872 they were officially confirmed as Medical Practitioners, and allowed to use the title of "Doctor."

George Prebble's son, William, from the age of about eleven was a constant companion to his father as he continued his medical administrations, and by the time he was fifteen he had decided that in two or three years time he would go away to medical school, take formal training, and become a medical doctor. His father spent a lot of time teaching him all that he knew, encouraging him to read the medical books, and learn as much as he could. Bill Prebble often told me stories of the cases that they had dealt with and how they had treated various conditions. One thing I remember clearly is his description of how his father made him learn, using real bones as much as he could, about the bones of the body. That way Bill would be able to recognise fractures when they occurred, would be able to recognise when they had been reduced, or put back into position, and would be able to put them into splints for the healing process to take place.

Unfortunately, George Prebble died when William was about sixteen, and William had to make a choice as to whether he would take over his father's business, which had grown considerably over the years and was quite apart from his medical activities, or go away and train as a medical doctor. The choice must have been an extremely difficult one, but eventually was resolved by the fact that William realised that if he left, the business would collapse and there would be no funds for him to pursue his medical education. Reluctantly, the choice having been made for him, he took over this father's business as a young man. Still, he was looked upon by the communities which remembered his father as an able medical assistant, and he was called upon for the rest of his life to render assistance on many occasions. Over the years he also acted as assistant to every doctor who came into Bonne Bay, either visiting physicians or as residence physicians, and he finally became the Secretary of the Bonne Bay Cottage Hospital which opened its doors of the area at the end of 1939.

When Bill finally "retired" he was well past retirement age, but his services were so valuable and he performed so well in his position as Secretary to the hospital that the Department of Health asked him to stay. Finally, he felt himself that he could no longer continue because of the difficulties of coming daily across the Bay from Woody Point to Norris Point, summer and winter, in all kinds of weather. It was really beginning to be too much for him. I don't remember ever seeing Bill Prebble get ruffled or angry, yet there were plenty of occasions when angry or difficult subscribers would argue with him, particularly when they hadn't paid their dues on time and were faced with a penalty. It was a sad day indeed when finally he announced his retirement and he made his last visit to the hospital and conducted the hospital business for the last time.

Many times William Prebble accompanied me as I made my trips along the Coast, or perhaps I accompanied him. I learned great respect for this man who had worked with so many doctors over the years, had learned so much on his own, and was always ready to give assistance to others. He was respected and known throughout the Coast. Often when we visited a settlement I would be referred to as Mr., but he would be referred to as Dr. Prebble. I was always delighted on these occasions because it meant that he was getting recognition for the many times that he had been the sole means of medical help for many people.

He knew everybody and everybody knew him, and more than just knowing everybody he often knew much about their medical conditions. I remember well a girl arriving at the hospital with a dislocated jaw. It was a simple matter to replace it, if one knew how to do it, and in a matter of a few seconds it had been reduced and everything was back to normal. Later in the morning, over a cup of coffee, I mentioned to him that I had treated a dislocated jaw that morning.

"Yes," he said, "I am well aware of it. As a matter of fact I came over on the ferry boat with your patient."

"Luckily it wasn't difficult and I was able to reduce it quickly," I told him.

"I'm glad to hear it," replied Bill Prebble. "By the way, that's the third time she has had a dislocated jaw."

I looked at him in amazement and then asked, "How do you know?"

He smiled as he replied, "I put it back the other times."

One of the earliest doctors who visited the area in William Prebble's time was Dr. Fisher who was practising in Corner Brook. Arrangements would be made to bring him by boat to Bonne Bay to see a serious case. I remember one case where Bill Prebble told me that he was asked by Dr. Fisher to accompany him to see a patient in Bonne Bay and he went with the Doctor to the house. The patient apparently had some kind of abdominal tumour and it was considered necessary to operate without delay. Dr. Fisher asked Bill Prebble if he would assist him, which he was only too willing to do, so the operation was performed successfully and the patient had an uneventful convalescence.

No complete list has been kept of the licensed doctors who practised in Bonne Bay. Amongst the early ones were Dr. Modsell, who came to the area before the First World War and who later became the head of the Department of Health and Welfare. He was also elected to the House of Assembly in which he served for a period. Later he became Deputy Minister of the Department of Health and Welfare. Dr. Campbell, who named the St. Barbe Coast "The Gold Coast," succeeded Dr. Modsell. He later set up practice in St. John's, was elected to the House of Assembly, and became a Cabinet Minister. As a young boy I can remember him well for his house was just across the street from ours on Duckworth Street in St. John's. However, little did I know at that time in the years to come I too would be a doctor and would be practicing in the area where he practised as a young man. The name "Gold Coast" was given because it was common practise in those days for the residents to be paid in gold coin, and in turn they would pay the doctor for his services in gold. Trading vessels carried the gold coins and as they purchased their fish they paid the fishermen with these coins. Many are the stories of the gold coins, of fires where the gold melted having been stored in small barrels in the house but the value was salvaged, for it was still gold even though melted and could be taken to a bank. Today the equivalent money in paper form would burn and there would be nothing to take to the bank. The ashes would not be acceptable legal tender.

Both Dr. Campbell and Dr. Modsell served in Bonne Bay, either just prior to or during the First World War. At the end of that period Dr. Milton Green started practise there and later moved to Deer Lake. He was followed by Dr. Templeton who stayed up to the time of the construction of the Bonne Bay Cottage Hospital in 1938-39.

The Commission of Government of Newfoundland, which took over from Responsible Government in 1934, introduced Cottage Hospitals at strategic points through the Colony. The construction of these hospitals during the depression days of the 1930s was dependent largely upon contributions of either money, materials, or labour from the local residents and others who would benefit by the presence of such a facility. Practically every family in the area contributed to the building of the hospital. The effort was spear-headed by a Hospital Building Committee with representatives from every community serving on it, and chaired by Mr. A. B. Harding of Norris Point. The Department of Health agreed that if the necessary contributions were forthcoming they would certainly help in the building and would take over the maintenance and staffing of the hospital when it was complete.

The Government agreed through the Department of Health and Welfare to provide some funds and also a foreman supervisor, Mr. Arthur Nichol, who was sent out from the Department of Public Works as supervisor and foreman to correlate the efforts being made locally.

There were a number of Cottage Hospitals already in existence in Newfoundland at that time, and the Department was able to provide the plans which now had been somewhat improved from their experiences in the other hospitals. The Bonne Bay Hospital was therefore at that time the most efficient and up to date hospital in the Province.

The site was about one mile inland from Norris Point itself, and the land on which the hospital was built and the grounds were donated by William Prebble, who served on the committee and, because of his long involvement with medicine in the area, became the first Secretary of the hospital. The plans produced by the government for the hospitals were being built to a more or less standard plan, and the committee then went to work to contact every family in the district and get from them a promise of either materials, labour, or money. Everybody pitched in and the hospital was complete and ready for opening at the end of 1939.

It was a three storey wooden building with a concrete basement. The basement contained a small section which was used as the Out-Patients Department consisting of a doctor's office, an examining room, a small drug room and laboratory combined, a small waiting room with the secretary's office attached, a laundry for the requirements of the hospital, a food store room, a workshop, the furnace room, and the coal cellar occupied the remainder of the basement. The main floor of the building contained two wards capable of handling ten beds in each with an attached bathroom containing a toilet and a small private room. Two slightly larger private rooms were located in the corridor outside the wards, each containing their own toilet. The x-ray room and its dark room, the operating room and its utility room, the kitchen, and the staff dining room with the main entrance and hall filled the remainder of this floor. The top floor consisted of three sections: the staff quarters consisting of four rooms and a bathroom, the nurses quarters, and a small doctor's suite which included bedroom, bathroom, and sitting room. The outbuildings consisted of a generator house containing three generators. One was exclusively for the use of the x-ray machine and was operated by remote control from the x-ray room. The other two 110 volt D.C. generators charged two banks of batteries which kept the hospital supplied with electricity. A small morgue stood by itself close to the generator house. Finally, a building which contained the ice house and a garage for the hospital truck stood just outside the hospital gate on the road to the doctor's house. The hospital grounds were fenced in and the sloping lawns in the front of the hospital had been used as a part of the war effort to grow potatoes. The furrows were still there for all to see in 1945 when the war ended. Laundry was to be done in the hospital and for this purpose outside help was brought in to assist the staff.

The hospital was situated approximately one mile from "the Point." The hospital's half-ton truck, which had certainly seen better days, was used by hospital staff to bring in supplies, mail, and patients over the rough road. Transportation in general around Norris Point and vicinity was slow. Since there were no roads, travel was largely by boat the majority of the year, and horse and sleigh during the winter time. Patients came from Chimney Cove to Ferolle Point, a distance of approximately 180 miles, and the hospital served a population of between 5,000 and 6,000 people. The hospital was intended to be operated by a doctor, one nurse, two ward aides, a cook, two maids, and a janitor.

The first doctor was Dr. Bob Dove, then a young unmarried man, who had experience in other parts of Newfoundland including a spell on the Newfoundland Hospital Ship, the *Lady Anderson*, which operated on the south coast. Dr. Dove moved into the Cottage Hospital just before it was ready for opening and took up residence in the Doctor's suite and began practising and admitting patients. Some people, not used to a hospital, were under the impression that one was only admitted to hospital if one's condition was terminal and therefore when the doctor advised hospitalization, it meant that it was the end. However, Dr. Dove's skills and ability in allaying the fears of the people developed an understanding and feeling for the hospital which spread throughout the district. He practiced there until nine months before I came in 1945.

The maintenance man, Martin Bugden, was a remarkable person. He kept every part of the hospital operating from maintaining the electrical supply to looking after the coal furnace, the plumbing, the requirements in the wards, the driving of the truck, the bringing in of patients, supplies and mail, and 101 other activities. He was proud of his work and was a perfectionist who always kept his cool. He never failed to keep all parts of the hospital operating in prime condition. In those early days he was single-handed but he actually performed the duties of three men. He was available on an around the clock basis and, in fact, there were no funds available from government to provide any assistance to him. In later years this changed and more staff was employed.

Martin accompanied me on all my trips along the coast in my boat, the *Tinker Bell*. He accompanied me along the coast in the first trip that we made by snowmobile. He cared for and nursed the hospital truck. He even drove the snowmobile until it proved obviously too much for one man to undertake all the duties and a driver was appointed for the snowmobile. Martin also took care of the maintenance of the mechanical side of the operation of the doctor's residence. He was responsible for the water supply and during the ten years that I was the Medical Officer, he became very much a friend and companion. Many a morning we would either be returning to the hospital at dawn from a call entailing boat work and we would end up in the hospital kitchen having a cup of tea, or perhaps I would be leaving the hospital after an all night session and would meet him as he came in to start his duties at around 6 a.m.

Our discussions ranged over every conceivable subject from local to provincial to national to international topics. He knew much about the folklore and legends about the coast and I always enjoyed coaxing these stories out of him. I only regret that tape recorders were not in existence in those days because I would have had a wonderful history of stories and reminiscences in his own voice. He devoted himself to seeing that the hospital ran smoothly and efficiently, partly out of pride in doing his own job well, but also with determination to provide the best services to the patients and staff at the hospital.

Occasionally there would be a difficult incident at the hospital, and Martin always played a valuable part in the dealing with it. On a number of occasions in the early days the door of the hospital would open and a man would walk in, usually a young man. Often such men had fortified themselves before they approached the hospital. They would then start to walk through the hospital going where they wanted and doing what they wanted until the Nurse in Charge would ask them what they wanted and they would advise that they had come to look at their hospital and didn't wish to be bothered. The nurse would then tell them that there were no visiting hours or that they had no right to move into the living quarters or into the wards if they had no business there. When they were asked to leave, the reply was always, "I own part of this building. I put time or labour or money into it and I'm entitled to come and go as I please."

My reaction to this was always that while everybody had done their share of building it, the building belonged to the district and not to any individual. While we were proud that anyone would care enough to come and see the hospital they had helped to build, certainly they had to abide by the rules and regulations which were important to the running of the hospital. This kind of talk got nowhere with the attitude that one was facing, and Martin often responded to our call for help, taking such men outside and away from the hospital because usually their voices would be loud, partly shouting, and it disturbed the patients and staff.

After two or three such incidents I came up with an idea which worked extremely well from that point on. When faced with this situation a positive approach always solved the problem and Martin was always asked to show the determined part-owner his part of the building. He was then taken to the morgue and told that he could stay there as long as he wanted and that *that* was *his* part of the building. Rarely did that particular individual try the same game again.

Chapter 5

CHANGES AT THE COTTAGE HOSPITAL

Being single-handed from the beginning of my stay at the Cottage Hospital, I realised I would face some problems. I had given this matter considerable thought ever since I had agreed to accept the position of doctor at the hospital. I was aware that I had to work out some kind of schedule which would enable me to deal with the Out-Patients Department, the in-patients under treatment, surgery, emergency surgical cases and deliveries which occur at unpredictable times, the operation of the x-ray department and the laboratory department, and finally the necessity of providing home care in the form of house calls and home deliveries. It had also occurred to me that quite apart from this load of work which dealt basically with day to day problems, there still remained the field of preventive medicine which I felt was vitally important and which included such things as school examinations, immunizations, and medical and health education. I decided that the first thing to do was to settle down and tackle the day to day operation of the hospital and get into a routine as much as possible to find out what the demands would be on my time. Later, after the settling in had been accomplished, I would assess what time was left over for any other programs.

Basically patients can be divided into two groups: those who require medical care and those who "enjoy ill health." This is true throughout the world and the latter group requires medical treatment just as much as the former. However, the test comes in determining who belongs in which group, giving the first group top priority, and remembering that little problems can become big problems if they are not dealt with in the right way. The clinic filled up very rapidly day after day as people who had been without the service of a doctor for nine months came seeking medical attention, and many, I am sure, out of idle curiosity to size up the new man. I had to remember to be very careful for first impressions were very important. If I wanted to make a success of my work at the hospital and in the district, then first I had to win the confidence of the people.

Once the Cottage Hospital was built it fell upon the people in the district to support it financially and this was done by means of an annual subscription. It was the responsibility of the Hospital Secretary to endeavour to pick up the annual subscriptions from everybody who was eligible but it must not be supposed that the amount of money collected would in fact maintain the operations of the hospital and pay the salaries of the staff and the doctor in charge. The family fee was $7.50 per year and for a single working person $5.00. Later this increased to $10.00 per family or $6.00 per single working person. A proportion of the amount collected, in fact, was paid to the doctor as his salary. And this in itself became an incentive both to the hospital secretary and the doctor. If the doctor wished to increase his salary, or even maintain it, then it became imperative to give good service and win the confidence of the people. Similarly the hospital secretary was anxious to get everyone in the district into the system to provide as much money as possible towards the doctor's salary and the rest to the hospital operation. On top of this there was an additional fee of $10.00 for deliveries, of which two thirds again went to the doctor. Another additional fee was for dental extractions, where the charge was fifty cents for each dental extraction and again two thirds of the fee was paid to the doctor.

The patients were responsible for providing their own transportation to and from the hospital, and were also responsible for providing transportation for the doctor should they request a home visit.

When I arrived at the hospital in 1945, the area had been without a doctor for nine months and the subscribers had dwindled, feeling that there was not much point in paying their subscription if there was no doctor in the area. My salary for the first year was approximately $4,000. As the time went by and we began to provide medical services and improve our ability the number of subscribers increased and within two or three years there were few people in the district who did not subscribe to the hospital.

There were penalties laid down for people who were not subscribers but did live in the district and who required medical attention. People were not allowed to pay up a delinquent fee, or perhaps several years delinquent fees, and obtain medical services immediately without paying the penalty. Many bitter arguments took place in the secretary's office as delinquent subscribers insisted on certain things which they believed they should have. Mr. Prebble, the secretary, always remained cool, firm, and above all fair. I always stayed out of these situations, for this department was not my responsibility. I never refused medical care to those who needed it because they did not hold a valid subscription. However, I was always guided by the secretary and the nurse who by regulation expected to see the cards of people applying for treatment. I also received some basic remuneration from the Department of Health which included a small stipend for acting as District Medical Officer, a Tuberculosis allowance, and a small living allowance. There were other peculiarities which sometimes were only discovered by talking to doctors who were working in other cottage hospital areas. For instance, for every six tonsils removed at operation the doctor would be paid the strange amount of $17.00. How anybody ever arrived at this figure I never discovered.

To the north of the Bonne Bay Cottage Hospital District, which included the immediate area and the two Nursing Districts of Trout River and Cow Head, lay the medical practice of Port Saunders. This district included the Port Saunders area and the Nursing District of Daniel's Harbour. There had not been a doctor in the Port Saunders Practice since 1942, and the patients therefore usually travelled to Bonne Bay for medical attention. Since this was an extra responsibility on my shoulders an arrangement was worked out with the Department of Health whereby an additional fee was paid for services rendered to the patients from that area.

For the first two or three years the majority of patients stayed at home for their deliveries although later this changed and in nearly every case the women came to the hospital. We averaged about 100 deliveries a year. As well, approximately 1,200 dental extractions were performed each year. We also averaged approximately 100 appendectomies each year with other surgical cases including tonsillectomies, hernia repairs, and various other surgical procedures.

One of the first difficulties, and luckily only a small difficulty, was trying to understand some of the local expressions. There were many expressions which the people used which were new to me and I had to be sure that I understood what they meant so that I could in turn understand what I was being told or asked. One of the earliest new expressions I met was one day when a patient came in and told me that he had "a wonderful pain" in his tummy. I countered by saying, "Don't you mean a terrible pain?" He replied "yes, it's a wonderful terrible pain." I didn't pursue the subject any further but took the first opportunity to find out what in fact it really meant and discovered that it is the Elizabethan use of the word meaning "a pain of such intensity as to be truly a wonder or wonderful." I met this expression many many times and it is still in use today in respect to a very severe pain. It is applied to headaches, toothache, earache, in fact, any pain of intensity.

Another expression which I recognised but when I first heard it was caught off guard was a patient who came in complaining "I can't glutch." It was years since I had heard this expression and it mean of course the patient couldn't swallow. The word uses phonetic associations to imitate the sound of swallowing.

It is quite common in certain areas of Newfoundland for our people to drop their "Hs" in one place and pick them up elsewhere. One gets used to hearing about "and a high up, 'erring" and "horanges." These are two good examples where the "Hs" have been exchanged, but to face a patient who says he has "galled 'is 'eel" can cause a temporary problem. The word "gall" was new to me but fortunately the offending heel was produced for my examination and I was able to quickly interpret myself.

Most men referred to their wives as "my woman" and to be invited to go and visit a woman who "is sick" usually meant that she is in fact in labour. I soon learned to be sure rather than sorry and after one or two unfortunate misunderstandings I always asked for as much information as could be given me concerning the kind of case I was going to see if I was going out on a house call. In my innocence in the early days to be invited to go see somebody who was "sick" suggested that it was merely somebody who was not feeling well. It was disastrous indeed to arrive at a house miles from the hospital after a trip perhaps by boat or horse and sleigh and find that one was facing a delivery without the necessary equipment. It only happened once and perhaps I could be forgiven for not understanding what in fact I was being told. I spent the first few months carefully making sure that I understood the expressions that were being used and, fortunately, I had a most understanding nurse who would often recognise my dilemma and get me out of trouble.

Four days a week, Monday, Tuesday, Thursday, and Friday, the out-patient clinic operated in the afternoons. This meant that my mornings were free for surgery, if any was scheduled, and to deal with the patients who were in the wards. It also provided some time for diagnostic work both in the x-ray department and the laboratory, and I had to learn to do many things in the x-ray department which I had never been taught, such as intravenous pylograms, kidney x-rays, gall bladder x-rays, Barium Series (upper gastrointestinal track), Barium Enema, amongst other things. It is relatively simple to take the x-rays, but it wasn't always easy to read them when one has been assisted over the years by having specialists available at all times. This was equally true of the laboratory. While I had done most of the work in my student days, I now had to depend on my ability to perform these tests with a degree of accuracy which was the equivalent of a good hospital laboratory with personnel specializing in this field. The amount of time available was limited and I was always annoyed at my inability to do many things that I wanted to do in the laboratory because there wasn't time available to do everything. I therefore built up in the laboratory a repertoire, if one can use that word in this association, of tests and procedures which gave me the maximum coverage for my patients with the minimum waste of precious time.

If I thought a patient was suffering from anemia there was no way of sending that patient for a blood test. I had to take the blood and do the test myself. It had to be fitted in with other work in the out-patient department, in the hospital, or in the district which at times meant that I worked very long hours to accomplish all the things that needed to be done.

The out-patients clinic lasted as long as there were patients there. At times, they would last for as much as eight hours for I was determined that every patient would be seen, and they were dealt with on a first come, first serve basis. It was impossible to introduce an appointment system although in the course of time I was able to develop certain days on which ante-natal cases could be seen which made it a little easier to set up for this type of case and streamline the process somewhat.

Since we had no maternity facility, the operating room had to serve multiple purposes. It was also the delivery room, and if we had a case in labour it meant that often a surgical case had to be postponed if the patient was near delivery. I liked to do my surgery early in the morning. And I preferred to do two or three cases in the same morning feeling that if you are going to do one case you might as well spend the morning doing such cases. Of course, this procedure was easier on the staff and we knew just where we stood for the day. I tried to start usually at 8 a.m. and muster the forces available.

Being single-handed I had to not only be surgeon but anesthetist as well. The Nurse in Charge of the hospital was not a trained anesthetist but soon learned under my supervision to continue the anesthesia which I would begin. The method we used consisted of my starting the anesthesia, which usually was open ether. I would pour ether over a cloth set on a metal mask and then put it over the patient's face. It was a miserable method of receiving an anesthesia, causing a terrible choking sensation. I had experienced it myself on several occasions and was very unhappy, but we had no other method for general anesthesia. However, I had been trained in the use of spinal anesthesia, and through sheer necessity found myself using this more and more for cases which did not strictly demand a general. I became fairly expert at judging the level to which I could put the spinal anesthesia and most of my appendix cases were done under this method. Occasionally, of course, one had a failure, the anesthesia for some reason didn't take, and we ended up resorting to open ether.

The procedure then was for me to start the anesthesia, wait until the patient was asleep, and then turn it over to the nurse who continued giving the anesthesia. I would then scrub up, robe for the operation and, assisted by one or sometimes both of the ward aides whom we trained in this procedure, I would then operate, keeping one eye on the patient while the surgery was being performed. Fortunately, I had received good training in the type of surgery that would be expected at a Cottage Hospital, and any major surgery would of course be sent to a bigger centre where they had more personnel and equipment. However, it was an expensive and often very difficult trip for patients to make. Where it was within my ability and we felt that we could handle the case, we tried to do what we could for our patients.

On a number of occasions patients had to go either to Corner Brook or, more rarely, to St. John's for a simple Cystoscopy where the doctor is able to look into a patient's bladder by inserting a small telescope-type instrument. However we didn't possess one and I appealed to the Department of Health to provide us with a cystoscope. Their answer was familiar, echoing the response we received for so many requests for equipment. That was when there were nearly twenty Cottage Hospitals and if one hospital got that piece of equipment they would all want one. They were quite blunt in telling me that there was no money for this type of equipment and that we would have to either get along without it or provide it ourselves. Once I sorted this out in my mind, it occurred to me that perhaps if we were to make an effort ourselves it might change their minds. Accordingly, I set up what I called a Hospital Improvement Committee. We set about raising funds to provide the extra equipment that would make our ability to help people ever greater. This began a series of concerts, plays, tea parties, card parties, and various other activities which brought in the needed dollars. I again approached the Department of Health about the cystoscope and suggested that we were now willing to pay half the cost if they would pay the other half. There was dead silence when I made my request, which I did in person on my next visit to St. John's. Finally, I was told that there was really no way that they could turn me down because it was very doubtful if the other hospitals would ever take such initiative. This began a period during which we managed to acquire various pieces of equipment and other items providing half the funds ourselves. It certainly did a great deal for the patients we treated by saving them the additional journeys and expenditure of money on fares.

Within a year the hospital was running smoothly. The number of in-patients which the hospital could handle efficiently had risen from twenty-two and four bassinets to about thirty-two for the demand for service had increased. More patients were coming by coastal boat seeking medical attention, more surgery was being performed, and it was not uncommon to have every bed occupied in the hospital and people boarding out in Norris Point waiting for an empty bed.

The second year I felt I was ready to start very gently tackling the preventive medicine side of our service. We began in Norris Point itself where there were two schools. In consultation with the principals of these schools it was agreed that we would give each child a general medical examination and a patch test. At the same time we would start an immunization program which would enable us to keep records of the immunizations given and build up our files on all the children. The children were brought in by grades and checked and tuberculosis patch tests applied.

We discovered a number of children who were infected with scabies (seven year itch) and others who had head infestations. The schools were advised that these children required medical treatment and it was suggested that their parents be told accordingly and asked to bring them in for necessary treatment. My preventive medicine program nearly collapsed at this point. I was immediately besieged by certain parents of the infected children, all now after my scalp for daring to suggest that they might not keep clean homes. Fortunately, I was able to persuade them that in fact not only can scabies be passed on but it can be caught from others. I pointed out that never had it been suggested that anyone had originated these conditions but in fact they should bear in mind that since their children mixed with the others they may well have caught what they had from somebody else. When they realised what I was saying the attitude changed and they sided with me in my efforts to find the real culprits and eradicate these conditions. They were all given treatment and sent on their way. This saw the beginning of the growing demand for an annual and sometimes term examination of the children to make sure that at least these conditions were eradicated. When the patch tests were read those children with positive tests were x-rayed. This entailed an extra load of work but it was indeed worth the effort for we did manage to pick up a few active cases and get them under treatment before they got out of control. Not only did this protect the youngsters themselves but prevented the further spread of Tuberculosis.

I was also surprised at the many conditions which we discovered in the course of our school examinations. These included skin infections, sight and hearing defects, dental defects, congenital defects such as heart defects, ruptures, ingrowing toenails and so on. Many of these problems the parents knew about but either didn't realise they could be helped or couldn't be bothered with them. It was a worthwhile program which started in a small way and spread as much as we could manage given my single-handed status. My first responsibility had to be to the patients in the hospital and those who were coming to the clinic seeking attention.

There were times of course when the load of work was almost too much for me. It seemed when I was overtired and completely exhausted another emergency inevitably would come in, almost proving to be the straw that broke the camel's back. However I managed somehow; the staff were always magnificent, and Edna was always there to support me, help me, and look after me. Edna played a very active part in the hospital for the first few years. She agreed to take on the responsibility of doing the x-ray work. During clinics she always came to the hospital and x-rayed all the patients. This meant a great saving of time for me because I didn't have to either keep the patients until I had finished my clinic, then x-ray them, and develop the plates and read them, or break from examinations after each patient and take that patient up for an x-ray, thus holding up other work. Edna's ability to do the x-ray work meant that I could see a patient, and then send that patient for an x-ray. In fifteen or twenty minutes, I would be able to slip out to the x-ray Department, read the x-ray, and give the patient the result and very often treatment, and have them on their way just as quickly as any hospital in the country could perform. Of course, Edna had her own responsibilities on top of this. She was running our house, looking after Edwina and educating her at home. Never being sure of my movements made it very difficult for her to plan meals and mealtimes. Fortunately, we had a maid and a handy man. Without these helpers, it would have been impossible for us to manage as well as we did.

Still, it was not uncommon for me to be so tired that when I was at the end of the day travelling either by boat or horse and sleigh on a call, I would fall asleep standing up. On the whole the people were most considerate and kindly. If I had eaten all the lunches and drunk all the cups of tea I had been offered over the years I would have been unable to cope for the people were generous beyond belief. They also had a great sense of humor and this I think I enjoyed more than anything else.

In 1949, the year that Newfoundland joined Confederation, the first Cottage Hospital Medical Officers Conference was organized. It was held in St. John's and was the first time that the medical officers from the Cottage Hospitals had been invited to sit down together with the Health Department officials and discuss the many common problems which existed. Apart from the opportunity of meeting the other Cottage Hospital Doctors we managed to put before the Department many problems and concerns which individually might not have meant much, but, when it was apparent they were common to all the doctors and all the hospitals, had a greater impact. Out of this conference came, I think, the most important action taken for many years. There was a unanimous demand by the doctors that to improve their ability to serve patients they needed a combined x-ray and laboratory technician. To my amazement, for I was the one who made the request formally, it was unanimously accepted and agreed to by the Department. Before the year was out every Cottage Hospital had a trained x-ray/laboratory technician. This new position changed the doctor's workload drastically and relieved him of many responsibilities so that he could concentrate on other areas.

This conference also saw the introduction of summer assistants. Cottage Hospitals were now supplied with available medical students who would come for the summer months and get not only experience, but be able to provide help in many ways. Over a number of years I had a total of three such assistants. The first was Gregory Nieman, a medical student from Corner Brook, who spent two months helping. I enjoyed having him and found his questions extremely refreshing and I found he kept me on my toes. However, I was still responsible for delivering medical services to the patients and to the hospital and I discovered that I didn't have nearly enough time to spend teaching him because I was too busy trying to deal with the day to day problems of my patients.

Two others, both from the United States, Perry Ottenberg and Dick Morgan, came in successive years and I believe that they enjoyed their stay and got something out of it. Certainly, I found that it took a load off me. They were able to take histories and assist in the operating room and even do deliveries under supervision. They also provided companionship. Perry Ottenberg during his day joined us on our epic climb to the top of Gros Morne. Dick Morgan during this stay came with me on a trip along the coast in the *Tinker Bell* and I am sure had fond memories of this. He still keeps in touch with me and has done very well.

In 1947 I was advised by the Department of Health that they had received a request from an American group who wished to do a nutritional survey at Norris Point based on the Cottage Hospital. They advised that they were anxious to have this done and would be pleased to authorize the survey but would like to know my feelings. I was delighted to think that we would be the centre for such an investigation. I felt that we would learn a great deal from it which would be most useful in our practise. I realised also that their findings would be important to the general health of Newfoundland.

In due course the team arrived and consisted of Dr. Ellen McDevitt, Dr. William Darby, and three associates. Their plan was to set up an office in the hospital where they would take a careful and detailed history of the families in the survey, take a careful and detailed account of all and every food which the family used, and carry out our medical examinations and other investigations looking for evidence of nutritional deficiencies. They were a most congenial group with a limited amount of time at their disposal for they had come a long way and had carefully prepared for this survey. They knew exactly what they were looking for and set about it with little delay. We welcomed their arrival not only from the aspect of the work they were doing but as visitors who were always welcome. Many evenings were spent at our house as we exchanged experiences and I greatly enjoyed picking their brains.

Ellen McDevitt was an old friend of Dr. and Mrs. R.F. Dove, and had visited Bonne Bay and Norris Point before. In fact, she had done some work in that area in this field previously. However, Dr. Darby, an American from the South, had never visited Newfoundland before and was greatly interested in our country, our people, and our customs. I did my best to prepare him so that he would understand our people when he was dealing with them and I am sure there were times when he felt I was pulling his leg. However, this feeling of his came to an abrupt ending one day while I was doing my clinic and he had a few spare moments and was standing in the waiting room outside. The patient who came in was a man and in response to my initial question, "what can I do for you?," he replied, "I want my eyes x-rayed!"

There are certain things of course which one cannot do and in the early days of the cottage hospital the use of some of our equipment and our ability to do certain things was not clearly understood by many people. In this particular case, this man was having some trouble with his eyes and he felt that if they were x-rayed I would be able to see the problem immediately and thereby cure him. I had been along this road many times before and knew it would take a lot of persuasion to convince the man that what he asked was an impossibility. However, I thought I could serve two purposes at once and so I told him that he was fortunate because we had a visiting doctor whom I believed might be in a better position to help him than me.

I left the room, took Bill Darby aside from the waiting room and explained to him that there was an extremely interesting case in my office, but that I did not wish to spoil the enjoyment he would get from the diagnosis. I asked if he would see the patient and help me accordingly. He was delighted to be of assistance and immediately went into my office to talk to my patient. I followed as far as the door and watched from the outside. Dr. Darby was a Southern gentleman, charming and gracious, gentle and quiet. He began by introducing himself and then saying, "what can I do for you?" I positioned myself so that I would not miss the expression on his face when the patient replied. Then came the words, "I want my eyes x-rayed," and I saw the look of astonishment on his face. He realised at once the impossibility of the request, but he also realised that this was a practical example of what I had been telling him, and he wasn't sure how to deal with it. He glanced out the door and saw me and I smiled. I shrugged my shoulders and he got the message clearly. It was now up to him to explain the situation to the patient. After that incident Billy Darby listened more carefully to what I would tell him.

The survey was carried out with a great deal of cooperation by the people. In fact, I was afraid that the people were too cooperative and, knowing that our people have a tendency to tell you what they think you want to hear, I kept a close eye on the survey for the first day or two to make sure that they were not being fed any misinformation. My suspicions were well-founded.

The carrying out of the interrogation covering the food stuff used in each household was a fairly lengthy process and consisted of one of the assistants filling out a large, carefully prepared sheet on which were listed all the various foodstuffs which might be obtained. I made it a point to have a look at the answers to a few of the first sheets which were filled out and was horrified to see listed there a number of items which I knew were erroneous. Foodstuffs were listed in various categories and these categories were then also broken down into canned or fresh foods. The supply of a variety of foods was very limited in our stores, yet there was no limit to the amount of the foods which the data indicated were available. And so to my dismay I discovered that people were replying in the affirmative to questions covering foodstuffs which had never been available in our area. Mostly our fresh fruits consisted of bananas, apples, and oranges, but of course the list contained many other fruits which, I found, were showing up as being used in the households. This was what really led me to do a more detailed coverage of the survey sheets and to point out that possibly their questions were being put as leading questions eliciting an affirmative answer whereas in fact if they were put in a different way the correct answers would be returned. It was indeed fortunate that I happened upon this because it might well have snarled up the entire survey.

At the time of the survey the majority of the people had a staple diet which varied little. Most houses existed on tea, canned milk, sugar (and often only molasses), bread which they made themselves, salt beef, salt pork, dried salt cod fish and pickled herring, potatoes, turnips, and carrots. This diet was supplemented by an occasional rabbit, piece of moose, fresh fish and, rarely, chicken. In the fall, sometimes people would have a piece of fresh beef but they were not fond of lamb or mutton. There was little spare cash and not too often could many of them supplement this diet with canned food from local stores. It was surprising then to come across a survey sheet showing that a household containing six or seven children and with very little cash had a wide variety of foods bought in the local stores.

We greatly enjoyed the nutritional surveyor's visit and it was with true regret that the time passed so quickly and they were gone. I found the report of this survey extremely interesting and believed that it was very important. Its findings helped to convince the Government of the necessity of further measures to improve the health and food standards of our people. It was as result of previous work that the Government had introduced measures whereby the flour sold in Newfoundland was enriched. The enrichment was responsible for certain conditions disappearing, specifically scurvy (lack of vitamin C).

The Bonne Bay area and the Northwest Coast, the St. Barbe District, were also selected for another experiment. This was the Red Cross Dental Clinic. It was decided that a dentist and an assistant (in this case his wife), would be stationed in the area, based at the Cottage Hospital, for one year. During the summer months he would be supplied with a boat and his equipment which was portable would be carried along the coast from settlement to settlement so that he could not only carry out a complete survey of the children, but also do what work he could. Accordingly Dr. and Mrs. Pownall, from Toronto, arrived to spend a year. We were delighted to see them for it added another facet to our ability to look after the people. The survey which Dr. Pownall was about to do was extremely important for there was a great deal of dental cases in the area. We were anxious to know as much as possible about its prevention.

Dr. Pownall felt that it would be almost impossible to do much more than carry out his survey and do extractions. In the early stages he confined himself to these two fields. Later, he undertook fillings, but the field was so vast that in the year at his disposal he was overwhelmed by the amount of work. He was extremely good with children and this was important because it was mainly the children with whom he was dealing. He soon won their confidence and became a good friend to all of them.

Dr. and Mrs. Pownall arrived early in the summer and, after orienting themselves, loaded their equipment in a cabin cruiser of about forty feet and set off for a fascinating summer of exploration and work in the St. Barbe District. When they arrived back at the end of August they were seasoned travelers, had made many friends on the coast, had tasted a variety of local dishes, and were well versed in Newfoundland expressions. There is surely no better way of getting to know Newfoundlander's and see how they live than in the manner in which this Red Cross Dental Clinic had operated. They then settled in for a winter of work at Norris Point. They carried out a detailed survey and a great deal of work on the local children. This program, although it was short, accomplished much and showed the urgent necessity of providing dental care and education for our people.

Around this time, another visitor appeared to enhance the lives of the patients. One day we received a visit at the hospital from a travelling movie operator. He had with him a 16 mm sound projector which he carried from settlement to settlement with a couple of movie films and a portable generator which provided the electricity to operate the machine. When he arrived at Norris Point he could locate no gasoline and appealed to us at the hospital for gas to operate his machine to provide a show that night at the Point. I was intrigued at the possibility and suggested that we were in no position to sell him or give him gasoline from our hospital supply but I felt that we could quite rightly give him gasoline to operate his machine if he was giving a show for the patients in the hospital. He gave this some thought, but being a good business man, he pointed out that normally he would expect some of the staff at the hospital to visit the show and pay an admission fee. He would lose this profit if they stayed at the hospital and saw the show there. A final agreement was reached that he would give a free show at the hospital for the patients whenever he was in the district, but the staff who attended in the hospital would pay a regular admission fee. In turn, we would supply him with the gasoline to operate his generator.

The visit of the movie man became established on a fairly regular basis and we all looked forward to the show. Many of the patients, particularly those from further north, had never seen movies before and they were intrigued and delighted. The average cost to the hospital was a gallon of gas about once every two or three weeks but the pleasure derived by the patients could never be counted in dollars and cents. The movies, of course, were old ones, but since there was no other entertainment available they were enjoyable nonetheless. Amongst our favorites, particularly the girls', were the Hopalong Cassidy movies which were very popular at that time. It was always like one big family as the staff and Edna, the girls and I, and the patients crowded into one of the wards for the movie show.

Chapter 6

THE NURSING STATIONS

The area covered by the Bonne Bay Cottage Hospital extended from the northern most point in the district, Reefs Harbour, St. Margaret's Bay, to the southern limit at Chimney Cove, just north of Cape St. Gregory near the entrance to Bay of Islands. The total distance covered was over 150 miles. In 1945 there were few roads in the area. Primitive roads from Deer Lake to Lomond in Bonne Bay, and from Woody Point to Glenburnie on the South side of Bonne Bay, served the area. The only other road, a dirt track from Norris Point to the hospital, covered a distance of approximately one mile. In the other parts of the coast there were paths, for they could be called little else, connecting most settlements to another, and used mainly in winter time when travel was possible by horse and sleigh. The people usually travelled by boat but when necessary would walk following these paths. However, these paths were not generally passable by motor vehicles. In any event, the only vehicle on the coast was the hospital truck, and it was restricted to the Norris Point area.

The coast was divided into areas covered by District Nurses who lived in these separate sections. The nurses were stationed at Port Saunders, Daniel's Harbour, Cow Head, Trout River, Woody Point, and Lomond. The nurses at Port Saunders, Daniel's Harbour, Cow Head, and Trout River were full time nurses. Port Saunders was a Nursing Station with approximately eight beds, a small operating room, an office, waiting room, kitchen, food storage area, and staff living quarters. The staff consisted of the Nurse in Charge, a ward aide, a maid, and a cook.

Daniel's Harbour, Cow Head, and Trout River had small clinics consisting of a waiting room, a combined office and examining room, and a small utility room. Woody Point and Lomond were staffed by part-time nurses, who did heroic work. These locations always posed the question: what part of the time is part-time? Among the nurses who worked in this area were Marie Butt and Hilda Gregory at Trout River, Mrs. Fowlow at Woody Point, Mrs. Bulley at Lomond, Jane Cluston at and Mrs. Honeygold at Cow Head, at Daniel's Harbour, Mrs. M.M. Bennett, and at Port Saunders, Mrs. Abernathy and Hilda Gallant. Of course, there were many others who came for varying periods and one of the later ones was Ms. Jakeman at Trout River who later made the epic journey from Trout River to Woody Point with a young girl in labour in the midst of winter and under the most difficult conditions. She saved her patient's life and earned the gratitude of the community for her courage and determination.

The Daniel's Harbour Nurse, Mrs. M.M. Bennett, M.B.E., S.R.N., S.C.N., was an English nurse who had come to Newfoundland after the First World War and had married and settled here. She had worked throughout her lifetime as a nurse, raised her family, and set up the clinic in her own home. Her kitchen was the waiting room and she had given up two other rooms in the house to an office and a storage room for supplies. Mrs. Bennett's devotion to duty over the years has been acknowledged many times and she stands as an example of a nurse who made an outstanding contribution to the district which she served. Many, many people in her area owe their lives to her and all of them have enjoyed better health because of her care and health education.

The area served by the cottage hospital and the nursing stations comprised approximately 6,000 people. It was impossible for me to reach these Nursing Districts every time they had a problem because I had responsibilities at the hospital. Also, the weather was unpredictable and would make travelling impossible at times. I made up my mind, however, that I would visit the coast at least once a year and more often if it was possible. Over the years it was my policy each year to take *Tinker Bell* from settlement to settlement and hold clinics, seeing particularly those cases which the nurses were anxious for me to examine. It was quite obvious that any urgent cases would have to be sent to the hospital, particularly if they were surgical or in need of investigation. And so the nurses carried out the work of day to day care and treatment of those cases which they could handle and referred to the hospital those cases which were more serious.

During the shipping season, which began usually in early May and finished around the end of December, it was relatively easy for patients to reach the hospital by coastal boat or in their own fishing boats. However, during the winter it became more difficult as the journey had to be made by horse and sleigh and many of the patients had a difficult and uncomfortable time reaching the hospital. At other times, illness would not wait for the coastal boat to arrive and often they had to make the journey in small boats in between or possibly during bad weather.

Difficulties and hardships were inevitable. For instance, in the late 1940s, a man woke up one morning at Hawke's Bay, yawned and found that he could not close his mouth; his jaw was locked in place. He was taken to the Port Saunders Nursing Station where the nurse tried to help him but couldn't. She felt that he should therefore go on to the hospital and he was put on a horse and sleigh, and taken to Daniel's Harbour where Nurse Bennett saw him. She was unable to help and advised him to continue on. By the time he reached Norris Point five days had elapsed; he was being fed by straws enabling him to sip fluids and his jaw was totally locked and open. I recognised this as a bilateral dislocation of the jaw and was able to reduce it in a few moments, but not without some difficulty because the spasm of the muscle had caused considerable tightening and it was much more difficult than if it had happened an hour or two earlier. He was a most grateful patient, but since he had spent five days en route I felt it advisable to keep him for a few days in the hospital. I made sure that his jaw would settle back permanently into the proper position and that a mouth infection which had developed was cleared up before he went home. Many similar examples can be told of patients with fractures, appendicitis, and other conditions who either had to wait for weather conditions to change or for other reasons took a long time to reach the hospital.

There were, of course, patients who had firmly made up their minds that they didn't intend to go to the hospital and had to be cajoled by the nurse into going in their own interest. Some of our people had preconceived ideas about the hospital. As I mentioned earlier, some didn't wish to be admitted to hospital because it was really a place to go to die. Over time, the fact that we took patients in who were sick and returned them in health to their homes changed people's views. The other strange thought, which still exists to a small extent, was that chest x-rays should be avoided because people were "afraid the doctor would find something." Presumably the thought was that what one doesn't know will go away. However, in the early days when Tuberculosis was rampant it was important to get as many x-rays done as possible, and one of the early procedures that we instituted at the hospital was a routine chest x-ray on every admission. These x-rays gave us a chance to screen all patients and we did in fact pick up every so often an active case of Pulmonary Tuberculosis.

My arrival at a nursing station was always well advertised in advance so that the nurse was able to advise people whom she wanted to be seen. Each nurse kept records of the patients seen, the diagnosis and the treatment, and this was a great help in dealing with cases. Often it only took the confirming word of the doctor to convince a patient that an x-ray or further investigation was needed, and my visits on the coast were always followed by large numbers of patients appearing on the next coastal boats. I had to be careful so that they didn't all arrive at the same time or we would be completely incapable of handling the crowds. However, I enjoyed visiting the areas and felt that not only was I helping the patients but it was probably good for the nurses to have a chance to talk to me and have a few hours when we could sit down and discuss the local problems.

Not only did I hold clinics in each of these areas but I also visited the other settlements on the coast and held clinics in the majority of these even though the nurse wouldn't necessarily be with me. Strangely each settlement had its own attitude and approach to problems. One settlement would see every house neat, clean, tidy, well painted with the boats and gear tidy and painted and the gardens well kept. Another settlement, perhaps even the next one, would be sloppy, dirty and unkept, the gardens would be overgrown, and the people perhaps apathetic. Largely this reflected the attitude of the leaders in the community. Either they were hard working industrious people, or perhaps they were the opposite. Sometimes it was nobody's fault. If there was no work in the area there would be no money and things would be very hard for the people who lived in these settlements.

One settlement would be ready and waiting for the doctor's visit with a line up of people all wanting dental extractions. Another settlement wouldn't want a single dental extraction. I found this difficult to explain although over the years I began to realise that it was often the poorer settlements that had more dental cases and often needed more medical care as nutritional deficiencies and diseases took their toll.

My trip in *Tinker Bell* usually took about a week and had to be carefully planned because for eighty miles from Norris Point to Port Saunders there were really only two places, Parson's Pond and Portland Creek, that I felt happy about mooring in for the night. Daniel's Harbour in the early days offered little shelter in its natural rock protected harbour, for it was shallow and small and filled with the boats of the men in the settlement. And so going north usually I would aim to visit Cow Head during the first day and then stop for the night at Parson's Pond, which had a good harbour but which could only be entered at high tide. The next day I could reach Port Saunders and do my work there. The return trip saw me visit Belburns and Daniel's Harbour, usually spending the night at Portland Creek. Eventually, Belburns had to be taken off the list because there was no office available and seeing patients onboard *Tinker Bell* was fraught with difficulties. There was always a swell on the harbour and the patients often got violently seasick. This put a swift end to our clinics. However, by giving adequate notice to Nurse Bennett, the people at Belburns were able to come to the nursing clinic to see me.

One of the problems that was always facing the Department of Health was the question of providing nurses to run the Nursing Stations. Throughout Newfoundland these Nursing Stations were located in areas far removed from the larger centres. They were usually located in the midst of the area that they served, and while they may have been located in a large settlement, the settlement was never very big. Such places did not offer much attraction to a young and energetic nurse who was ready to join in and enjoy social activities which she had learned to appreciate during her years of training.

While some of the nurses were married and pursued their profession having the companionship of their husbands and often family, many were young and single, and found life in the settlements very lonely, especially during the winter. It was also at times very arduous and the nurse often had to make difficult and sometimes dangerous journeys by boat or by horse and sleigh. Their dedication to their work was quite outstanding.

When a nurse who had served for a period of time gave notice to the Department either that she wished to transfer to another area or that she was leaving, perhaps to get married, there was always a problem for the Department to find a replacement. The Nursing Districts could not be left without a nurse because the people had come to depend upon their nurse to provide them with medical services. The isolation of the communities also demanded some form of local service if at all possible. The people always caused an uproar when it was announced that the nurse was leaving, especially if a replacement could not be found immediately. The people felt neglected and were frightened that in time of emergency there would be no one to aid them. An example of the strong feeling generated by the transfer of a nurse happened in Trout River in 1951. The Bonne Bay Cottage Hospital was losing its nurse and the Department had tried to find a replacement without disturbing the nursing equilibrium in our area. They had hoped to send in a new nurse to take charge of the hospital but could find no one. Finally they made their decision and sent me a telegram advising me that Miss Hilda Gregory, R.N., who had been sent to Trout River about a year previously and had worked continuously there, had been selected to assume the role of nurse in charge of the Cottage Hospital. The Department requested that I arrange to fetch her.

I understood that this announcement was greeted with a great deal of dismay by the people of Trout River. The Department offered no indication of a replacement. Trout River, containing approximately 600 people and being isolated on the coast during the winter, was determined that if they couldn't have a replacement they wouldn't allow the nurse to leave. Faced with this situation I felt it wise to go myself to Trout River, if possible reason with the people, and bring the nurse to the hospital.

Accordingly, I advised Miss Gregory that I would be coming and to be prepared to leave on the next fine day. Martin Bugden and I set off in the *Tinker Bell* and it was indeed a pleasant sunny day and the trip was uneventful. However, on entering Trout River and dropping our anchor about 100 yards from the shoreline, I noticed a large group of men on the beach apparently gathered to discuss something. I felt there was little doubt they were discussing the nursing situation, for they all recognised my boat, and they were aware that the nurse was under orders to leave. It had always been customary when my boat entered Trout River that somebody on the beach would put off in a dory and come alongside and take us ashore. It was only necessary for us to throw out our anchor, assure ourselves that she was safely moored and would not drag, and then go ashore. This day nobody put off and Martin suggested to me, knowing the situation, that it was very doubtful that a dory would come to fetch us. We did, however, carry our own dinghy and could easily launch this and go ashore ourselves. However, the distance was so short and there were so many dories and dinghies around that we felt it was unnecessary. We waiting for what seemed a long time until finally Martin attracted a man who was by himself on the beach and asked him to fetch us, which he kindly did. We then went ashore.

I told Martin that I would be going to the Dispensary to meet the nurse and do whatever work was necessary before we left again. I suggested he talk with the men and, if necessary, I'd be pleased to talk to them also. I arrived at the Dispensary and found Miss Gregory there. She was aware of the situation and told me that the people had said that there was no way they would allow her to leave until either her replacement arrived or some assurance was given them that a replacement would arrive shortly. In the meantime, her trunk was packed and she was ready to leave but doubted that anyone would help carry her trunk to the beach and load it on the boat. She also had patients she wished me to see. We set about our work, first seeing patients who came to the Dispensary, and then making a large number of house calls to people who were unable to leave their homes.

Having finished our work, which took several hours, we then went to her boarding house where we had a lunch and Martin was able to tell me what he had learned. He confirmed what we already knew. The feeling of the men was intense and at one point it had almost touched off real trouble. In the heart of the discussion Martin was told that the men were inclined to put the doctor and himself back on the boat and tell them to get back to the hospital and mind their own business. Of course, their intention was to keep the nurse in Trout River. Martin knew well how to talk to the people and he explained that just as he was acting under orders from me, so I in my turn was acting under orders from the Department of Health in St. John's. We both could only do what we were told. He assured the men that we were just as anxious to see the community with its own nurse as they were, but they must recognise the fact that the hospital was now without a nurse and we couldn't play our part in providing medical services to the district if we couldn't operate. The cooler heads in the group accepted this reasoning at face value, along with his assurance that we would do everything possible to see that they got a nurse as soon as one was available, even if it meant making another journey to bring her ourselves.

Miss Gregory took over as Nurse in Charge of the hospital and shortly thereafter the Department did manage to find a nurse who was sent to Trout River after a short period of orientation at the Cottage Hospital.

In the early days of course there were many difficulties for the nurses, the loneliness and isolation being the biggest problem. The Department of Health was limited by its budget, but there were some things which I felt strongly they should have done to help make life more bearable for the nurses. One of the simplest and most important of these was the provision of a radio for the use of the nurse in each Nursing Station. However, the Department couldn't see this and there was no way that we could convince them of the importance of this simple piece of equipment. It took a small incident to change their way of thinking.

It was the custom for top Department officials to visit around the Province during the summer months and in due course Mr. D.L. Butler, who was then the Administrator of the Department, made a visit to my district and decided to visit the Nursing Stations by boat. He planned to go to Cow Head and Daniel's Harbour and Port Saunders by hiring local boats and then catching the coastal boat back. Accordingly he set off and we looked for his return with the coastal boat in approximately five days time. However, the weather changed and it became very stormy. We knew from our radio reports that the coastal boat was stormbound and, since the bad weather continued for several days, instead of the four or five days he expected to be away it was ten days before he arrived on the coastal boat from Port Saunders. He immediately came to the hospital where we had a discussion on conditions generally in the Nursing Districts and there was no argument about what was the most important discovery of his trip.

His trip went uneventfully until he reached Port Saunders where he believed he would have perhaps two days before the coastal boat arrived. However, because of the weather and the boat's delay, he found himself there for approximately one week. He lived in the small hospital and had all the comforts of home in so far as the hospital could provide them, but the nurse had no radio and there was therefore no way of either receiving news, weather or shipping reports, or entertainment. He found that he had to go to the house next door where Father Nixon, the parish priest lived, knock on the door, and ask if he could come in and listen to the radio to keep in touch with the world. Not only was he annoyed at having to make this journey and frustrated at being stormbound but he now got a good taste of what it must be like to be in a Nursing Station without a radio. He assured me that the next boat going north would carry with it a radio for the nurse at Port Saunders. I was delighted at this new insight into one aspect of the life of the nurses in the more isolated areas and a new attitude which had developed overnight in the Department of Health.

Chapter 7

TREETOPS

The doctor's residence at Norris Point was situated approximately one quarter of a mile from the hospital up a private road and deep in the forest. The location had been chosen for its proximity to the hospital, its privacy, and the view. Set in the forest, it was shaded by evergreens and birch and protected by the trees in winter time. Behind the house was a great hill covered in trees which rose steeply and offered further protection from the North. The house itself fronted on Wild Cove, which was on the northern side of the entrance to Bonne Bay, so the view from the front of the house looked across to the town of Woody Point and Curzon Village. Winterhouse Brook could be clearly seen, with Table Mountain dominating the background. To the right lay the rugged hills running out on the southern part of the Bay to the Western Head. The main section of the Bay separating Norris Point and Woody Point could be clearly seen from the house. There was always something to watch on the Bay. We named the house "Treetops," which seemed most fitting, and we put up a large sign by the gate proclaiming this.

The house itself had been built by Dr. Dove, and was designed by Payne of Montreal, the man who later was the designer of both the Western Memorial Hospital and the West Coast Sanatorium in Corner Brook. The house was a two-storey wooden structure on a concrete basement and contained a large living room, a study, a dining room and kitchen, with an entrance foyer and hall with an open staircase leading up to the bedrooms on the floor above. Upstairs, there were four bedrooms, a dressing room, a linen room, and a bathroom. Steps led from the linen room to the attic which was large enough for storage purposes.

The concrete basement could be reached by two sets of steps, one leading down from the main floor and the other from the outside at the back. It contained a coal room capable of holding approximately twenty-five tons of coal, a coal furnace room, a laundry, the generator room, which contained a 32 volt gasoline drive generator and a bank of batteries, a wood room capable of holding about four cords of cut and split birch wood, a workshop, and a food cellar which was always cool and helped to preserve food.

At the time we moved in, the frontage had been dug up as part of the war effort and used to grow potatoes. However, an orchard containing ten or twelve apple trees lay out front, although in the ten year period of our stay it never once produced anything which could be called an apple. Through the grounds flowed a small stream which we later developed into a little pond. As we cleared and worked on the grounds, we planted a lawn, flower bed, swings for the children and kept it all as nice and tidy as we could. About 100 yards up the garden was a hen house and a run which we were to find most valuable.

The house was finished on the outside but not inside. The floors were merely rough lumber papered over. The staircase had no bannisters or railings, and there still remained quite a lot of work to be done. One of the first things we discovered was that we were going to be bothered by flies, black flies, mosquitoes, and sand flies. Early on in the game, the Department of Health made it quite plain that they did not supply fly screens for doctor's residences. In turn, I made it quite plain that there would be no doctor if there were no fly screens, and in due course fly screens were produced.

We started out living in the doctor's suite at the hospital, but we made plans to move into the house as soon as possible. This plan, of course, depended on the arrival of our furniture and supplies from St. John's, and also on the arrival of our own effects which we had shipped out with us but had not seen since we landed in Port aux Basques. The whole lot, some twenty pieces, including boxes, trunks, and cases, arrived on the first coastal boat after a six week wait. In spite of the fact that we had travelled so far relatively little damage had been caused by the many handlings that had taken place. The worst damage was that a metal trunk containing some of my equipment had been ripped open along its bottom, but since it was metal, nothing was lost.

With help from Bryant Harding and Bill Prebble, I was able to arrange to get in gasoline to operate the generator, stove oil to operate the cooker, coal for the furnace, birch wood for the two fireplaces, and a dozen hens to put in the henhouse, which would provide us with fresh eggs and later with something to eat. I also took into my employ a local man, Joe Roberts, who was to act as handy man and gardener, and generally look after the running of the house and grounds.

In spite of the fact that there were no floors finished in the house, we had purchased carpets for the main rooms and were able to make do and get our furniture into position. At least we were able to make a start. We were fortunate in finding a girl who would live in and help my wife, for it was a large house and we really needed this assistance.

The milk was delivered daily, fresh milk from the only cows available, and was brought in a container and transferred then to our own pots and pans. Edna now had to face that we had no refrigerator, merely a pantry, which in summertime could in no way be called cool. This was to present problems of its own. However, the hospital did put ice buried in sawdust in an icehouse and we did manage to procure an icebox. Every two or three days ice would be brought up from the hospital and put in the ice box which certainly helped to preserve our food a little longer. Still, pretty well everything had to be made in our own kitchen. Edna had to tackle the problem of making her own bread. She found that by bringing the milk to a boil and letting it cool, she could provide cream daily. We had as much milk as we wanted, fresh cream every day, and butter was in fair supply. Sometimes it was impossible to get anything except very salty butter, however, and fresh vegetables and meat were very scarce, only available once a week when a shipment was brought from Corner Brook. Again the problem was one of keeping fresh food both in the stores and in our home, as the stores had no refrigeration nor any way of keeping fresh foods for any length of time.

Quite apart from my work at the hospital there was now a considerable challenge in tackling living under these conditions, and while we were comfortable and had many facilities that others didn't, we were still at considerable disadvantage in the type of electrical supply, 32 volt, the lack of refrigeration, and the lack of fresh foods generally available. I put out feelers immediately and within a year I had acquired a Servel kerosene refrigerator which worked like magic and was a complete life-saver during our stay in Bonne Bay. Not only did it preserve our food but it provided ice and the many other facilities available through a refrigerator. It was a most efficient and remarkable machine.

Our oil stove was something that we had to "learn." This was new to us and it became a problem, with a forty-five gallon drum of stove oil set on a stand on its side outside the kitchen door. Fuel had to be taken into a can from this fuel tank, which was then inverted and automatically ran into a burner pot which was controlled by a carburetor. It could therefore be turned up or turned down, but at the most unlikely time would blow out completely. We did manage to "learn it" and once learned, it proved most effective.

However, it wasn't long before I realised how difficult it was to depend on a forty-five gallon drum of oil which inevitably would give out when we found it extremely difficult to replace. The local men had no difficulty as they knew how to handle these casks of fuel oil or gas. As far as I was concerned, it was rather like trying to manoeuver one of the pyramids. There were times when we had to tackle it alone, but it was an unhappy time and I set about finding ways of getting rid of it. Eventually I built an oil shed about fifty feet away from the kitchen, slightly up the bank, and put an oil tank underneath the shed which had a direct line feeding into the stove. This oil shed not only contained drums of fuel oil and could therefore be manoeuvered in winter time because they were under cover, but it also contained gasoline and kerosene for the generator and the refrigerator. It proved to be worth its weight in gold.

The road from the house to the hospital, running through the forest, was lonely and very dark at night. Edna did not feel at all happy about this. Shortly, we set up two or three poles and ran lights from our own house's electrical system down as far as our gate. We could light our way with these when we needed them or when guests were coming to visit. They made a tremendous difference to our feelings of being isolated.

The hospital truck would bring supplies up to the house and occasionally take us down to the Point. But it was an awful nuisance opening and closing the gate. The gate kept horses out of the grounds, for they wandered freely all over the district. Eventually we decided that we would put a cattle trap at the gate, and this we did, and it was most effective for a while. It prevented the horses and cows from wandering into the property, but it also caused one or two accidents. After several years, it was removed.

As we got into our stride and settled into the house, the curtains were put up and our carpets were put down. The house was still unfinished but we were living in it, and we were negotiating with the Department of Health, who in turn negotiated with the Department of Public Works, to finish the house. The following year it was finally completed.

The hens were something entirely new to us. Feeding them morning and night was an interesting experience. The excitement of finding eggs increased when we realised that there were no fresh eggs to be bought in the district, and we were dependent on these for our own use. It can be imagined how carefully we looked after our hens and coaxed them to lay eggs. Pretty soon I discovered that we had company in the hen house. Some of the largest rats I have ever seen began chewing holes in all parts of the house to get at the feed. We were also the target of a hen hawk which the girl who was working at the house saw attacking one of the hens. She dashed into the house one morning shouting "the 'awk 'as got the 'en." When I deciphered this message, which she shrieked over and over again standing in the hall with a hen tucked underneath her arm, I dashed up to the garden and found a hen hawk flying away with its victim. I sought out our man, Joe Roberts, and told him. He assured me that he would make short work of the hawk, for he was an expert shot, and with a .22 could down a sparrow anytime I wanted. After lunch he appeared with his .22, and if ever I saw a rusty rifle which I didn't really believe was fit to use, it was his.

I was extremely worried about Joe's gun and decided that I would lend him one of my 12 gauge shotguns. As he worked, I put a shotgun and supply of shells beside him, and went off to my work. Later that afternoon I heard a shot as I was on my way back to the house and hurrying up I arrived in time to see Joe looking at the side of the hen house, which was a mass of holes. The hen hawk, in the meantime, had safely flown out of reach and was sitting far up in the trees looking at us. I must have looked a bit puzzled as Joe explained that the hawk had been sitting on the fence post, eyeing its prey, when he spotted it and crept up, took aim and fired. He then paused, pushed his cap back and scratched his head, saying "I think she's out of line and pulls to the left." I assured him that it was a brand new shotgun which had never been fired before and I doubted very much that it was out of alignment. Joe scratched his head again and said "Well, my own rifle, I lets her go to the right and I did the same with this, so I guess she's out of line." I let it go at that, as it was quite evident which one was out of line.

The next day, while I was in the garden, I spotted the hen hawk in the trees ready to come down and ran for the house to get my gun. As I dashed back up the garden the hen hawk was overhead. Although I fired at it, only one solitary feather fell, and the hawk went gracefully off in search of further adventures elsewhere. While I didn't kill it, I didn't see it again, so I guess I succeeded in giving it one heck of a fright.

Meanwhile we were busy with our .22 rifle and traps trying to get rid of the rats. At the same time we used metal plates to close the holes that the rats had gnawed in the hen house. In short order we had this menace under control but not before one or two of the rats had managed to get into the house through the open basement door being left ajar accidentally. The story of our chasing them through the basement loaded with coal and three or four cords of split birch wood is a complete nightmare. However, once we set out to get a rat, knowing there was one in the house, we were persistent. Even though it meant hours of hard work, moving perhaps several cords of wood to get at the rat's hiding place deep down, we were always successful.

Edna performed miracles, not only making our house a home, but providing meals out of food that we weren't use to. Above all, she coped with my peculiar hours, for I never knew from one minute to the next if I would be at home or miles away. Before I brought her to Newfoundland, I had spent many hours trying to tell her, over the years that we had been married, about Newfoundland, about our customs and about the new situations and challenges that we would be meeting. One of the things that I had talked about often was bakeapple, a berry with a peculiar taste and odour, which is a great favourite in Newfoundland, and of which I was very fond. That first summer I was offered a couple of bottles of bakeapples, and I was delighted and carried them home with a great deal of enthusiasm and told Edna that this was the famous bakeapple that I had been telling her about. I suggested that perhaps the next day we might open a bottle and have it.

I enjoyed looking forward to this rare treat, and I arrived home the next evening excited at the meal that I was about to have. However, when it came time for dessert Edna placed a can of peaches on the table to my amazement and I couldn't prevent myself from asking her what happened to the bakeapples. She explained apologetically that she realised that I would be bitterly disappointed, but when she opened the first bottle it was obvious to her from the smell that they had gone off, and were not fit to eat. She had thrown them away. I realised at once the mistake had been mine, for she had never seen, smelled or tasted bakeapple, and it was quite understandable that a stranger to this particular delicacy might come to the conclusion that they had gone off. We immediately opened the other bottle and I was able to assure her that this is how they were supposed to smell. We tasted them. They were delicious. I was delighted and Edna soon learned to enjoy them herself.

Getting ready for winter was something that we had been warned about, and it took a considerable amount of preparation and ordering of supplies. We had been advised that we had best get into the house approximately six months supply of all the staple foods that we would need. These included sacks of flour, butter, vegetables, canned foods, jams, preserves, and so on. Salt meat could be obtained any time of the year through the local stores, but the best time to buy potatoes and vegetables was in the fall when the gardens were dug up and there was a good supply available. Fresh meat, we were told, should be bought around about the beginning of December and hung up in the porch leading to the basement. It would be cold enough for the meat to freeze and we could then cut it as we needed it.

We did as we were told and Bill Prebble very kindly made arrangements when he ordered meat for the hospital to get some for us. If I recollect, the first year we had two quarters of beef and a full sheep. These were hung up in our porch and that was when the fun began. The theory of cutting the proper cuts of meat is fine when you are dealing with unfrozen meat. But it's a completely different matter when you are dealing with a piece of cement which is basically what the meat becomes when it is frozen solid, and has been hanging in position for perhaps a month. It was no laughing matter when Edna asked me if I would cut some meat.

The meat was hung from the rafters by rope and the position of the steps going down into the basement made it extremely difficult to reach up into the rafters, undo the rope and let a side of beef or half a side of beef or half a sheep down gently. Remember that it was frozen solid and weighed what felt like a ton. Once the meat had been taken down, it was then a question of staggering into the kitchen with the chosen hunk and setting to work with a saw, a hack saw, an ax or anything which could cut off a piece of meat and provide a meal. By this time there would never be any question of a choice cut or particular cut. It was a question of simply getting some meat.

We used our knowledge to the best of our ability to try and get cuts that would make suitable roasts, but the difficulties which presented themselves can be imagined. The effort led to both a great deal of rejoicing that any meat was obtained and complete exhaustion by the time the operation was finished and the meat rehung before it thawed out. This latter concern, of course, was extremely unnecessary because it was always frozen so solid. We learned a lot that first winter. Particularly, we learned the tricks of how to deal with meat. The next winter we were much better prepared. We had our meat precut into manageable sizes and never again faced the disastrous situation that occurred the first year.

The laundry presented another problem. There was no outside laundry to send our clothes to, and, therefore, they had to be cleaned in the house. We were fortunate in having the help of Mrs. Carrie Hiscock, who looked after us over the years and played a considerable part in our lives during our stay. She came regularly and particularly took care of the laundry. The work was made easier by our 32 volt washer which operated quite well and took care of the mechanical side. The laundry room itself had twin basins. It was a large room which was capable of handling clothes lines to aid in drying during the winter months. Once we succeeded in getting a 32 volt electric iron with an ironing board, we were in business. When the iron eventually gave out we found that it could not be replaced. We then had to fall back on flat irons. These, of course, consist of a handle with three detachable heavy iron bases which are placed on top of the stove and used one after the other, there always being one ready for ironing when a cold one was put back.

It became very apparent that one had to be a handyman. I enjoyed puttering around the house and garden in what spare time I had, which frankly wasn't very much. However, I did learn to put glass in a window, do some painting, lay out the vegetable garden, and generally do the things around the house which in a city one simply passes on to the local fix-it man or specialists. One had to repair electrical equipment, mechanical equipment, and anything else as best one could and gained a great insight into the reason for the ingenuity of Newfoundlanders. It is born out of dire necessity and bears out in fact the old saying "necessity is the mother of invention."

Over the ensuing years our way of life changed little but the subtle changes that were made were the result of our experience. They were for easier living and easier ways of doing things. For instance the hens increased from a dozen to approximately sixty, and we found that in this way we not only had chicken to eat when we needed it, but we had a plentiful supply of eggs. It was not uncommon that Edna would take a dozen eggs and make a beautiful omelette which always astonished our visitors. We also found ourselves in a position to help the hospital if it desperately needed fresh eggs and couldn't get them. While we were never in the egg business, we did find that our excess eggs could be sold to the hospital at the going rate and this helped defray the cost of feeding our hens. We brought seafood shell from the Labrador through the kindness of the Organ Brothers who operated a store in Red Bay but lived in Norris Point. Every fall, they brought us down two or three barrels of crushed shell which was important to the diet of the hens. We tried lobster shells and found that not only did the colour of the eggs change to a pinkish salmon colour, but there was a distinct taste which we were not too happy about. However, necessity sometimes was the reason for such measures and we had to use whatever we could get hold of.

There was nowhere in Bonne Bay that one could go to buy a magazine or book, nor was there a public library, and we found that we had to become self sufficient and we set about immediately ordering various books and magazines. Eventually we had a steady flow of material coming into the house and subscribed to some fifty newspapers, periodicals, magazines, and book clubs. It meant that every mail brought something, and that the long winter days were eased by the availability in the house of plenty of reading material.

Edwina was not forgotten and we had children's newspapers and magazines and books coming in for her. Edna probed the availability of local education and found that in those days it left a lot to be desired. She made contact with the Calvert Correspondence School, known throughout the world for the wonderful courses provided for children in situations such as ours, and with her own teaching experience she was able to put together a grounding for Edwina. The courses started her off better than in any other way I can imagine, even the big city schools, and gave her a great foundation in education. It entailed a great deal of work on Edna's part and constant supervision which she gave willingly and with great dedication. The teacher-pupil relationship brought the two of them together in a way which I don't think would have been possible anywhere else.

Living alone in the Doctor's house was lonely for Edwina and not being at school, for she was too young, didn't give her much opportunity to meet children. However, Mrs. Hiscock who was a woman in her fifties, had a little girl about a year older than Edwina, who was the youngest of her large family. This child, Gerine, occasionally accompanied her mother to play with Edwina and they got on tremendously well together.

Two years later Edwina asked if she could have Gerine up for a weekend, and we were very happy to have this happen. In due course, Gerine arrived to spend the weekend. She never went home again, but stayed on as a permanent member of the family, of course with her mother's permission. They felt that as long as she was welcome in our house she would benefit more and in turn enjoy the friendship of another child her age for she was the youngest of a large family with a considerable age gap between herself and her next sister.

Gerine became so much one of the family that when we went on holiday or pretty well anywhere we took her with us. We now had two children instead of one. In later years Gerine, at her own insistence, asked permission to change her name to Murphy, which she did legally when she entered St. Clare's Mercy Hospital to train as a nurse. This gave me great pleasure, for my father, Dr. John Murphy, was one of the founders of St. Clare's Mercy Hospital in St. John's, and it had always been my intention to return to St. John's, start medical practise, and be on the staff of that same hospital. Since my destiny appeared to be elsewhere I was delighted that Gerine was now going to at least represent the family in the hospital.

Gerine's entry into our lives certainly changed the lonely aspect that we had been worrying about for Edwina. It gave her a constant and compatible companion. The two not only worked and played well together but insisted on dressing alike almost as if they were twin sisters. For many years we let this go on, but eventually felt that they should be more individual and we helped them provide their own individuality in due course.

·Gerine, the shy, skinny little girl who first came to visit with her mother and wouldn't speak a word all afternoon, eventually became not only a member of the family but also graduated as an R.N. and assisted me many times in my practice. After nursing in Canada and the United States, Gerine married, produced beautiful twin girls, and settled into a position with Bowaters Paper Mill Limited in Corner Brook as Industrial Nurse.

Chapter 8

THE WINTERS

The winters on the coast were hard and long. In Western Newfoundland, the people have come to expect at least five months of snow and wintery weather. Because of the possibility of early snowfall and the difficulties of land transportation to bring in supplies, it was wise to be ready for winter not later than the end of October. We had to look forward then to try to plan our requirements for the winter months and this included not only food supplies but also fuel and other items.

The hospital and Doctor's residence used coal, so when the order for the hospital coal was made it included our order as well. We had a coal storage room in the basement of the house which would accommodate about twenty-five tons of coal, and the only vehicle in the area was the hospital truck. We needed men who would load the truck from the boat at the Point, and then unload it into our coal cellar. This was a slow cumbersome business, and after the first year we prayed for fine weather because the truck would only handle about two tons at a time. If the weather was bad between hauling the hospital coal and ours, the road would be ruined for the rest of the year. It was most unfortunate when it was very wet because the road between the hospital and the house would then become deeply rutted and ruined and make life miserable as we all tramped mud into the house and over the carpets.

We learned the first year to close all the windows and doors when the coal was being put into the house and to seal the cellar door into the basement because the house would be pervaded with coal dust. It was a great nuisance and took a great deal of work to remove. The oil for the oil stove of course was transported in barrels, as was the gasoline for the generator and later kerosene for the refrigerator. It was important to make sure that the full order arrived and was stored, not only close to the house, but where it could easily be reached during the winter months.

Large quantities of foodstuff, flour, vegetables, potatoes, canned foods, and so on were brought into the house and stored in the vegetable cellar in the basement. Several cords of birch wood were cut. These were sawed into the right size length to fit the fireplace in the lounge. We stored them in the basement where they took up a large amount of room. Storing the wood in the basement kept it dry and easy to get at in winter. Being birch, of course, the junks burned with a good heat and left little residue.

However, the art of keeping the furnace going day and night was something we had to acquire and we learned this out of sheer necessity. During the cold winter nights if the furnace went out, not only did the house get very cold and take some time to warm up, but we had to start the fire again. There was always the possibility that some section of the house would freeze. It became necessary then before going to bed at night to bank the furnace in such a way that it would give out enough warmth and stay alight throughout the night so that first thing in the morning it could be stirred to life again and brought rapidly to full heat. We became most proficient at this over the years.

The first snow flurries usually came sometime in September, but no snow stayed that early at Norris Point. The high hills and particularly Table Mountain, however, which faced the front of the house, became snow covered in September and usually remained that way until June. October often saw the snow lie on the ground for some time, and well before Christmas the mantle was down for the long winter. However, I do remember one year when we had only enough snow to give us a white Christmas Day, and then the snow did not come until the January 10, which I believe may have been a record. Certainly I don't recollect it ever having been as late since that date.

Once the snow settled it was there for the rest of the winter and the hospital truck and my jeep were no longer usable. There was no means of snow clearing, so the trip from the hospital to the Point had to be made either by foot or on a horse and sleigh, and part from the necessity of bringing patients in or supplies, the hospital had no means of transportation. I did in fact build a fine plough which mounted on the bumper of the jeep, rode on metal runners, and was of hardwood reinforced with steel. However, the depth and the weight of the snow was more than the jeep could handle, and while it worked for the first ten or twelve inches, the first time we were facing drifts of more than two or three feet it was rendered useless. Our winter transportation problems were not solved until the winter of 1949-50 when we acquired a snowmobile. This machine completely changed travel, not only for us at the hospital, but for the whole province. But that's a story in itself.

The difficulties of moving around during the winter and the necessity of being warmly dressed changed our pattern of living. Of course I had to be on the go, so I found myself doing a lot of walking and travelling on sleighs. But Edna, the first year or two, had no necessity to be out all the time and in fact very rarely did get out. We made it a point of going to visit Bryant Harding once a week, but Edwina wasn't at school, being taught by Edna at home, and there was really nowhere else to go.

The snow seemed to collect around the house and there was always a vast quantity which appealed to Edwina as it would to any child. She and Edna spent a lot of time playing in the garden, tobogganing down the hill behind the house, making snowmen and so on. They were of course aided and abetted by Molly, the St. Bernard, who was Edwina's constant companion, and they always had fun playing in the snow. Molly loved the snow and would bury herself and then shake the snow off so that everyone got a share of it.

None of us had ever skied and this first winter we felt that we had a wonderful opportunity to learn. It would be useful as well. When we visited Corner Brook in October to buy supplies for the winter, as well as buying heavy clothes, parka, and such like, we bought skis. Our first attempts would have made Charlie Chaplin look like a beginner, and we all ended up in various inextricable positions in various parts of the garden, for we chose the privacy of our garden in which to learn. However, after a half a dozen runs, each one a little more dangerous than the previous one, it occurred to me that if I had an accident and broke my ankle or my leg or my neck, the nearest doctor was about fifty miles away, Dr. Green in Deer Lake, and the nearest hospital was eighty miles distant in Corner Brook. Without any further discussion I unstrapped my skis and told Edna that I wouldn't be trying to learn any more because of the danger of this type of accident, but that I thought she and Edwina should continue. In fact I never did get on my skis again although the sport appealed to me in those days as good fun and good exercise. Strangely enough nobody in the area was interested in skiing, and in all the time we were on the Coast, apart from one or two people in later years, I never saw anybody on skis.

The men who worked in the woods made and carried snow shoes with them, and this was something which we felt we should try. Snow shoes, of course, are large oval shaped plaques which tie onto one's boots. By the sheer fact that they are so broad, they spread the weight of the body over the whole shoe. They are made with wooden rims which are steamed and bent round to form this oval shape, with a tail extending from the back and then a web of leather thonging woven to provide a net-like surface. They are fairly light but difficult to learn to manoeuver because one has to learn a movement different from walking. Otherwise, one snowshoe will come down on top of the edge of the other and you will crash down every second step. It was fun trying it but we didn't use them for any length of time.

Neddy's Harbour froze over as soon as the weather got cold enough and being a protected harbour it became an ideal skating rink. It was fascinating to see everybody out skating, particularly the children whose parents had made skates out of wood blocks. These homemade skates had a section of a bucksaw blade embedded in the bottom with straps to hold the skate on the boot. They were fine, inexpensive little skates and the children performed magnificently on them. The grownups of course used regular skates, although there were many examples of the old type which locked onto one's boots rather than being screwed on to the bottom of proper skating boots. During our time there was no organized hockey, but the kids did amuse themselves with their own form of ice hockey and many an enjoyable day was spent in this manner.

Some of the ponds in the area contained trout, and it was quite common during the winter to organize a small group who would walk, or more usually, all pile aboard a horse and sleigh and head for a pond, drill holes in the ice, set up windbreaks by cutting branches from the trees, and settle down to a few hours of trout fishing. Some of the trout were sizable and it was not only fun but productive as well.

Many of the families had horses or ponies which they used particularly during the winter for hauling wood. Most of the homes depended on wood for warmth and for cooking, and it meant a continuous battle to keep the stocks of wood outside the house replenished. Two or three times a week, and sometimes daily, if a man only had dogs and a small country sleigh, he would go into the woods and be gone most of the day cutting wood, loading it and hauling it out. It then had to be cut up into junks using a bucksaw. This was an arduous and time-consuming business.

The road from the hospital to the Point was well travelled because not only did the local people use it, but patients coming from across the bay, who came over by ferry, used it, there being no bus service or other vehicle in the early days. I would have thought that the traffic would help to keep the road smooth, but in fact it a series of gullies developed from the hospital to the wharf. Of course, the same existed on every road where there is snow with the sleighs using it. These gullies and hills were known as "Yes Ma'ams." I was always fascinated by this name and tried to find out where it came from. Nobody could be sure but I had the feeling that as a sleigh bounced around the road the ladies would be upset by the bumping and probably suggest to the driver either that the road was rough or that he go slower. He would always reply "Yes Ma'am" and so they got their name.

Another thing that often happened was "sidling." By mid-winter, instead of the road being flat, snow drifts packed down by the sleigh would cause the sleigh to slide across it and the road would then be sloped off at an angle into the ditch. Between the "Yes Ma'ams" and the sidlings a trip even of one mile or so to the Point was always an adventure and at the same time a bit of a hazard.

The main problem which presented during winter time was the question of transportation. For the first year we were dependent on horse and sleigh to enable us to move around. When I went on house calls, I either walked or used a sleigh. Very occasionally when a man didn't have a horse he would come with a dog team which usually consisted of two or three dogs tied by a long line to a small country sleigh but he would have to run alongside and I found on the whole it was easier to put my bag on the sleigh and run alongside the owner.

Moving about by sleigh over distances as much as ten miles was a very slow business. There were no roads, one followed the tracks that other sleighs had made, and there was no way that the horse could travel at any speed for any length of time. The usual thing was that the horse plodded its way along and it was simply a question of the length of time it would take to make the journey and return to the hospital. The cold was a major concern. It became my custom to always take a blanket or two in spite of the fact that I was well wrapped in warm clothes and wore a heavy overcoat with a fur collar and a warm cap. Later I was to find greater freedom of movement and more warmth by dressing as the local people did with a parka. During bad weather it was particularly difficult travelling by sleigh and some of the journeys were really quite desperate.

I always worried when I was on one of these long trips to a house somewhere about what was happening at the hospital in my absence and what I would have to deal with on my return. If I was away five or six hours, there could be quite a considerable backlog and no matter how tired I was it still had to be faced. These primitive methods seemed a very time consuming and wasteful way of getting around the district, so it wasn't long before I started to look for a better one. I learned that there was now in existence a motor toboggan which had been developed in the United States, and found to my surprise that one of the garages in Corner Brook was the agent for this machine.

I examined the machine on my next visit to Corner Brook, and it looked at that time as if it might be the answer, so it was sent to me to try out. However it proved unsuitable. It had no reverse gear so that when one slid off the road a tremendous muscular effort was needed to pull this very heavy machine back into the road and get it moving again. It had a very wide turning circle and in the small narrow tracks it was difficult to manoeuver. However, it appeared to have cracked across the main body of the machine and had been welded. This combined with its other characteristics of literally shaking itself apart every couple of days proved too much when one was looking for a dependable machine. It became necessary to carry a spanner at all times to keep tightening up bolts which were forever coming loose, and its foot kicker starting handle proved extremely difficult and tiring to start. I needed a dependable machine and there was no point in having one I couldn't trust to take me over isolated land between settlements. Once I contemplated all these drawbacks, I returned the toboggan.

We settled down to using horse and sleigh. For our own amusement and occasional use, we developed our own dog team consisting to two St. Bernards and a sleigh. On a visit I made to St. John's, I went into Rings, the harness maker on Water Street, and asked him if he would make me two harnesses for my dogs. He refused blankly and said he was much too busy with other things to waste time on trivia such as that. However, I put on the table in front of him a diagram I had drawn showing what I wanted, and this attracted his attention to the point that after studying it for a few minutes he told me he would be only too pleased to build the harnesses. It was at this point, I think, that he recognised me. He had been there many years and as a small boy I had always spent much time gazing at the model of the horse which stood in the window, and often going in to get the smell which is peculiar to a harness store.

I had designed the sleigh in such a way that it had three shafts, and the harnesses which were made for the dogs allowed them to be hooked on to the shafts. The reins went back far enough that one could sit on a box which I screwed on the sleigh and which was big enough to take me and my medical bag. The picture then is of a sleigh with a box on which the driver could ride capable of carrying either the medical bag or mail or food or whatever, and the two St. Bernards side by side in shafts to keep them in position.

This proved a most effective and pleasant way of travelling around, provided one had the clear understanding that very often the dogs would sit down and refuse to move until you showed them that you were willing to walk ahead of them. We discovered that the thing to do was to wait for a horse and sleigh to pass and then give the dogs their head. Their objective now was to catch up with the sleigh in front and climb in! This they did on many occasions and it became an exciting game to let them tear down the road after a sleigh and hold them back just enough so that they couldn't climb in. This resulted in high speed travelling for as far as the sleigh ahead was going.

Edna used this method quite often to take the girls to school. The St. Bernards were very happy in the snow, very large and very powerful; they made short work of getting to school and back again. I can remember occasions when in the bad weather Edna would be driving with the girls sitting on the back, and she would arrive at school to find that one had slipped off and was somewhere back on the road.

There were other hazards involved in using a St. Bernard dog team. One of the most exciting happened to me one day when I was doing a house call at Norris Point. I had turned into the front garden of the house I was visiting, tied the dogs to the fence, and gone in to make my house calls. When I finished I came out, put my bag in the box, untied the dogs, and started out into the road. At this time there was a big bank of snow across the front fence and it was impossible to see either right or left into the road so I had no idea what was out in the road. As I approached the gap leading to the road, I urged the dogs to go left for I was planning to go back to the hospital, but to my amazement they turned sharp right and at high speed took off down the road. As I came into the road on the sleigh I saw immediately what had happened. Only ten yards from us the mailman's ten or twelve dog team was rushing towards us.

Before I could stop my pair they had moved into the middle of this pack of dogs and the fight began. Dogs were yelping and barking and flying through the air as my two laid into them and it became apparent that I would have to move swiftly or there would be real trouble. Afterwards I couldn't really explain how or why I did what I did, but I moved into the middle of this fighting mass of dogs and grabbing my two St. Bernards, I literally lifted them out from amidst the other dog team, took them across the road into a field, and tied them on to the fence. I walked back into the road and was horrified by what I saw. The snow had flecks of blood over a considerable distance, there were dogs lying all over the place licking their wounds and yelping, and the mailman was scratching his head and surveying the damage in dismay. I could only assure him as to how sorry I was that this had happened and that I had been taken by surprise since I had just come out of the house a little way up the road and didn't have time to control my team. He shrugged his shoulders and philosophically informed me that this was the luck of the game. He had been the loser this time, but perhaps next time I would be the loser. He assured me that this is the way it had always been and no doubt always would be. He wasn't able to ease my guilt at all and to this day I haven't forgotten the incident which, I believe, could have been avoided.

With Confederation in 1949 came the first of the blessings from Ottawa, and the most important one that came for us was a Federal Grant to provide snowmobiles. I was informed by the Department of Health that this grant was the first for the Province and would provide a Bombardier snowmobile which would be delivered as soon as it was available. The machine itself arrived at about Christmas time 1949. It was a large machine capable of seating approximately twelve people, was equipped with skis in front and rubber metal tracks for propulsion with a Chrysler engine mounted in the rear. It had a door on each side in front and the driver's seat in the middle of the machine was flanked on each side by another seat. Behind this were two benches lengthwise down the machine so that passengers sat facing one another with room for two at the back facing forward. There was a large door at the back, and the engine could be reached by doors on each side. It appeared to be a large and cumbersome machine but once we learned how to use it we found it remarkable with tremendous ability in snow. Over the ice it was capable of a speed of about 45 miles per hour, but there were few stretches of road on the coast where one could get up this kind of speed. In fact one was navigating through small narrow roads designed, if they were designed at all, to accommodate small horse and sleighs.

The snowmobile changed our whole outlook on winter travel, made it fast and made it pleasant. The machine was well heated and it was now no trouble to carry patients, make house calls, or carry supplies. Day or night the machine was always ready to serve. We tried to operate it ourselves, but there were times when it was impossible for either Martin Bugden or myself to be available. After a year we were able to impress the Department of Health to the point that they provided funds for a full-time driver. The driver made a big difference as he could provide an extra service to patients who visited from across the bay and had no transportation on the hospital side.

Of course, we had to learn about the capabilities and limitations of the Bombardier. It was attractive when travelling any distance to try and get away from the narrow trails, which in the early days we often had to make wider ourselves using an ax and a bucksaw. It had been common practice to cross ponds but we learned that the weight of the engine in the rear of the machine tended to drag it down if the ice was in any way soft.

I well remember an incident where we had the patients aboard and had picked up some meat to bring to the hospital. In travelling across a pond, which appeared to be quite safe, we got close to some soft ice along the bank and the back of the machine went through. We were in danger of sinking. Quickly I got everybody and the meat, which was a considerable weight, out of the back of the machine. While this was being done Martin had taken the ax and cut a tree which we placed across underneath the front of the tracks. We tied this in position with strong cord so that the tree projected out some ten or twelve feet on each side of our snowmobile. I now started the engine and putting the machine into forward gear allowed it to crawl up out of the hole using this tree as a lever. When the tree came to the back of the tracks and started to move up when it hit the back of the machine, the cord was arranged in such a way that it snapped immediately. By then the tracks were on firm ice, the tree broke clear, and by giving her full throttle I had her on firm land. Once we reloaded the meat and supplies and patients, we were again on our way. This trick we had learned from reading all we could about snowmobile activities elsewhere and also from stories we had heard about the trials of other snowmobile owners in Newfoundland.

On another occasion we were travelling by snowmobile from Norris Point to Cow Head and we had aboard three or four patients including a mother and a ten day old baby. We had picked up a guide at Sally's Cove who was going to take us as far as Cow Head. He had never been in one of these machines before and it was a very exciting experience from him. By this time I had removed the two seats on each side of the driver's seat because I found that with passengers sitting there it was difficult to manoeuver the wheel. It was much better for the driver to have the driving compartment free for himself. He could then concentrate and have complete freedom of movement. An added benefit was that these two passengers could sit on the edge of the two benches a couple of feet back and assist at watching and directing.

As we went through the woods at one point we came upon a tremendous snow bank at a considerable angle. It was a grim looking sight as I put the machine onto this bank of snow trying to edge across it. Examining the angle of the snow drift, I was quite sure that if we did it gently we would get through safely, but I didn't count on the excitement of our guide. As we edged up the most acute angle of the snow bank he couldn't stand it any longer and suddenly threw his hands around my neck and said, "we'll never make it." As he grabbed me around the neck and pulled me backwards, this in turn forced my foot down on the accelerator and the sudden spurt of speed turned the machine on its side. We found ourselves lying downhill at about a forty-five degree angle.

I immediately switched off the engine and we set about trying to find out how we would get out. The door on the underside of the machine was on the ground and we couldn't open it. The door on the upper side to our amazement was now wedged tightly under the lowest branch of a tree under which we had slid. The trap door in the roof was almost right against the trunk of the tree. The rear door was on the ground. We were trapped inside the machine. With a hot engine and gas and oil spilling out, it was an unhappy situation and we had to move swiftly.

We managed to open the trap door in the roof just enough for Martin to get his hand out and with a small ax he started swinging at the tree branch until he had luckily managed to cut it off and make enough room to get the upper side door open. We pushed Martin out first. He jumped to the ground, ran around to the back and cut off the gasoline in hopes of avoiding a fire. He then came back and we got everybody out of the machine, moved the woman and child to a safe spot and made them comfortable. Luckily it was a clear day and although it was cold it was quite pleasant.

We then went back to the snowmobile and I had a good look at it. It was lying in a downhill position wedged under the lowest branches of a tree and getting it back in the upright position was obviously going to present considerable problems. We carried in the machine, in addition to an ax and a bucksaw, shovels, and spare gas and oil to assist in a situation like this one. On this trip, Martin, myself, our guide and one other man made up our total manpower. Martin himself was worth all of ten men. At that time, however, I weighed approximately 145 pounds, and frankly could hardly lift a 100 pound sack of flour, let alone a snowmobile. However, we put our minds to the problem and set to work first of all to dig out the snow bank on the upper side so that at least we would have something level on which to put the machine upright. When this was complete we then tried to lift the machine and found that between the four men we could lift it probably six inches.

We proceeded then to lift the machine six inches at a time. Martin told us that if we could lift it, he would hold it while we changed our grips so that we could then lift it further. He would then hold it in the next position, and this is exactly how we lifted that machine. It was evident that we had to get it up or we would be left out in the isolated area now some halfway between Sally's Cove and St. Paul's Inlet. The possibility that anyone would come along was very remote and even if they did it would be a horse and sleigh capable of perhaps only looking after one person. By a super human effort we managed to lift that machine six inches at a time, and each time Martin would take the weight and hold it. To my amazement, in a very short time, we had the machine back in the upright position.

Now came the question of whether we had lost too much gas, oil or anti-freeze, and whether we could get the machine going again. We took the spare gas and put it into the tank, we checked the oil in the engine and replenished it, and we refilled the engine with anti-freeze. Low and behold, when I pressed the button, the Bombardier roared to life. Martin was a perfectionist and a first class engineer and while he would allow the engine to run and warm the machine up and let the passengers get inside again, he insisted on checking the machine thoroughly, particularly the engine. He didn't want us to start and then break down for the lack of some small adjustment which should be made before we began. When he was satisfied, we prepared to set off again. Before we did, I solemnly advised my guide that dreadful things would befall him if he grabbed me again at a moment such as that. The remainder of the trip to Cow Head was made without incident and we were happy to arrive in one piece. When it was time to return I asked the guide if he was coming with me and he assured me that there was no way he was going to travel in one of those new fangled machines again ever!

I think probably the highlight of the snowmobile's career and its power to change the course of winter travel came in March of 1950 when we attempted to take the machine to Port Saunders. The trip was initiated, first, to prove that it could be done, and, secondly, to enable me to reach the Nursing Stations during the winter. Martin and I carefully planned our trip. We took aboard extra gas, oil and anti-freeze, axes, shovels, bucksaw, rope and tackle, and a quantity of food and sleeping bags in case we broke down somewhere along the way. March is a month when usually the weather is more settled and the days are beginning to get longer, so we picked a fine day according to the weather forecast and left at the crack of dawn. We had approximately 100 miles to travel and didn't know what difficulties we would have in getting across rivers and ponds as we went North.

By this time we were both well versed in the operation of the machine, and experienced in driving and manoeuvering it. We made good time as we travelled up the Coast and we stopped at Cow Head and Daniel's Harbour just to let the nurses know that in fact we were on our way North and also for a lunch in each place. It was getting dark by the time we reached River of Ponds and, apart from the fact that in some places we had found the trail too narrow and had to get out and cut some branches to get the machine through, we found that most of the trails between settlements were wide enough to take a horse and sleigh. Luckily, the snowmobile is not a wide machine. There were times as we travelled through the paths, however, that the branches of the trees on each side were scraping the sides of the machine. Nor are these little roads straight. They do a great deal of winding as they go through the forest, and it became a slow, tedious and arduous business guiding the machine. We wanted to keep up as fast a speed as possible and yet at the same time we had to be careful not to have an accident. I found that I could manoeuver the machine through the forest and the narrow trails using my foot on the accelerator to bounce the machine down onto the skis as I turned a corner. This method gave a great grip to the skis and turned her more sharply. If I did not do this, she had a tendency to turn more slowly and one was more likely to hit trees. It must have made a somewhat rough ride for the passengers we had picked up as we went from settlement to settlement. At the back of our minds, we felt that in this way we would have manpower on board in case we ran into difficulties.

It was an uneventful trip until we reached Spirity Cove, which lies south of Port Saunders with Keppel Island in between. At this point Hawke's Bay cuts across the direct line and we were faced with the prospect now of either having to go inland to Hawke's Bay and out again, which would put approximately another twenty or twenty-five miles on the trip, or tackling the ice across to Keppel Island and from there across to Port Saunders, a direct run of about two miles.

The local men assured me that the ice was quite safe, very thick and solid, but they felt that Keppel Island was going to present problems because of the steep drop caused by the rafting ice on the other side. Knowing it would only take a short time to have a look we decided that we would go across to Keppel Island. Crossing from Spirity Cove to Keppel Island was no problem and when we got on to the Cod's Tail at the top of Keppel Island, there in front of us across the ice were the lights of Port Saunders. However, we found ourselves facing a twelve foot drop almost straight down on the north side of the Island. It seemed to me that there was sufficient curvature that even though it was a steep and fairly sharp drop the machine would probably go down and curve out at the bottom and it would save a great deal of time. Everybody got out of the machine and gently I took it to the edge and slid her over. She slid down just as I had hoped and came out of the sharp turn at the bottom as if she had been built for that type of operation. The passengers were quickly aboard and we sped across the last mile to Port Saunders. As we came up onto the road from the ice with our headlights illuminating the area, heads were looking out of every window and the men were appearing from all over. It was now about 9 p.m. and quite dark. The people had seen the headlights of the machine on Keppel Island and had heard the noise of the engine. In the still night of Port Saunders it could be heard for a considerable distance. It wasn't long before the whole settlement was out to have a look at us and our new machine, the snowmobile, for this was the first one that had travelled the Coast. We parked the machine in the garden of the Nursing Station. We were greeted by the nurse who informed us that they knew where we were at all times because our journey had excited such interest on the Coast that the telegraph operators had passed the word from settlement to settlement. Our progress was followed with great interest all the way.

I discovered later that our arrival at Port Saunders had been signalled back to Bonne Bay and they knew literally the moment we arrived in Port Saunders. This was the first trip that had been made up the Coast by snowmobile and I was proud and happy to have had the opportunity, with Martin Bugden, to make this first trip. I was also very tired from the journey.

Strangely enough within a few minutes of arriving an accident case, a man who had caught his hand in some barrels of fuel causing severe lacerations and tendon injuries, was brought in. For the next several hours I found myself in the operating room repairing the damage. I was so grateful that I happened to be on the scene at the time I was needed. After spending a day in Port Saunders and seeing some patients, we set out for the return journey, which was completely uneventful. Again we picked up people travelling from one settlement to another, but we arrived back in good style and with no further adventure.

The snowmobile received continuous use during the winter months and proved the most valuable piece of equipment that an isolated hospital could have. It was used up and down the coast, but particularly in the Norris Point-Rocky Harbour region. On occasions when the ice was good we went across to the Woody Point part of the Bay and even up the Main Arm to Lomond. I can remember on one occasion needing supplies urgently and going through to Deer Lake, having travelled up the Main Arm to Lomond. I remember it was a beautiful sunny day, cold but clear, as we made the trip to Deer Lake in excellent time, and without any trouble. The road was completely buried in snow, and there was no traffic so we were able to maintain a good speed. If I remember correctly we reached Deer Lake within the hour from Lomond. Having picked up our supplies, we returned to Lomond and there to our surprise found two other snowmobiles at the edge of the ice. It was still a beautiful sunny afternoon, and since the other two machines were heading towards Norris Point we agreed to have a race. We allowed ten minutes for all hands to tune up their machines and then at a given signal the three machines set off. I simply put my foot on the accelerator and pushed it as far down as it would go and our machine leaped out over the ice. I watched out on each side, for I was the middle machine, to see keep track of the competition. We roared into Neddy's Harbour a few minutes ahead of either of the other machines, a tribute to Martin's skill at maintaining and tuning our Bombardier. Some woodsmen who had been in the hills surrounding the Main Arm told us how they watched the three machines tearing up the ice with a plume of snow thrown up behind each machine looking for all the world like three animals with huge tails as they moved at high speed in the direction of Neddy's Harbour.

There weren't many opportunities for this type of activity and I don't remember another occasion when we had the opportunity to try our machine against any other. We did however have many opportunities to cross rivers and ponds which gave us anxious moments. Inevitably, there were times when we had either engine failure through such things as a fan belt breaking or a plugged gas line or ice in the carburetor or some such mishap. We always carried tools and enough equipment and I never remember being unable to return to base.

The introduction of the snowmobile saw the end of the dog team as the mail carrying vehicle. It wasn't very long before snowmobiles, having proved themselves, were accepted throughout the Province, and, in fact, throughout Canada. They made a big difference to transportation and mobility throughout our Province, particularly on the Northern Peninsula which had always been so isolated during the winter. The mail now travelled the North more quickly and became very efficient. Of course we were delighted when the mail started being delivered from Deer Lake to Bonne Bay by snowmobile because it became much more dependable. The distance from Deer Lake to Woody Point over the "struggle," which is a high hill behind

Glenburnie, sometimes took two or three days to accomplish by dog team. Along the route, at about fifteen mile intervals were lean-tos, small shelters built largely for the mailman so that at least he and his dogs had somewhere to go for shelter if the weather was very stormy. While the mail had originally been delivered once a week and sometimes wouldn't get through for two weeks or even longer, now with improved service it was sometimes delivered twice a week. There still remained the problem of bringing the mail from Woody Point across to the northern side of the Bay, and this depended on either the ability of the ferry to get through the ice; if there was ice in the Bay, the ability of the mailman to come across the frozen surface which had to be strong enough to carry his weight and the weight of the mail. It was usual for the mailman to be the first man to cross the ice because his job was such that he had to get the mail across at the earliest possible moment. I am sure he took many risks but he always delivered the mail.

It became obvious to me that the snowmobile, while an extremely valuable piece of equipment, was at the same time somewhat large for myself making a house call, and I felt that a smaller machine would be even more valuable. I contacted the distributors who in turn contacted the manufacturers and eventually I got word that they were working on such a machine but they expected it to be a year or two before it was ready. They believed it would carry two people and this seemed completely ideal to me and I waited impatiently. I left Bonne Bay before this small machine was on the market. It is known today as the Bombardier Skidoo! There is no doubt that in my time it would have been most helpful to us. Today of course the roads are built to Provincial standards and kept plowed all winter, and such a machine can be used only off road. The skidoo is used mainly for amusement, since regular motor vehicles can travel throughout the year and throughout the whole district.

One other form of winter transportation deserves mention because it was the forerunner in many ways of the snowmobile. Quite simply, it was an ox hauling a sleigh. A typical example of Newfoundland humour is the quick way in which Newfoundlanders react. The snowmobile was a machine of great wonder when it first appeared and was viewed from every angle and with great interest by everybody. At the same time, I remember an ox trudging slowly along hauling a sleigh and some wit immediately saying, "Look here comes the slowmobile." What an apt expression and how very fitting. However in its turn the slowmobile had proved a wonderful machine for those who owned them because the strength of the ox in hauling wood was tremendous even though the ox had more difficulties because of its weight in deep snow. The majority of the people, because they couldn't afford anything else, had small horses weighing between 400 and 500 pounds. These were easier to maintain during the winter and were ideal for hauling firewood. However, some of the woods camps which used the largest horses would sell off these horses and the men occasionally would buy one and bring it home to use for heavy hauling.

It became quite common for a family to have either half a dozen dogs or a small horse or, if the workload was heavier, a big horse. They also had a few hens, and some sheep and often a cow. Strangely, I recollect seeing few pigs and they were the exception rather than the rule. All these animals would be loose in wintertime, but would stay close to their homes because of feeding. It was truly a case of knowing on which side their bread was buttered.

An interesting custom to which we were introduced the first winter was that of Janneying or Mummering. This is a ritual, I suppose one would call it, which takes place mostly in the outports between Christmas Day and Old Christmas, January 6. It is a custom which has been brought mostly from Britain but in fact is found across Europe, and consists largely of dressing up and disguising oneself and then knocking on doors after dark and expecting some refreshment. We were not prepared at all for what was happening and were taken by surprise on the first night.

Our oil stove in the kitchen was operated by a carburetor. To raise the heat one simply turned the small dial and to lower it again it was turned in the opposite direction. It was not a large kitchen but it was brightly painted in white and red, with a black and white stove. It contained three or four chairs and a small table apart from the sink and the counter. The first night there was a knock on the door and upon opening it half a dozen figures were seen outside heavily disguised and talking in squeaky voices asking if we would let in "any

Janneys in the night." We were only too pleased to invite them in, guessing it was some kind of custom and they sat silently in the kitchen looking at us and giggling to themselves while we didn't know quite what was expected of us. After fifteen or twenty minutes they left and were promptly replaced by another group and this went on from approximately seven in the evening until midnight. We had no liquor in the house and the only thing we could offer the visitors was fruit juice and cookies. By midnight we were exhausted having sat through a large number of Janneys, none of whom we had recognised and all of whom were extremely shy. Frankly, we felt that we had not lived up to whatever expectations there were from the groups who visited us.

The next day I went to see Bryant Harding and asked him about this and he roared with laughter and explained that there was really nothing for us to do except be civil, provide refreshment if we wished to, and possibly try to guess who the visitors were. Edna and I had a conference later in the day and wondered how we were going to deal with the situation if it happened again. We prepared by getting in more juice, liquor not being obtainable, and a good supply of candies and cookies. We decided that we couldn't possibly manage twelve nights continuously like this, and that something would have to be done about it.

That evening when the first group arrived I had made with Edna a decision as to how we would handle the situation. The first group was invited in and was informed that they would have to help us guess who they were otherwise there would be no refreshments. This obviously stopped them in their tracks for the moment and they didn't quite know what to do. I explained that to help us identify them they would have to perform and really make an effort to help us guess who they were because since we were new to the district we would have difficulty in putting names to them even if they hadn't got masks on. They appreciated this. Then the fun began. Each individual made a great effort to try and help us guess their name, aided and abetted by the others. Eventually it developed into a fun game which everybody played. However, it was again obvious that we couldn't manage five hours and since they were all heavily disguised and wrapped up in sheets and blankets and coats and anything they could lay their hands on including often pillows tucked up inside their coats, I found that by walking past the stove and turning it up full in about twenty minutes the heat would prove too much and the evening ended much earlier than previously.

After three nights we agreed that we had had enough. Edna of course would be on her own many nights while I worked and she did-n't want to handle the mummers by herself and so we agreed that we would only invite visitors for the last night, January 6. This was passed around by word of mouth and the supply dried up until the last night when we had a good crowd come to the house and every-body had a good time.

This first experience gave me a great deal of food for thought, and as we discussed it, it became apparent that it was going to hap-pen every year. There were twelve nights on which Janneys could or would visit the house. With a few changes, we saw that it could be turned into a good evening of entertainment for everybody. The next year we had turned the basement around in such a way that I now had a large workshop. We rearranged it so that the Janneys came down the basement steps from the back of the house, which was out-doors, to find themselves on a platform I had built which in effect was a stage for their performances. Not only had I built a stage, but I had equipped it with lights. We equipped the room with all the chairs and benches we could lay our hands on. We let it be known that we would only receive Janneys on the last night, January 6 but that all would be welcome. More than this we did not say and decided that a lot of the fun would be in them not knowing what was going to happen. We were now better prepared both to receive the Janneys and to provide refreshments.

When the great night finally arrived the first group came down the stairs and having been directed that way by signs that were lit up outside, found themselves on the platform looking into the glare of lights with Edna and myself and the maid, and Edwina and Gerine and some of their friends and some of our friends ready to greet visi-tors. The format was made quite plain to them. They now had to per-form and help us guess their identity, at which point they would take off their masks and not only receive refreshment but join the audi-ence and try and guess the identities of those who followed.

It isn't difficult to imagine the fun that developed and for three or four hours group after group came in and put on some kind of performance. Everybody tried to guess who they were, and then after some refreshment, everybody settled down to do the same with the next group. We kept this up every year that we were there and while the custom is gradually dying out, I think it was a most convenient way for us to handle the situation and give everybody a little bit of extra fun.

One year I decided to fool the family and under the pretense of answering the telephone, I slipped away and dressed up myself and then appeared at the door. I went through a performance and nobody guessed my identity. Finally the heat was too much for me and I had to retreat but I retreated happy in the thought that nobody had recognised me. I reentered the house through the den door and upon appearing was greeted by the girls who told me I had missed a great performance and that nobody had been able to guess who it was. They found it difficult to believe later when I told them that I had fooled them, but when I produced the clothes and sheets they were convinced.

The subject of Janneying is one that has created a great deal of interest over the years. Books have been written about the origins and customs of Mummering in Newfoundland. We look back with interest on the opportunity that we had to take part in this custom and enjoy the good fun that it brought.

Apart from the difficulties of facing heavy snowfalls and the difficulties of moving from house to the hospital and the house to the Point, there were times when I found it very satisfying to be living relatively quietly. However, when the storms came, and sometimes they were extremely bad with heavy snowfalls, one did worry about what might happen. A failure, for instance, of the furnace would result in the pipes of the house freezing and then bursting. Bearing in mind one lived so far from a major centre, such a prospect was frightening. It would be a considerable time before parts could be obtained and more damage would be ensuing all the time. On only one occasion did the pipe freeze in the house. That was in the ceiling over the den and we were fortunate in being able to locate the exact spot. We cut a hole in the ceiling, located the particular piece of pipe which had frozen and burst and which was flooding the house, and were able to repair it. The possibility of fire was also ever present and we were extremely cautious both at the house and at the hospital to see that there were no fire hazards and that everybody knew exactly what to do in the event of fire.

Snow clearing around the house was always a bit of a problem but we only used the back door during the winter time and it didn't take long to shovel this clear. However, the hens had to be fed and while we didn't shovel a path up the garden to the hen house, sometimes the snow was up to our waists as we went up morning and night to feed the hens and collect the eggs. One of the big problems here was in providing water for them and keeping the hen house clean. To keep the water from freezing we used special containers that had an oil lamp built underneath and while I originally felt they were perhaps dangerous, in actual fact we never had any problems or incidents. I was always afraid that perhaps the hens would fight and knock one over but they were heavily weighted and difficult to upset. This kept the water from freezing. The feed we kept in self-operating bins built into the hen house itself. As the hens ate at the bottom of the bin more feed came down. Still, it needed supervision. We kept a good supply of shavings from the local sawmill on hand and used these liberally on the floor cleaning the hen house at intervals to keep it sanitary. In this way, while the quantity of eggs diminished during the winter, the hens were kept warm and fed and productive.

We had a good supply of magazines, periodicals, books, and other reading material coming in all the time through the mails so that there was always plenty to read. We had a piano which I was fortunate in being able to buy when we first arrived and had it sent out from St. John's. This became very important as we had to make our own entertainment. Edna enjoyed playing the piano and I always enjoyed fiddling with it too. We enjoyed singing and often had the nurses and a few friends in for an evening of fun and entertainment.

However, the long winter evenings presented some problems. I realized that too often I was busy at the hospital or out on calls and the family would have gone crazy with nothing to do. So I purchased a radio. When we arrived at the end of the war there were no more than half a dozen radios at Norris Point. They were expensive, costing close to $100 which was a lot of money in those days. They operated on a battery which was a large heavy thing and which of course had a durability which depended directly on how much it was used.

The radio which we bought locally gave good service with an aerial which I rigged outdoors. We found that the local station in Corner Brook, VOWN, provided us with news and entertainment, but tended to fade in the evenings. This was infuriating if it faded right in the middle of the news but we had to accept this fact. However, as it got dark, we found that we were pulling in loud and clear stations from the Maritimes and the United States, and I began to chart all the stations we could hear. We began to list down programs which came on regularly every week.

At the first opportunity I bought the best radio I could find, a Zenith which had short wave as well. This machine also was battery operated and gave even better results than the other radio. Now with Short Wave we were able to listen to Britain at night time, for we could pick up the BBC Overseas service and listen to many of the shows which we had enjoyed while we were in Britain. Using this newer radio constantly we built up a schedule of programing and gradually put together a radio entertainment which was admirable in those days.

Certain things stand out in my memory. In 1944, while the war was still on in the Pacific, I learned to listen to Gabriel Heater, the American commentator who came on each night and usually prefaced his remarks by either "good news tonight" or "bad news tonight." We also listened to the Lux Radio Theatre, the Canadian weekly play, Truth and Consequences, several serials, and several thriller programs.

However, the most important programs were still the news programs from Corner Brook and the weather forecast. The show to which everybody listened without fail was the Gerald S. Doyle News Bulletin, not only for the news content, but for the messages. When Newfoundland entered Confederation in 1949 the broadcasting system, known then as the Dominion Broadcasting Company and operated by the Commission of Government, was taken over by the Canadian Broadcasting Corporation and became part of the Trans-Canada Network. The policy of the Canadian Broadcasting

Corporation of course was that their news programs were not sponsored but were provided by the National Network. However, the Gerald S. Doyle News Bulletin had become such an institution in Newfoundland that an exception was made. The Gerald S. Doyle Bulletin, familiarly known as the 'Dial Bulletin,' was allowed to carry on, and for many years the CBC Provincial News was presented as the Gerald S. Doyle News Bulletin. It performed a wonderful service over the years in providing free messages. People could advise their families of their whereabouts and their movements. Families would get reports from patients in hospital. People would be advised that things were being shipped by boat or by train. Some extremely funny messages, some intentional and some unintentional, came out over the years over the air. Many of these have been collected, others have gone down to posterity and become part of our history. But the passing of the Gerald S. Doyle Bulletin was mourned by every Newfoundland and it is remembered to this day.

I think the most outstanding and memorable thing that came over the radio over those years was the full broadcast daily of the proceedings of the National Convention which took place in St. John's in 1947-48. This Convention led up to the plebiscite to decide Newfoundland's future, and was resulted ultimately in Confederation with Canada and the first general election. Every night the National Convention Proceedings were on the air and we listened with a great deal of interest to the debates and followed the course of our history in the making. I doubt if anybody realised in those early days that J. R. Smallwood, who seemed to follow every speaker, was taking his place as a man who would eventually lead the Province for over twenty years as its first Premier.

When the weather was really bad and we felt completely cut off at the house, even though I had to get to the hospital to do my work, we still had the telephone. This was something without which we couldn't have existed. Not only could Edna and I keep in touch with one another so that if any problems arose she could contact me, she could also ask me to bring home certain things if she needed them. I could in turn tell her when she could expect me back for meals and so on. The telephone put us in touch with Bryant Harding and the post office, and also enabled the patients who were phoning in to talk to me directly, for the nurse could plug the call through from the hospital. It was an old crank type magneto telephone and it was a party line on which all those people who had phones were connected. It started at the Point with the post office and Bryant Harding and ran to the hospital and the Doctor's house and then to Rocky Harbour and along the Coast as far as Sally's Cove. It was a wonderful help to the people who lived further out for they could phone in for medical advice, to advise the hospital that they were coming, or to request house calls. It kept us all in touch. During the war years it was important for the local defence of the area and not only was word passed along the telephone line as to news items coming over the radio but also it enabled the watches on the coast to phone in information to the telegraph office at Norris Point.

It was quite understandable that when the hospital number rang, natural curiosity would cause most people to take off their receivers and listen to the conversation. If the call was from the far end of the line somewhere the taking off of all the receivers tended to drop the available power and the voice at the other end would be sometimes so distant that it would be almost unintelligible. I recognised why this was and on occasions would simply shout into the telephone "everybody off the line please, I can't hear what's going on" and then I would hear click, click, click all the way along as people replaced their receivers, and the voice would then come in loud and clear. I quickly learned that our people are very adept and wise when it comes to making a diagnosis. On several occasions I received calls telling me what they believed was the matter with a patient. Sometimes, when the patient was seen, it turned out to be just as the nosy caller suspected. Several times I was advised that a patient had Meningitis and this proved to be the correct diagnosis. Of course, there were many other times when the diagnosis made by one of the laymen couldn't be more wrong, but on the whole I would say the batting average was pretty good.

Chapter 9

THE COASTAL BOAT

From the time of the earliest settlers in Bonne Bay in the early nineteenth century and for the next 125 years there were no roads in the Bonne Bay and Great Northern Peninsula areas. Transportation of people and supplies was therefore done by water. Before the advent of engines for boats water travel depended upon sails. Large schooners from Canada and the United States used Bonne Bay as a base of operations for fishing. They brought supplies with them and either fished themselves or bought from the local fishermen the fish which they had caught. Locally many of the inhabitants built small schooners and the inshore fishery was prosecuted in the traditional dory. The men equipped their dories with sails and became adept at sailing.

In the early days, Bonne Bay was a more important place than the Bay of Islands. The coastal boat service, supplied and operated by the Newfoundland Government, went from St. John's around the northern part of the Island to Bonne Bay then completed the circuit by continuing to Port aux Basques and along the South Coast back to the Avalon Peninsula. Later a service operated on the northern route between St. John's and Corner Brook, returning by the same route. This was supplemented by a boat which sailed from Humbermouth, Bay of Islands to Battle Harbour, servicing specifically the northwest coast and southern part of Labrador.

Both the east and west coasts of the Great Northern Peninsula are difficult to navigate and often stormy and hazardous. Many have been the ships which have been wrecked on these shores. Perhaps the most famous was the loss of the S.S. *Ethie* in December of 1919 at Martin's Point near Sally's Cove north of Bonne Bay.

It is indeed a thrilling story of courage. A Newfoundland dog which was on board the *Ethie* after she was wrecked swam ashore with a line from the vessel. The men on shore used this line to haul ashore a larger line and by this means everyone on the *Ethie* was rescued. A baby on board was transported safely in a mail bag and didn't even get wet. The rusty plates of the *Ethie* are still visible fifty years after she went aground.

The men who sailed the coastal boats gained for themselves a reputation of good seamanship and determination. They knew how important it was for the coastal boats to make their regular ports of call to deliver and pick up the mail, to deliver and pick up supplies, to deliver and pick up passengers. They did everything within reason and safety to make sure that their schedule was complete. It was only for totally adverse weather conditions that they would fail to stop at a designated place.

Many times, because of weather, the boat would be stormbound somewhere on the coast for as much as twenty-one days at a time. I can remember the last boat of the year being stormbound at Woody Point for three weeks over Christmas and the New Year, but determined to make the final voyage because the boat carried mail and supplies which would be badly needed during the ensuing winter.

The captains of the coastal vessels were a breed apart. The coastal boat captains had served their apprenticeships, had their tickets, and had served for many years before they were appointed to the responsible position of captain of one of these ships. However, the captains of many of the local schooners were captains in name only, being perhaps the owners and operators of their own ships, having learned their trade from their fathers or from other local captains under whom they had served. Often they navigated "by guess or by God." They could in fact be compared with the early pilots of aircraft who flew "by the seat of their pants." They may not have known too much about the use of charts and parallel rules, but they could smell their way by day or by night in fog or snow, in fair or foul weather. They knew every shoal, every rock, and every harbour. They often travelled outside Newfoundland waters becoming famous the world over for their ability to handle ships and sail the seas.

In 1945 two ships served the northwest coast. The *Northern Ranger* plied the route from St. John's to Battle Harbour to Corner Brook and return. She was a regular steel hull vessel built in Scotland and delivered in 1936, and was perhaps the most modern of the fleet at that time. The other ship, *Clarenville*, launched in 1944, was the first of the ships known as the "splinter fleet." This was a group of ten wooden hull vessels built during the war, as part of the war effort, at Clarenville in Newfoundland, and designed really for the fishing trade. These were excellent sea boats about 100 feet long and capable of carrying eight passengers.

By 1946, the demand for increased service was growing and so *Clarenville* was used for the run between Corner Brook and Battle Harbour only. The *Northern Ranger*, being a larger vessel, with better accommodation for passengers and sleeping quarters for approximately thirty-two, was greatly in demand during the summer months by tourists who made the trip around the northern part of the Island and southern part of Labrador. The service given by these two boats was quite remarkable when one looks back at the difficulties, but of course there were times when their schedules were disrupted by weather conditions and this tended to frustrate people who were dependent on their service. However, one developed an attitude that if the weather delayed the boat there was nothing anyone could do about it. The *Northern Ranger* under normal circumstances made the round trip in approximately twenty-one days. The *Clarenville* managed her route approximately every ten days.

The arrival of the coastal boat at Norris Point was always a time of great excitement. Proceeding north from Corner Brook the boat would bring long awaited packages and supplies. The boats were always met by almost the entire population at every port of call and it was in fact almost a gala event. As soon as the boat made fast, the children and many adults would climb aboard to talk to the passengers and crew. The unloading would proceed with everybody watching with interest to see what was being landed and to whom it was consigned. Often fresh foods, meat, and vegetables would be seen arriving and people would head for the stores to make their purchases.

When the boats arrived inward bound to Corner Brook they always brought patients heading for the hospital. Often we were aware of the arrival of certain patients for we had been warned of their coming and transportation had been requested. If the case demanded it, I would be there myself to meet the boat to supervise the unloading of a patient. We would get ample warning of the arrival of the boat for we would receive a phone call either from Sally's Cove or Baker's Brook, or from the lighthouse keeper, George Young, at the Rocky Harbour Lighthouse at the entrance to Bonne Bay. From there the vessel would proceed directly to Norris Point and we would know that within an hour the boat would dock. The more work we did in the hospital, and the more confidence the people had in our ability, the more patients arrived. I can well remember the day that the *Clarenville*, with accommodation for eight people, arrived with 120 passengers on board. They had been picked up at all points on the Coast and about eighty got off at Norris Point to visit the hospital. That was a busy day.

It was quite common for the boats to arrive in the middle of the night and in the early days many patients expected to be seen immediately upon arrival. However, it was impossible to rouse the hospital staff in the middle of the night to accommodate the routine investigation of patients who were anxious then to go on to Corner Brook, do their shopping, and be ready to catch the return trip of the coastal boat two or three days later. Often this procedure was reversed and patients would go to Corner Brook, do their shopping, come to Norris Point a few hours before the boat was due and expect to be seen even if it was midnight, so that they could catch the boat and go home. I had to be very firm in laying down certain rules and we would not see routine cases and investigate them to suit their convenience after they had had several days on the town.

Each boat, apart from the crew, carried a mailman. The mailman had his own office aboard where he sorted the mail for delivery at the various settlements as the boat made its trip, and at the same time picked up mail which he would take back for delivery elsewhere. In a small vessel the size of the *Clarenville*, the mailman shared the same cabin as the Purser. I well remember one incident when I was called to the *Clarenville* because there was a very sick woman on board.

When the vessel docked I went aboard and was taken to the Purser's cabin where I found the mailman busy in this little cabin trying to sort the mail and do his work. Lying in the lower bunk was a woman who was unable to move because she was so sick. She weighed approximately 300 pounds. The mailman kindly vacated the cabin while I examined the patient. I ascertained that she needed hospitalization and was completely unable to assist herself. I retreated to the corridor outside and explained the position to the Purser and suggested that he would have to somehow get three or four strong men to help get her on the stretcher which we had brought with us in the hospital truck. I decided that this was a time for brawn and I watched from a safe position outside the cabin at the efforts of the men to get the patient on the stretcher. But for the fact that we were dealing with a very sick woman the efforts of the men to get the patient on the stretcher would have been hilarious. It took nearly half an hour. I thought that I would have at least two of the men as patients for they were in imminent danger of being crushed several times. Then came the difficulty of manoeuvering the stretcher through the cabin door at right angles to turn down the corridor and out onto the deck. Eventually it was accomplished with a great deal of wriggling, shouting, pushing, and with no tempers lost. The patient was then passed over the side of the boat and into the back of the truck which we had backed up to the edge of the wharf.

I knew that we had to face the difficulty of getting this patient into the hospital and so I called for volunteers. Everybody piled into the back of the truck and we took off for the hospital. There was no point in trying to bring the patient through the front door of the hospital. It just was too small. The emergency doors into the ward were opened and the patient made a triumphant entry on her stretcher carried by four strong men who deposited her on the hospital bed. Many other emergency cases arrived on the coastal boats. Patients with surgical emergencies, fractures, severe lacerations, and so on. When the boats arrived during the night with cases such as these, of course, there was no argument. They were dealt with immediately.

I came to know the captains and pursers of the ships quite well and developed a friendship with Captain Walter Blackwood, the skipper for many years of the *Clarenville*. Blackwood was a remarkable man, a great seaman, with deep feeling for people and their problems. I loved the times that he could spare an hour or two and come to the hospital and sit down over a lunch and tell yarns of experiences on the Coast. One day Captain Blackwood arrived and told me he had a severe cold and asked if there was anything I could give him. He didn't want to be knocked off his feet since it was important to keep the vessel on schedule. At this time the use of Vitamin C (Ascorbic Acid) had recently been suggested as a good form of treatment for the common cold. I had used it on a number of patients with what I felt was a degree of success. Certainly it could do no harm because there were no known side effects to the use of this vitamin as a drug, it would not affect one's ability of judgement, or produce any drowsiness. The recommended dose was approximately 500 mg three times a day.

Having treated a number of patients, my stock of 100 mg tablets was depleted, and so I found that I only had 25 mg tablets left. This meant that to take 500 mg I would have to prescribe twenty tablets three times a day. However, when I told Captain Blackwood to take twenty tablets three times a day, his hair stood on end. He was very doubtful about the advisability of acting as captain of the vessel and taking such an apparently stupendous dose so often. I tried to reassure him and explained that he could come to no harm in any way by taking the tablets but that in fact it might do him a great deal of good. And so scratching his head, still somewhat doubtful, he left taking his box of tablets. I looked forward to seeing him on his return to find out what effect they had on him. It was ten days later before the *Clarenville* returned and I made a point of going to see him. He chuckled as I asked him how his cold was. He told me that he trusted me completely but felt so strongly about his responsibility that he took no more than five tablets at a time to make sure that he felt no adverse effects and had gradually increased the dose until he found out as I had told him that he felt no different. He assured me that he felt the treatment had shortened the course of his cold but suggested that I get a supply of the correct strength of drug. He felt that it was probably normal to be unwilling, even scared, to take the quantity I had recommended.

Some months later I had to take him ashore and hospitalize him for a bleeding ulcer, brought on in the first place, I always felt sure, because he was so conscientious and worried about his job. He responded to treatment and was later transferred to an office job in St. John's. I saw him several times when I visited St. John's and, while he was glad for his health to be shore-bound, I know that he missed the excitement of being captain of a coastal vessel.

In the 1950s, the demand still increasing, an even newer vessel, the *Springdale*, was put on the service operating between Lewisporte and Corner Brook. She was able to do this run in approximately eight days and the service improved by that much more. We looked forward to the visit of the *Northern Ranger* and the *Springdale* in summertime for they always carried many tourists, many of them Newfoundlanders and people whom we knew. It was exciting to meet the boats knowing that friends were aboard.

Chapter 10

A. B. HARDING

The Leader, the man who was looked up to by the whole community, and the man whose advice and help in making decisions was sought by all, was A. Bryant Harding. An extremely interesting man who had spent his entire life at Norris Point, he had many positions apart from his main occupation of business man and merchant. He was the Commissioner of Wrecks for the Coast, he was Chairman of the Hospital Committee, he was the Advisor in the area on many matters to the Government, and he was the instigator of many projects over the years.

His father John Harding had come from the South Coast before the end of the nineteenth century and had settled at Norris Point. He was a merchant and appeared to have done very well. At some point he appears to have rendered a valuable service either to the Crown or the British Navy, although the details are very scarce, and as a result he was made the official agent for the British Navy in Newfoundland. This appointment meant that all supplies obtained by the British Navy in Newfoundland would be done through John Harding. Apparently, even if he was not on the spot to deal with the supplying, the commission was credited to his account.

Certainly he was extremely active on the West Coast of Newfoundland where there were two main areas used by the British Navy for fueling and supplying. One was Bonne Bay itself where there was both an official anchorage, this being in the South East Arm, and the other was the fueling depot in Neddy's Harbour.

To this day the markers set up by the British Navy to show the holding grounds exist and can be seen in the South East Arm. In Neddy's Harbour, set into the cliff on the south side of the Harbour and cemented into position can still be found the rings used for the ship's lines. It was in Neddy's Harbour that they took on coal, for in those days the warships were coal fired. John Harding also had built great ovens in which bread was baked and while these no longer exist they were well remembered.

News of the coming of ships often arrived several weeks ahead and preparations were then made for fueling and food supplies to be ready. To provide meat the cattle would be driven south from as far north as River of Ponds, and slaughtered and butchered when the ships arrived. There were occasions when owing to weather or short notice the cattle did not arrive and the ships left without fresh meat. However, the bakery was always able to provide loaves of bread. Whatever vegetables could be found, fish, and other foods were also loaded at these points. A similar situation existed in St. George's Bay which was the other depot used by the British Navy and, therefore, it was necessary for John Harding to make trips to this area to look after the Navy's needs as well.

In this period, the last twenty-five years of the nineteenth century, the West Coast was unspoiled, still in its natural state, and abounding in fish and game. The Navy was aware of this plenty and the ships took advantage of these opportunities to indulge in salmon fishing and hunting and shooting. Local guides were used and it was as a result of being stationed in the West Coast area that eventually saw so many ex-Naval people settle in West Newfoundland. One of the most interesting highlights of this period was the visit to Bonne Bay of the then Prince of Wales, later to become King Edward VII on the death of his mother, Queen Victoria. He was a hearty, fun loving man, and parties were often given on the visiting ships, the outstanding ones of course being when the Prince of Wales himself made his visit. Bryant's mother, Nan, often recounted stories of the parties and the good times that were enjoyed by the local people who were invited. She was proud to relate how she was the belle of the ball and danced with the Prince of Wales. It struck me in later years that there was a great likeness between King Edward VII and A. B. Bryant. All Bryant needed was a beard.

Bryant had over the years collected photographs of the warships which had visited Bonne Bay and had a collection of these photos with the names of the ships. It was always interesting to look at them because they were the early British Naval vessels with both masts and funnels. It was a remarkable record. He also kept a daily diary and had done so all his life. It was a remarkable document and recorded the weather, the state of the fishery, any visiting vessels, and general activities in the area. It was by itself quite a history of his life and times in Bonne Bay.

When he was a young man of about eighteen or nineteen his father died and Bryant immediately took control of the business, went to Canada where he took his course in Business Administration and Commerce, and returned to Norris Point to put into practise what he had learned. He ran a very tight ship and, as he often told me, at the end of each day his records were correct so that if anything happened to him everything was up to date. There were no loose ends dangling. It was after all just plain good business, and the lessons he had learned on the Mainland held him in good stead all his life. He had the ability to detach himself from small things and see the bigger picture. This was important when one lives in a small community. Because of his ability he was accepted and respected as the Leader.

Bryant read a lot and subscribed to newspapers and magazines which kept him abreast of business and news from elsewhere. He built his home during the First World War, and installed one of the earliest coal furnaces on the Coast with radiator hot water heating systems. He also installed the first lighting plant, a gasoline powered generator, which charged wet cell batteries providing 32 volt D.C. current to his home. He had one of the first Kodak 16 mm movie cameras and his films today would be a most valuable record. I can remember seeing one particularly that was a record of a hunting trip made in the 1920s. The advent of radio saw him again in the lead with the first radio on the Coast. He became a source of the news for the community. Bryant was also instrumental in having the telephone line set up from Norris Point to Sally's Cove, and of course had a telephone in his own house.

He had always had his own boat and at the time of our stay in Bonne Bay he had a sleek fast boat named *Tuna*. He used this for business trips to Lomond and to Woody Point, and in years gone by for trips to Curling to visit the bank. In the early days it was common for people to use gold as currency. This resulted in a situation where a man like Bryant Harding, who did business up and down the coast, would find himself with a large amount of money in gold coin, and he often told me of the worry of putting this in a boat and taking it to the bank in Curling and having it counted and deposited. It was Bryant, in fact, who told me the story of the man on the Coast who had stored his money, gold coins, in a small nail keg in his house when it caught on fire. When the searches went through the house ruins they found the remains of this keg and of course the heat had melted the gold. They thought it was useless and the man thought he was ruined. However, it was taken to the bank and, since gold is gold no matter in what form, its worth was still realised.

Bryant's mind was always looking at new ways of making money and at one period he set up a fox ranch at Gad's Harbour. The important part of his thinking was to choose the peninsula that runs out forming Gad's Harbour as location for the ranch. He placed fencing across the narrowest point and buried the wire three feet into the ground. Then he turned the foxes loose on the man-made island from which they could not escape. It now only became a question of watching over them and feeding them and they could survive in a natural habitat. The problem was feeding them, but this was accomplished largely by providing tuna and whale meat, both of which abounded in the Bay. One of Bryant's movies showed the catching of the tuna which was done in a way similar to whaling for he had mounted on the bow of the *Tuna* a platform extending out over the water from which a man could throw an iron tip spear with a rope attached. The boat would move up into a school of tuna and the man would then spear a tuna which would promptly dive taking the line with it. However, on the end of the line was a metal drum brightly painted and when the tuna was spent and died the can would mark the spot and it could be retrieved at leisure and the tuna hauled aboard. Using this method meant that the boat could then follow the school and perhaps kill several tuna in one foray. Interestingly, tuna fishing at that time was not used as a sport by many people. President Franklin D. Roosevelt apparently had visited Bonne Bay in the 1930s to indulge in tuna fishing and presumably was successful. Still, the main use of the tuna was to feed the foxes. While the market for fox skins remained good, it was a lucrative business but eventually the fad passed and with it the fox ranch went out of existence also.

Bryant married during the First World War. His wife Emma was from Woody Point and had been a telegraph operator for a short time while we were living at Norris Point. They had two sons, Milton and John. Milton joined the R.C.A.F. in 1940, was later shot down and captured, and spent two years as a prisoner of war in Germany. He returned when released after the war's end and went to live in British Columbia. The other son John was a sickly boy, pale and thin, and with little strength. Bryant and Em looked after him carefully and no cost was too much in helping him gather his strength and fight off illness.

One of the greatest achievements of Bryant's life was his convincing of the Commission of Government during the 1930s of the necessity to build a hospital in Bonne Bay. He chaired the committee which decided that the hospital should be built at Norris Point on the north side of the Bay to provide the greatest coverage and easiest accessability for those people whom it would serve living on the Northwest Coast. If the hospital were placed on the Woody Point side, for six weeks of the year it would be impossible to reach and would deny services to those people living north of Bonne Bay. However if the hospital were in Norris Point, it would not deprive the people on the Woody Point side as much because they could, although with some difficulty, at least reach Deer Lake or Corner Brook where medical services were available. It was agreed by the Commission of Government that the people would be given a hospital but at the same time they had to undertake certain things themselves.

As Chairman of the Hospital Committee, Bryant was responsible for seeing that everybody in the district contributed either money, materials, or labour, so that it truly became a project belonging to all the people in the area. The word was sent out and from every community somebody was put on the committee and was responsible for seeing that the people did their share.

The construction of the Bonne Bay Hospital began in 1938, and the hospital was complete and finished at the end of 1939. Many are the stories told by Bryant about the construction and effort contributed by the people. Many times fittings or bits and pieces would be found missing or the orders had not been given. Sometimes somebody had forgotten to order something and Bryant himself often came to the rescue with bits and pieces he dug up in his own store or basement. However the hospital was completed, the people did take part, and looking back there is no doubt that he was the driving spirit behind this outstanding example of a regional effort which was so beneficial to the whole area. Bryant knew everybody in the district, knew them up and down the Coast, knew their fathers and grandfathers, and was most helpful in providing information and assistance in many aspects of running the hospital.

Occasionally we ran into problems in our own house and he was always ready and willing to be of assistance. His home was open to us at all times, and I can't remember visiting the Point without dropping in, even though it was just for a brief ten second visit, at least to say hello to him and his wife. He was full of stories and had an infectious laugh, hearty and deep. He enjoyed telling stories and enjoyed hearing them in turn. To my amazement he had investigated me fully and when I arrived at Norris Point he already knew all about my family and was able to tell me a great deal about myself which surprised me. He was delighted that I was a Newfoundlander. While the people of the area were desperately anxious to have a doctor, they were even more pleased to find out that the doctor was one of their own.

Bryant's concern and assistance went in all directions and one of the most obvious was his concern for the sick. He was always around to meet the ferry and to be of assistance if anybody needed shelter or transportation or accommodation. This generosity applied to the coastal boats and Bryant was known throughout Newfoundland by business men who travelled that way. As well, he himself made business trips to Corner Brook, St. John's, and Canada.

Chapter 11

PRE-CONFEDERATION

The years immediately following the end of the war in 1945 were the end of an era, but little did anyone realise it at the time. Since Newfoundland's discovery by John Cabot in 1497 and the first attempts of colonization by John Guy in 1610, we had been Britain's first colony and therefore the oldest member of the British Empire. We had gained Dominion status and stood shoulder to shoulder with other Dominions such as Canada, Australia, New Zealand, South Africa, India, and were proud of our recognition. Our Prime Minister took his place at the Empire Conference of Prime Ministers and had the same authority and voting power as the others.

Then came financial disaster in 1933 with the resulting loss of Responsible Government. Newfoundland was bankrupt. Commission of Government was installed in 1934, consisting of three men appointed by Great Britain and three Newfoundlanders chosen in consultation with the Governor. The six members were chaired by the Governor of Newfoundland. The Commission had to deal with the financial crisis, which was worsened by the Great Depression.

The task which faced the Commission of Government was extremely difficult. With little money to run the country and unemployment at its height, times were indeed very hard for our people. At the worst point of the crisis the unemployed received the magnificent sum of six cents per day per person. It was a miracle that we survived. The war, however, brought employment and prosperity to Newfoundland. The fishery was prosecuted at full strength, for food was desperately needed. The two paper mills in Grand Falls and Corner Brook were in full operation for their products were required. Men worked long hours in the forest for timber and at the pit props.

Many thousands of Newfoundlanders flocked to the colours to serve in all theatres of war in every arm of the forces. They joined the Armed Forces of Great Britain, Canada, and the United States. Most sought after were the Seamen, who Winston Churchill described as "the best small boat men in the world."

While rationing was introduced in Newfoundland and many goods were in short supply, at least there was full employment and the country prospered. By 1949 when Newfoundland entered Confederation with Canada there was a surplus in the bank of twenty million dollars. This was indeed a large amount of money at that time.

When I returned from the war in 1945 to take up my duties in Bonne Bay, I had come from Britain where all manner of goods were in very short supply. Particularly food was scarce and it was with amazement and delight that we found a great deal more available in Canada and Newfoundland than we had received overseas. While there may not have been a great variety of foods at least there was plenty to eat and we felt that it made up in some way for our isolation. I well remember the first steak which I had after arriving back, something we had been unable to get for five years. By present day standards it was indeed very small but by the standards at that time it was a large steak. Because we had conditioned ourselves to rationing I was unable to eat it all. It seemed criminal that I would have to leave any part of it on my plate and I felt very guilty but had no alternative. I was extremely worried about my inability to deal with that piece of meat for many months afterwards and even today I have my doubts.

However, in 1945 Newfoundland was still independent and general conditions were still very poor. This situation was immediately evident in the degree of apathy which was evident in the people. It was quite a common sight to see a row of men sitting on their heels with their backs to a fence or railing idly passing the time of day and quite content not to move for hours. Time meant very little and was used in a common expression, "there's plenty of time." Another expression which clearly indicated a degree of apathy was "Come here I want you," for they had neither the inclination nor the energy to move but expected someone else to do it instead. There was no rush to do anything because it really didn't matter whether it was done today, tomorrow, or next week or next month.

Many of these people had not had the educational opportunities which exist today nor was the Legislation in existence which kept them at school beyond twelve or thirteen years of age. It was common for a man to take his boys out of school when they were old enough to help in the boats or in the fields and they had to pull their weight as soon as they were old enough to do so. Many of them never got beyond grade three or four at school and illiteracy was quite common.

Being a fisherman or woodsman was hard work and the years of the Depression and War had taken their toll through illness or lack of nutrition with the result that the people aged early and men looked worn out before they were forty. On the other hand the birth rate in Newfoundland was extremely high and by the time a woman was thirty she often had ten or twelve children and herself looked like a woman of fifty or sixty. It was not easy to support a large family on the small incomes that were available in those days. The average income for a hard working Newfoundlander was about $500 a year. Many, of course, made less than this and most neither felt nor saw the actual cash.

In each settlement there were usually two or three merchants who sold food and supplies and bought the fish and lumber as the case may be. The people were in effect employed by the merchants because whatever they earned went on the books and they took it back in the form of purchases. This system received severe criticism over the years for it was felt that the merchants were using people in a feudalistic manner. But in fact to understand the system one had to live in the midst of it and see how it worked. I found that the majority of the local merchants were honest men caught in a sort of trap, trying to make a living, but responsible for supporting many families who had no other means of support. The trap was particularly evident when a man died, for there was no way that the merchant could get any return on money owed from the widow and children. In this case it was common practice to write off the account and support the widow and family as best could be managed.

It was a very different story when one considered the merchants in St. John's who supplied the merchants in the outports. The St. John's merchants really did want their pound of flesh and saw that they got it. If there was a villain anywhere it was the one in St. John's for he had no feeling or interest in the difficulties of people affected by death or illness or inability to provide a living and pay bills. The merchants away indeed got rich and lived in luxury. I gained a great respect for the local merchants who played such a large part in supporting their communities. When things were good they had good times but when things were bad they suffered with the people in their own community. They fought the battles for their people with the merchants in St. John's to provide the necessities of life for all.

Newfoundland's Old Age Pensions at this time consisted of fifteen dollars per quarter per couple. This was sixty dollars for a couple for a year. They were not eligible for the pension until they were seventy-five or over, they had to undergo a form of means test, and they had to provide a certificate of inability to work for which the doctor was entitled to charge them twenty-five cents. I would never bring myself to charge any of these old people twenty-five cents knowing it had to come out of such a small sum on which they had somehow to survive from one year to the next. As they grew old and less able to help themselves, they had to survive on practically nothing and it was recognised that their families would help supply them. One would often see a daughter going to the house with a bowl of soup or a pie or a loaf of bread or something which would help to keep them supplied for a day or two. The hardest hit of course was the widow or widower living alone who had to make do on even less. They suffered terribly. Not only had they to feed and clothe themselves but during the winter they had to somehow provide fuel for warmth and oil for light.

The ordinary family whose earner was sick or unemployed was also in an extremely difficult position. The rules at that time gave the welfare officer no leeway whatsoever and the regulations stated clearly that to be eligible for welfare assistance the recipient had to have nothing. This meant even greater hardship for they were forced to sell a cow if they had one, the hens, the sheep, the horse, anything that could be sold until they were in fact completely destitute at which point they could receive some assistance. The assistance was extremely meager and nickerly. It was common to see the children without shoes, the girls wearing dresses made out of flour sacks. In fact, the flour came in sacks with the pattern already printed on it. They were used for curtains, for pillow cases, for tablecloths, and for clothing. It was common also to see the children going to school carrying a couple of logs which would be used to keep the school warm during the day.

The diet which most families enjoyed was a hard one, but one which they had grown up with and to which they were used. Regularly every family had tea, molasses, flour, potatoes, turnips, cabbage, canned milk, and some sugar. Salt beef, salt pork, salt fish were the main sources of protein. Cod, salmon, trout, herring in season, with seal and lobster when available supplemented the staples. Sometimes an occasional beaver was added to the menu and, with luck, occasionally a duck or some bull birds.

Each family had its own garden and raised its own potatoes, turnips, and cabbage. Most families had a horse to help bring in the firewood. There were scattered hens and sheep in each settlement. The sheep, of course, provided the wool which was used to knit socks and sweaters. Some families were fortunate in having a cow, which provided milk, and the odd house had a goat. Strangely, I don't recollect seeing any pigs although I knew that it was in years gone by the recognised thing to have a pig which was killed for Christmas. Christmas itself didn't mean turkey and plum pudding; it just meant another day as usual as far as food was concerned.

The homes were wooden and were usually constructed on wooden posts consisting of one story bungalows with the main entrance always being through the kitchen. The newer houses had a front door facing the road but never had steps completed. That was always to be done when they got around to it. I learned early that the front steps of houses were to be avoided. The older homes had often been built with front steps and a small veranda or porch. However, it was customary for everyone to use the kitchen door located at either the side or the back of the house and the front door was usually kept for a visit from either the minister or the doctor, and so was rarely used. After I had put my foot through either the steps or the planking on the veranda in a couple of houses I decided that it would be wise to follow the route used by everybody else, so, to the dismay of many families, I insisted on using the same door as the rest of the family.

The porch or veranda was often called a bridge. This term led to some difficulty in the early days before I became used to the expression for it was not uncommon that a child would fall off the railing of this bridge and perhaps sustain some injury. I was greatly concerned when I was told that a child had fallen off a bridge, figuring that they meant a bridge over a river which would be a considerable drop. However, it didn't take long to recognise this expression. While certainly some people sustained severe injuries, the majority of them were minor.

The kitchen in every house served as the main gathering room. In winter time this was the warmest room, for the fire was kept going and the cooking was done here. Mostly wood stoves were used, which usually had a line hung up over them on which mitts and socks and other articles of clothing were hung to dry. It was not uncommon to find a dog or a cat, or even both, lying underneath the stove enjoying the warmth. Wedged behind or at the side between the stove and the wall was often a wooden box made into a cot containing a baby. There was no doubt that any child would keep warm there, but it is amazing that more of them weren't cooked. A small entrance porch by the kitchen door usually contained a supply of wood and splits, a bucket or two of water, the garbage pail, rubber boots and bucksaw, and many other items used daily.

In winter time the hens and sheep would not be far from the door and, because of the depth of snow, often one walked into the garden of the house over a fence without realising it lay underneath. The main reason the houses were raised on posts was not only to keep them off the ground and away from the damp, but to raise them sufficiently that the necessity of continuous digging out during winter was removed. Few houses had proper basements, the open space beneath the house usually being boarded around to protect it from the cold winter winds. It also provided shelter for the animals and took the place, in many cases, of a barn. Wood for use in heating and cooking was stacked in a standing pile similar to a wigwam and there was a continuous chore often left to the children and sometimes the wife of cutting this wood in suitable lengths using a bucksaw.

Most men had a shotgun or rifle and sometimes both. These weapons were either hung in the kitchen or just thrown in the porch. Too often they were uncared for, never cleaned or oiled, and left to rust from one season to the next. As a result of this lack of care, occasionally combined with the tampering of the charge in a cartridge (which they often opened and doubled), there would be a bad accident when a gun would explode. Injuries were sustained to hands, faces, and eyes particularly. However, people learned rapidly that the manufacturers knew how to make the shells. After a few mishaps, they left the cartridges alone. There were still a few "swiling" guns still around. These were extremely long barrels, sometimes as much as six feet, and operated with the use of a stick with a fork which was used for resting the barrel. They were muzzle loaders and so the hunter went with his horn of powder and his bag of shot and did his own loading.

Most men looked forward to taking a week or ten days in the fall and joining with a few of their companions on a rabbit hunt. They would leave for their favourite hunting spots and set up camp, set out their snares, or slips as they were called, which they then visited daily. Sometimes they could bag a moose or two and combine the hunt with some birds as well. There was of course difficulty bringing the meat out and the wiser hunters tried to bag their kill in an appropriate spot. In winter time often the men came across moose which were "yarded." This is a self-explanatory word. In the deep snow the animals had pounded it down resulting in a wall of snow being left on the perimeter. They had in fact walled themselves in and put themselves in a yard. They were easy prey for the hunters who simply appeared on the edge of the snow and shot them.

The hardest working men were continually on the go all year around. While they may have had little, at least they lived fairly well with a varied diet of fish and meat which they could often obtain themselves, vegetables which they grew themselves, heat which they obtained from wood they cut themselves, and many of the clothes which they made themselves. There was no such thing as store bought bread. Every household made its own. Butter was rarely available and every family ate margarine. Jams they made themselves for the family turned out in force at berry picking time when they went to their favourite spot for blueberries, raspberries, strawberries, and bakeapples. Partridge berries were scarce and usually we got our supply from Labrador, brought in the fall by the Organs when they returned from Red Bay for the winter.

It had been suggested to us that it would be wise to bottle meat and chicken every year in the fall and for the first two or three years we tackled this tremendous task. At the end of three years we had such an uneaten supply of bottled chicken that it did us for the next five years and we found that it was just as simple to wait until we needed a chicken before we killed and ate it.

Few homes had indoor toilet facilities or running water. Equally as few had electricity. It was common practise for several homes to use a common spring or well and the water was fetched in buckets. Lighting was of course by oil lamp, and the Aladdin Lamp particularly was very powerful. Most homes had a storm lantern for emergency purposes as well as candles and flashlights. However, it was rare to meet anybody even on the darkest night who was carrying a lantern. There were no street lights but in winter time the lights from the homes on the road would reflect on the snow and it was surprising how one adapted to the dark and made use of even the slightest glimmer. Winter time could be quite pleasant at night with a clear sky, a bright moon, and the stars in the sky and the crisp snow underfoot. It was beautiful and exhilarating.

I was surprised at the general feeling about Government. As it was explained to me, people in the outports of Newfoundland had always looked to Government to provide certain things, and they knew from experience that the best time to ask for and expect to receive what they wanted was just prior to an election when campaigning was in full swing and promises were being made in all directions. One of the most sought after benefits from Government was a well in one's own garden. It took me a long time to understand why this particular thing was being asked from Government as a personal request when it seemed only right that this became an individual responsibility and should not have rested on Government shoulders.

However, looking at the general picture, there was very little that Government actually did for so many people.

Government was responsible for the provision of a Government Wharf, for the post and telegraph office and the delivery of mail, for welfare such as it was, and, prior to the Cottage Hospital, for a very small portion of health services. The lighthouses and beacon were the responsibility of the Marine Department of Government, as was the Coastal Boat Service. The Newfoundland Railway was owned and operated by the Government. There was no trans-insular road connecting Port aux Basques to St. John's. Such a road was not completed until the 1960s. However, there were local roads and that was shared responsibility. A local roads committee or board existed in most areas, was given a grant each year by Government, and to this the local people made their contribution in kind, for the rate paid to road workers under these grants was about half what was the normal wage rate. Their work consisted in little more than ditching and filling of pot holes and, except for a few major projects, could only be referred to as maintenance work. There were few new roads built outside the Avalon Peninsula before Confederation.

Until Confederation, Newfoundland used the British rule of the road with all vehicles driving on the left hand side. Since most of the vehicles were imported from the United States this meant that the driver was sitting on the left hand side of his vehicle and driving on the left hand side of the road which put him at a disadvantage when trying to pass another vehicle going in the same direction. When we joined Confederation we changed this rule and drive now on the right hand side of the road. The rule really never bothered me because at most we had the hospital truck and the jeep and over the years always managed to miss one another!

The Public Works Department was responsible for the maintenance of buildings which consisted largely of post and telegraph offices, magistrates houses, Cottage Hospitals once they had been built, doctors' houses, nursing stations, Newfoundland Constabulary Buildings, and the General Hospital and the Hospital for Mental Diseases. A few other public buildings, including the magistrates' courses, were also their responsibility.

The Newfoundland Constabulary and the Newfoundland Ranger Force were the responsibility of Government, the former being in the major centres, and the latter existing in the outports. With our entry into Confederation the Ranger Force became integrated and absorbed by the Royal Canadian Mounted Police, and the Government of Newfoundland entered into a contract with the RCMP to police the entire province. The Newfoundland Constabulary withdrew from the rest of the Province and became the St. John's Police Force.

When we were a separate country we operated our own customs and excise department. Located in various parts were the official Ports of Entry with an office and Customs Officers. While we operated our own Income Tax Department the majority of Newfoundlanders didn't make enough money in the course of a year to be eligible to pay any taxes. However, there were hidden taxes with a Government Tax on such things as liquor, tobacco, and gasoline.

The arrival in the area of a representative of Government always stirred up a great deal of interest but because of the difficulties which the Government had faced since the Commission took over there was a great deal of discontent. It must also be borne in mind that Newfoundland had always been independent and people resented the imposition of any form of government upon them which they had not chosen themselves. One incident occurred in Bonne Bay when one of the Commissioners visited and incurred the wrath of the local people because the Commissioners had refused a request which had been made to them. To make their point and nail it down without any doubt the men decided that they would take a form of action which could not be misunderstood. When the Commissioners' boat arrived and he refused, in any way, to agree to their demand the men promptly hauled the boat high on the beach and said that there it would remain until the Government agreed to their request. The boat, which was a large cabin cruiser and had brought the Commission from Bay of Islands, was more than the small crew of two or three could launch single-handed. The local men were adamant, no agreement no boat. It was resolved eventually when a promise was given by the Commissioner that without fail on his return he would do all he could to change the Commission's mind on this particular request. Accepting this as better than nothing the boat was refloated and he was allowed to go on his way. He kept his word, so that in due course the Commission complied with the request.

Prior to the building of the Pulp and Paper Mill in Corner Brook in 1923 and its coming into operation in 1925, the main industry in the area had been the fishery. The West Coast abounds with all kinds of fish and a lucrative area was the Lobster Fishery. Most families were involved. However, the demand for men to work in the woods had come as another source of income for many men. At the beginning, it was impossible for men to work at the fishery during certain seasons and then during the cutting and driving season to work in the woods. Over the years, some had shown a preference for the fishery and others for the woods. Some, however, tried to combine both which made a very hard and difficult life.

Both forms of work, the fishery and the woods, were extremely hard and the men tended to age very rapidly. The fishery was prosecuted in almost any weather, and under sometimes most difficult conditions. Strangely few people had ever learned to swim. Wrapped in their heavy oilskins the men often faced the hazard of falling overboard.

Working in the woods had its problems as well for the men were plagued with flies during the summer months and with difficult snow and ice conditions in winter. Their living conditions were very primitive and their meals crude. Their work was done with an ax and a bucksaw which represented the hardest kind of manual labour. The men were unused to being away from home for any length of time and the families were unused to being without their men. It was not unusual for a man to only manage three weeks at a time before he had to take time off and go home to see that his family was well and look to their needs. This made difficulties for camp operators, for the men would decide on the spur of the moment very often that they would be leaving so the operator could never be sure how many men he would have from one week to the next. The wood was cut, limbed, piled, and scaled. It was then hauled by horse and sleigh to river points where it was driven down river in the spring. It was collected in booms at the mouth of the river and transferred to towing booms which were hauled by tug to Corner Brook. A large operation took place for many years in the Bonne Bay area with the wood being driven down the Lomond River and thence taken by tug to Corner Brook. This same operation was of course taking place in other parts of the West Coast, the other big operation being at Hawke's Bay. An equally big operation was taking place near Deer Lake with the logs being driven down the Upper Humber River, towed across Deer Lake, and driven down the Lower Humber to the holding booms at the mouth of the river. Many men from the Bonne Bay and St. Barbe areas worked in the camps in these two areas. Saturday night was always a big night on the ferry as the men came out of the woods and headed for home either for the weekend or a longer period.

The Lobster Fishery was prosecuted in the spring of the year and the lobsters were caught and brought to collection points where they were picked up by boats from Gloucester, Massachusetts, where there was an ever-growing demand for lobsters. In a good season men who worked hard and had a successful year were known to have made as much as $3000 in an eight week period. This amount may sound large but it had to be shared between two men, a portion went to the holding area, and they had their expenses of gas, twine, bait, the lobster pots, and the maintenance of their boats. When all this was taken into consideration, lobster certainly was a good source of income but would not see them through the year without other additional means of earning money.

At Norris Point, Arthur Caines had a fish plant and spent a lifetime developing and refining methods of curing and packing fish. He imported a fish drying machine and also devised a method for canning caplin which was very successful. After trying many different ways of preserving this fish he found that cotton seed oil appeared to be the one vehicle which could contain caplin without deterioration. The plant packed all kinds of fish and included seal meat as well. With Arthur's son, Gordon, and Clarence Laing the three were a going concern. Clarence was the engineer, imaginative and inventive, and he kept the equipment and machinery in operation at all times. Arthur and Gordon served as researchers and marketers. Their plant employed a large number of men and women and bought fish from all around the bay, whatever was in season.

Just as they began to make their mark, tragedy struck. Gordon learned that he was a diabetic, became depressed, and disappeared one night never to be found. The whole settlement was saddened by his unfortunate loss. Shortly afterwards his father, Arthur, developed a blood condition which proved incurable. He was soon gone also. There was no one to carry on the business, the doors were closed, and it slowly rusted and disintegrated. A powerful source of employment and income was gone from the district.

We had always been fond of fish and were extremely fond of herring roes. In the early days after our arrival in 1945 the herring fishery was prosecuted in Bonne Bay, in the spring and in the fall when the herring struck in. At these times all the boats were occupied with fishing and all hands in the settlement set to work cleaning and packing the herring. The herring fishery was done under the massive United Nations Relief and Rehabilitation Administration (UNRRA) Program which provided food for countries across the world in dire need. I used to watch the men and women work at cleaning the herring and I noticed that the roes were always discarded along with heads and entrails. I asked about this, for this is a great delicacy and most nutritious. I was told that only rarely would the people eat this and that I was very welcome to whatever I wanted. There was always amazement when I would go into the shed and ask if the roes could be dropped in a bucket which I took with me. With a shrug of their shoulders the workers would be only too pleased to comply and in no time my bucket would be full of roes. It would be a great night at our house and in fact for several days we would gorge ourselves on these delicious roes.

Strangely, within three years the herring had deserted Bonne Bay and for the rest of our time there they never struck in the bay again. However, they were found at the mouth of the bay and outside. A similar thing happened, I am told, in Bay of Islands and no one could ever produce an explanation as to why this happened. I doubt that it was pollution because the pollution problem had not arisen in those days in the Bonne Bay Area. It was a loss, to say the least.

Little farming was done on a scale bigger than the family plot. Some families had a field each which they used for cultivating potatoes, cabbage, turnips which were the mainstay of their diet. It was common practice to plant the potatoes on May 24 or thereabouts and to dig them approximately the end of October. Usually the children were taken out of school for planting and digging times and the workforce consisted of the entire family. The planting was quite simple. A horse and plough operated usually by the man of the house made a furrow, and the family followed planting the potatoes which had been carefully prepared. The eyes of the seed potatoes were cut out and placed in position gently. A second furrow turned over on top of the first and this automatically buried the seed, prepared it, and left it growing until harvest. The harvesting could be done simply by running the plough up the furrow which threw the grown potatoes onto the surface of the earth. However, some people used older methods which consisted of digging a trench and placing the earth on top of the seeds which were laid in position on the ground. This process meant a series of high mounds were built containing the seed, with deep ditches on either side. This was a slow and labour intensive method and an effort was made by Government to help the people develop and use the easier method. An Agricultural Councillor was placed in the district whose job it was to explain and demonstrate to farmers how to grow their food more easily. His was a long job for they were slow to accept newer methods preferring to stick to their known and tried ways. He finally convinced them by a practical demonstration whereby he himself ploughed a field, set his potatoes, and then at the end of the year dug the field and compared his return with theirs. Of course, every planting was accompanied by fertilizer, usually synthetic but often kelp collected from the beaches. The presence of the Councillor helped to improve the consistency of farming and allowed the people some measure of security. They would have vegetables during the summer and a store put down for the winter months.

People typically spent most of their indoor time in the kitchen. The front room, which was a dining room or lounge, was rarely used. However, the front room did serve as a place to receive a visit from the Minister or by the doctor, but mostly for weddings or funerals. A funeral was a very special time. The body was laid in its coffin in the front room and the community gathered to pay tribute and talk about the deceased. Children ran in and out curious to see what was going on and look at the corpse. They would gather outside and whisper and giggle. There were rarely fresh flowers available and it was common practice for the women to make wreaths artificially. They were simple but fitting tributes and they stood up to the weather on the grave. Often there was no minister available for the funeral service, so the local teacher would have to perform it. The coffin was handmade by a local carpenter, for there was never any money to be spent unnecessarily. It was simple and dignified but stark in its reality. When it was the wage earner who had died I always worried and wondered how the widow and children would manage. Times would be difficult for them. But usually their relatives and friends rallied around and they always managed to make out. The oldest boy or boys at this point would suddenly become men and have to take on the burden and responsibility. They would leave school and get to work many years before they should rightly have done so. It was accepted as a part of life.

One of the biggest events which could happen in any settlement was a wedding. Until recent years there was a great deal of inter-marriage in settlements brought about mainly because of the difficulties of transportation. It was many miles from one settlement to the next, often without roads, and since travel was mainly done by water there were times when it was very difficult or impractical to make the trip on a regular basis. There was little entertainment in those days, for few people had radios and the travelling movie might only come once or twice a year. These people were not given to reading much but they did enjoy a good time. And so the expression came into being whenever there was going to be a party or a dance or a wedding that there was going to be a "time." The whole community looked forward to a "time" and everybody turned out in their best clothes to take part. The older men and women often spent the entire evening just sitting around the sides of the hall watching the proceedings for the whole evening. The children from the youngest up were all welcome and usually made a fair nuisance of themselves in the early hours as they ran around the hall regardless of people who were trying to dance. The music was usually supplied by a fiddler; a settlement might have two or three so that usually one was available. There was no such thing as a band or orchestra nor had the travelling groups of musicians started yet. A common form of dancing was square dancing which involved the majority of those present at the "time." However, a very popular item was a tap dance or shoe dance which is common in our outports and is usually done to the fast rhythm of a jig.

The "time" would start at 9 or 10 p.m. and would go through the night as long as the fiddler had the energy to keep playing and the dancers had strength enough left to dance. Tea and coffee and other refreshments would be served by the women, and the men would slip out for something a little stronger which was hidden not too far away. Rarely did trouble develop at these affairs and apart from being tired, the people showed few untoward effects the next day.

When a "time" was proceeded by a wedding, the wedding itself usually took place in the afternoon in the church and the wedding party, family, and invited guests then repaired to the bride's home for the wedding supper. The food which was prepared was sufficient for anyone who cared to drop in, although the bridal party and especially invited guests were seated and served first. From the time they had finished eating until the supply of food ran out anyone was welcome and, in fact, was expected to sit down and have a hearty meal. The table was always piled high with food and the women were busy in the kitchen keeping up with the demand.

On occasion the bride and groom, who were always seated at the head of the table, would be flanked by one or more of their children. Marriage ceremonies often had to await the arrival of a minister on his visits, which were not always frequent. Nobody ever took any notice of this and I never heard it mentioned.

Although I was nearly always invited as a special guest to these affairs, I found that my presence tended to dampen the gaiety of the occasion. Presumably because I represented some kind of authority being the doctor in charge of the hospital, too often the people felt they had to behave in a very dignified manner when I was there. Approaching the hall we would hear the sounds of revelry and dancing but as we entered the room there would be an awkward feeling as the people weren't sure whether they should carry on or not. We always felt that the best thing to do was to pay our respects and leave quickly so that everybody knew we had done them the courtesy of the visit but would not inflict ourselves and diminish the enjoyment which came all to infrequently.

The first wedding I ever attended in the outports was in 1945 at Port Saunders. I had arrived there on my first visit and been extremely busy seeing patients. After a day's work, I was tired but delighted to receive an invitation to the wedding banquet. I knew nobody in the area but the nurse suggested it would be a good form of public relations and that the people would be very honoured to have the doctor drop in and have a meal. After I finished my work, I made my way to the house which wasn't difficult to find because the entire settlement was converging on that particular house and the noise could be heard for a great distance. When I arrived at the front door there was a fair crowd waiting to get in but the passageway opened immediately as I was recognised and voices passed the word from one to one "the doctor's here." Somebody appeared in the doorway and shook my hand and invited me in and immediately on entering the house the noise and conversation subsided and I was taken to meet the bride. A pretty girl dressed in her white wedding gown greeted me very shyly and I expressed my best wishes and asked where her husband was. A great deal of whispering ensued and finally the young man was produced supported on each side by two of his friends and it was apparent at once that he was in a complete stupor from drunkenness. Having literally shown me the bridegroom they then deposited him back on a couch and I was invited to take my place at the table. The fact that somebody was already sitting on the seat and eating a meal meant nothing. He was yanked out and his plate removed and I was invited to sit in that place. I was embarrassed at this happening but knew it would be worse if I refused. I took my place at the table full of strangers. They were perhaps even more embarrassed than I, if that was the possible, but made the best efforts they could to make me feel at home. I was showered with salt and pepper, mustard and pickles, milk, bread, and sugar from all parts of the table as they tried to make sure that I had everything I needed. From the kitchen was produced the largest plate of food I think I had ever seen and I must admit that I did justice to their efforts. My policy had been that being the only doctor I didn't drink, so I stuck to my tea and after a suitable period, having talked to a few people and knowing that I had a heavy day ahead of me on the morrow, I thanked them, again wished them well, and left.

A similar format for wedding banquets was observed in all the settlements. A great deal of work went into the preparation and serving of the food and the objective was to have everybody come in for the occasion and enjoy themselves. They were truly memorable days for the bride and groom, although it was usually the bride who had the memories. Too often the groom celebrated too well and remembered little afterwards.

Chapter 12

CONFEDERATION

The war was over, things were rapidly getting back to normal, Newfoundland had a healthy surplus in the bank, and there was a general feeling spreading across the country that we should now consider governing our own affairs once again. It was now twelve years since we had lost the right of self-government. We had played an important part in the world conflict which had just ended, for not only had thousands of our men and women served in the Armed Forces, but Newfoundland itself had become a strategic centre as a naval guardian of the Atlantic. As well, the massive Trans-Atlantic air base at Gander had ferried thousands of planes to Britain to maintain Allied air supremacy. Newfoundland had contributed a great deal, both in men and resources, towards the war effort.

It was agreed, therefore, that a National Convention would be called into session to determine the future path of Newfoundland. For this purpose election of members to sit at the National Convention would take place. This was the first election held since 1932, and the art of politics, elections, and all the backroom strategy had become an almost lost art. In due course a date was set so that the people of Newfoundland would elect from their districts members who would represent them at the National Convention.

I was extremely interested in this whole business and desperately anxious to become involved. I had very strong feelings on the matter but there was no way that I could see which would enable me to take an active part. In my position as doctor in charge of the hospital I had responsibilities which I could not neglect, and although it was the general opinion that the National Convention would probably only be in session for a maximum of six weeks, there was always the possibility that it would take longer. Although I had been in Bonne Bay for about a year and a half, I still felt that I did not have the experience to be acceptable as a candidate for the district. I also felt an even greater responsibility to continue with my work in the medical field instead. I discarded the idea of taking part, although it was with a considerable degree of reluctance.

There was no talk in the district of a candidate and none appeared from elsewhere to offer himself as a candidate for St. Barbe. There was a rumour that Ed Roberts, a merchant at Woody Point, would offer himself but it was apparently no more than a rumour. Nomination day at last arrived with the deadline set for 2 p.m. We were all anxious that afternoon to hear if in fact anybody had been nominated. It was with relief that we learned by telegraph message shortly afterward that Ed Roberts had walked in ten minutes before the deadline and been officially nominated. Since his was the only nomination, there would be no voting. He was thereby elected by acclamation. I was disappointed on the one hand for I felt it better to have a contest. On the other hand, I was relieved to know that at least we had a representative who would sit at the National Convention and represent our district.

In the meantime, before the National Convention convened, a great deal of discussion took place throughout Newfoundland as to what might develop. There appeared to be two choices. Continuation of the present form of Commission Government or a return to Responsible Government. The doubts expressed by many people concerned the ability of Newfoundlanders to provide the men who were capable and responsible enough to operate our own government. The political patronage which had been the custom in previous years had obviously done a fair amount of harm and led to a degree of corruption which was no longer acceptable. We had suffered severely in the depression and people were not happy at the thought that we once again might face similar hard times. The Conservative Party which had been in power in 1932 had earned the reputation which labelled "Tory times as hard times." This suggested that people might not be willing to accept a Conservative Government. It was also considered that the Conservative Party was made up largely of the merchants from St. John's. This confirmed the people's worst fears that times might get harder as the merchants tried to line their own pockets. In due course, the National Convention convened in session. The Newfoundland Broadcasting Corporation arranged daily broadcasts. Although there was a fair amount of newspaper coverage, in those days the paper was published once a week in Corner Brook and was always four or five days reaching us.

However, the radio produced for us each evening coverage of the days' proceedings of the Convention which was taking place in the House of Assembly chamber in the Colonial Building, St. John's. The recordings were played each night and engendered a great deal of interest. People gathered wherever there was a radio to listen. I am sure that many people bought radios to hear the broadcasts, this being the lever many families needed to convince themselves that they needed a radio.

Instead of the National Convention sitting for six weeks, or perhaps even twelve, the debate raged on and the Convention dragged out for eighteen months. The issues were no longer plain choice between a continuation of Commission Government or a return to Responsible Government, but now two other issues were thrown in: Confederation with Canada or economic union with the United States. The latter issue was not taken very seriously, for Newfoundland by tradition was both independent and tightly tied to the Mother Country, Britain.

The new issue of Confederation with Canada had been dealt with twice previously in 1868 and again in 1895 and had been rejected both times. It seemed likely now that it would be rejected again. However, a new factor had emerged to sway the people: the voice of J. R. Smallwood, the National Convention Representative from the Gander District. A well-read man, a journalist, and union organizer, a broadcaster known throughout Newfoundland and latterly a farmer–for during the war he was in the business of pig farming at Gander–he was extremely well-grounded in our history and knew many thousands of Newfoundlanders, many of those by first name.

Deeply convinced that Newfoundland could and should no longer remain independent, he saw a great future for our people if he could convince them to join Canada and enjoy the many benefits which this rich neighbor would lavish upon us. He argued that it would not be a one way street for we would, in joining Canada, bring with us into Confederation nearly half a million hearty people, largely of British origin. Not only these human resources but also vast natural resources in the sea, the forests, and the minerals were now becoming evident as being contained not only in the Island of Newfoundland but in the vast, largely unexplored territory of Labrador.

A trend soon developed at the National Convention as Smallwood began to hammer home day after day after day the various points leading, he hoped, to Confederation with Canada. Any member who spoke against it was always followed by Smallwood repudiating and rejecting the points which had been made by the previous speaker. Fierce indeed were many of the debates and many incidents once or twice almost led to fights on the floor of the House. As the time came for the Convention to make its decision, their difficulty was obvious. The choice which they would recommend appeared to be either continuation of Commission of Government or a return to Responsible Government. Their recommendation if accepted would be put in the form of a Referendum to the people of Newfoundland who would make their choice when they voted. But Smallwood and some others were not satisfied. They were not happy to think that to reach Confederation we would have to return to Responsible Government and elect a government in favour of Confederation who would then go and negotiate the terms. They wanted Confederation put on the ballot paper as an alternative for the Referendum.

I could see no way that Newfoundland would enter Confederation without the truly democratic method of electing first a Responsible Government. This Government would represent Newfoundland in any negotiations with Canada, having been given a mandate by the Newfoundland people. I was convinced that the correct method was to vote for a return of Responsible Government and then, having elected a government, if the people wished Confederation they would elect a party which was committed to Confederation.

The National Convention recommended the two alternatives but left out Confederation. Smallwood and a group of others made a special trip to London to request the British Government to include Confederation on the ballot paper. The British Government, frightened that a return to Responsible Government would eventually result in bankruptcy again and not anxious to continue their own involvement and contribution through Commission of Government, would in the final analysis be glad to see Newfoundland absorbed into Canada. They agreed with the Smallwood group, therefore, and directed that the third alternative be on the ballot paper.

It was agreed before the Referendum that since there were three alternatives, unless there was a clear majority, the alternative which received the least number of votes would be dropped and there would therefore be a second Referendum.

By the time the first Referendum was held in 1948, almost two years had elapsed since the calling of the National Convention. The arguments for and against the three alternatives which were on the first ballot paper had been discussed over and over again. Without any fuss the people went to the polls and when the results were announced it was seen that they had rejected a continuation of Commission of Government giving it a mere fifteen percent of the vote. The other two choices were almost equal. There would be a second Referendum.

The second Referendum was held about six weeks after the first. The true battle began as those on the two sides began gathering support. The Prime Minister of Canada, Louis St. Laurent, made an announcement that Canada would not accept Newfoundland into Confederation unless it showed by a clear majority that it wished to become the Tenth Province. Now we saw a return to the old style political meetings, publishing of pamphlets, newspaper reports and advertisements, and addresses on radio. The loudest voice by far was that of Smallwood who was the leading exponent of Confederation. Bitter arguments split families as they argued for or against the two choices. Finally, on the day of decision, the voters went to the polls, and, when the result was announced, Newfoundland had voted for Confederation, but by a slim margin of about four percentage points. However, most of the anti-Confederate vote had come from the

Avalon Peninsula. On the West Coast, St. Barbe district had voted strongly for Confederation, with seventy percent of the votes cast in favour.

However, there was not a great deal of rejoicing amongst the people who had supported Confederation because they were not sure exactly what they had accomplished beyond the fact that they had given up their independence and thrown in their lot with Canada. Still, the leaders of the Confederation Movement were jubilant. On the other hand, there was a great deal of sorrow evident amongst those who had voted for a return of Responsible Government, for we had lost our hard fought independence and self-determination. The Prime Minister of Canada immediately broadcast a speech of welcome and congratulated Newfoundland on its clear cut decision.

The Governor now appointed a committee which would go to Ottawa to arrange the terms under which Newfoundland would enter Confederation. It was a difficult situation. While the people had voted to join Confederation, the committee was in no way a government trying to make or get suitable terms. It had no more right to reject Confederation because it didn't like the terms than to make certain demands under the threat of returning without signing any agreement. The die had been cast and the committee had to do the best it could. There must have been moments of grave doubt amongst some of the members and one at least, Chesley Crosbie, refused to agree to the terms which were offered saying that they were financially unsound. He resigned from the committee and returned to Newfoundland. After a slow and somewhat shabby start in Ottawa, for they were left sitting in their hotel unable to begin the discussions for several days, at last they sat down to hear the terms. Many were the rumours which spread through Newfoundland during this period, but by December of 1948 the Terms of Union were worked out. March 31, 1949, at one minute before midnight was chosen as the time Newfoundland would enter Confederation and the agreement was signed. The next day, J. R. Smallwood was sworn in as the first Premier of Newfoundland, forming an interim Provincial government until a general election could be held. For the first nine months, the unelected Smallwood and his Confederate associates ran the government.

For those Newfoundlanders in favour of Responsible Government, April 1, 1949, was day of gloom. They greeted our entry into Confederation by hanging black crepe on their doors or flying their flags at half mast. Many wept openly as we became Canadians.

The changeover took place smoothly. Many departments of government were absorbed by Canadian departments. The Newfoundland customs and excise department, for instance, became the Canadian Customs and Excise Department. We would now pay Canadian Income Tax, and certain goods which were imported would be subject to different rates of tax, either higher or lower, depending on the Canadian prices. If the goods were manufactured in Canada the price was usually lower or perhaps higher if they were imported from other countries. We changed our traffic regulations to conform to the Canadian standards, particularly driving on the right side of the road. The Canadian Broadcasting Corporation took over the Newfoundland Radio Network and we now received national programs on the local CBC station. The Newfoundland Ranger Force was absorbed by the Royal Canadian Mounted Police which now became the official policy agency of the Province. The biggest immediate change was governmental. We prepared to elect our first Provincial Government, our first members of Parliament, and W. L. McKenzie King, the Prime Minister of Canada, appointed our first Senators.

Two political parties emerged. The Conservatives, headed by Harry Mews of St. John's, who basically had been the supporters of return of Responsible Government, and the Liberals, headed by Smallwood. Smallwood was in the stronger position. He was not only acting Premier, but also a well-known political figure who had in effect already won his first victory by leading Newfoundland into Confederation and forming the interim government. The issue was simple. It was an appeal to Newfoundlanders to elect a government consisting of men who had fought for Confederation and who could now work with Ottawa and bring to Newfoundland the full benefits of Confederation. The Liberals warned that Tory times were "hard times." The people had not forgotten the Depression days of the 1930s and held the Tories responsible. They wanted no return to those conditions. The Liberals were returned with a large majority of seats and J. R. Smallwood became the first elected premier of Canada's Tenth Province.

The changes which were brought about by Newfoundland's entry into Confederation with Canada were slow to take effect across the province. If people expected a sudden overnight change then they were surprised. The most striking benefit which was evident immediately was the arrival of the first Family Allowance cheques. This was a tremendous windfall for the majority of families, and it was almost too much for many of them to understand and cope with. Suddenly, depending upon the number of children in the family, extra money was in the mother's hand. At first many of the children convinced their mothers that the money was intended for them and that they should be allowed to have it and spend it. In the first few months, parents did let this happen in many cases and the children had a great time buying candy and other things which took their fancy. However, the people soon settled down and realised the allowances were for parents to provide for the needs of the children. They brought about the most obvious and striking change, the ability of the families to clothe and feed their children much better than ever before. For the first time many families were getting real cash in their hands which they could choose to spend where they liked, and they were no longer tied to a particular store, or merchant, as in the past. I saw no evidence of this bonanza producing a different outlook on the wage earner, but it certainly helped to take some of the load of worrying about providing adequately for the families from off their shoulders.

The Old Age Pensioners, who had suffered badly in the past, now didn't know what to do with the allowance which was theirs by right of being Canadians. The original allowance in Newfoundland was $15 for a man and his wife each quarter providing they were seventy-five or over. Now at age sixty-five they were receiving $45 each and every month. This worked out to $1,080 a year compared to the pathetic $60 a year previously, and included the sixty-five to seventy-five age group. Many of the older people were bewildered by the money which was showered upon them and certainly, for the first time in their lives, they were able to live in comfort and dignity. In a similar way veterans who had received Veterans' Allowance previously now received a much larger allowance and were a great deal better off than before. Not only did these benefits help the people, but they gave a tremendous boost to the Newfoundland economy, for a large amount of money now flowed into the Province. This money alone provided more employment which was an additional economic gain by itself.

There was some benefit to being Canadians in that there was no Customs Duty now on goods imported from Canada. Not only did this do away with the nuisance and sometimes difficulties involved in clearing goods through Customs, but in many cases it meant a reduction in the cost of goods. There is no doubt, however, that in the early days of Confederation a great deal of second class goods were dumped in the Province from mainland Canada. There were many examples of us receiving seconds, but even this was straightened out with time as Newfoundlanders refused to be second class citizens and made this quite plain in their dealings with business firms on the Mainland.

For some time prior to Confederation various Federal Government agencies had sent representatives to Newfoundland largely to deal with government departments in St. John's regarding the changeover and effect of operating under Canadian jurisdictions. However, it was not until after Confederation that the first Federal representatives arrived in our area. Among the first to arrive was the Inspector from the Narcotics Division of the Health Department in Ottawa. He made a trip to Bonne Bay to visit me to inspect our facilities and to advise us on the new procedures. He took the road from Deer Lake to Lomond and then came by ferry to Norris Point. The only other way in or out of Bonne Bay was by coastal boat.

The Inspector, after examining our setup, advised me that we would now have to build a special cupboard which must be kept locked at all times and which would contain our supply of drugs. Not only was the cupboard to be locked but the drugs were to be kept inside a container also locked within the locked cupboard! This requirement did not present any difficulties. However, I was not prepared for the next item of the Inspector's agenda, and this was a matter of how to deal with drug addicts. After questioning me as to whether we had any drug addicts in the district, to which I was able to reply in the negative, he then told me that there were drug addicts in Canada who would go to great lengths to obtain drugs and we should be on guard and prepared with this situation should it arise. He advised me that if any of the Mainland addicts came to Newfoundland they would probably head for a hospital such as ours and were usually pretty desperate people. He suggested that we offer no resistance but let them take whatever they wanted to get clear of them as soon as possible.

I don't think he understood why I burst out laughing at the suggestion that we would do anything else until I explained to him how impossible it would be for a drug addict to be successful in raiding the hospital. I only had to remind him of the difficulties he had faced in reaching us and that he would now have to reverse the procedure to get back to Deer Lake or Corner Brook. It was not difficult to imagine how far a person who had carried out a raid on the hospital might get. It was doubtful that he would get anywhere because a phone call to the Point would ensure that no boat was available and a second message would bring the police to take care of the matter. This was the first experience the Narcotic Inspector had had with such an isolated place and he too joined in my laughter when he realised that it would literally be an impossibility as I had suggested.

We had visits from Health Officials from the Federal Health Department and were subjected to a great deal of questioning as to the method of operating the hospital. I was quite happy to give them all the information they wanted, but I got angry at one point when a medical doctor who was looking over the hospital setup gave me a list of our shortcomings at the end of the visit and suggested that I should be doing a great deal more laboratory work than I was presently doing. At that time I was responsible for everything at the hospital and was the only medical doctor available. The nurse was responsible for the nursing side of the activities and my wife helped in the x-ray department. With my work in the hospital, the outpatients clinic, the district calls, the reading of the x-rays, and the laboratory work, I found that my day lasted sixteen hours on average and very often twenty hours or more. There was no way that I could undertake more laboratory work than I was already doing and it was foolish for anyone from Ottawa, particularly a member of the profession, to come to our Cottage Hospital and tell me I should be doing more. Already I knew that all Cottage Hospitals provided more work than any of the doctors could do properly. I made a counter-suggestion that Ottawa should now provide the necessary funds for the extra personnel which would in turn provide the additional services which we so desperately needed. I think when I had finished making my points and explained to the visiting doctor what I and the other doctors were required to do that new light was thrown on the subject.

I like to think the visit that was made to my hospital and the suggestions which I made were in some way responsible for grants which later were made available and which did in fact improve the service in Newfoundland. Certainly it wasn't long after this that over $1,000 worth of equipment arrived for the laboratory. None of this had been requested by me, but had been provided through a grant to the Province for all the Cottage Hospitals. Newly introduced equipment was followed by the laboratory/x-ray technician, which made our ability to do investigations ten times better than it had been in the past.

It took between one or two years for the full changeover to take effect and to allow the new services to settle down. The coastal boats were now operated by the Canadian National Railways and the service improved somewhat. The mail was now part of the Canada Post Office and the service improved. The Canadian National Airline, TCA (Trans Canada Airways) had been operating into Newfoundland from the Mainland prior to Confederation, but following Confederation improved their services. Federal grants which were available to the Province to all Departments now began to show an effect and money was available to start building a network of roads, to improve welfare benefits, and so on, and gradually the change became noticeable right across Newfoundland.

The Labrador boundary question, which had been disputed for years by Quebec, was finally settled by Confederation, for the Federal Government recognized Newfoundland territorial boundaries and accepted them as provincial boundaries when we entered Confederation. While Quebec has never accepted either the Privy

Council decision of 1927 awarding Labrador to Newfoundland the Federal Government's acceptance of our boundaries of 1949, in fact the boundaries are quite firm in Canadian Law, and can only be changed, as is the case throughout Canada, by agreement between the two provinces involved and the Federal Government. I doubt that this issue will ever arise again, even though Quebec continued to print the maps of its Province showing all of Labrador as being a part of Quebec.

The era of having to make it on our own was over. Newfoundland now faced a future with the promise of massive grants from Federal sources to assist all departments and all our people. The standards of all facets of life improved almost beyond recognition over the next few years and the per capita income, which was drastically below Canadian levels in 1949, began to rise year by year. It would be many years before we would reach the National average but each year was an improvement over the previous one, and the benefits could be seen everywhere. Health standards improved, communications and transportation improved, but the independent spirit still lives on.

Chapter 13

TINKER BELL

My first experience being asked to do a house call in Bonne Bay was early one morning when a man appeared at the hospital and told me that his wife was sick and would I come visit his home across the Bay. I agreed to do this and we set off for the Point where he had a motorboat. It was an ordinary fisherman's type boat powered by an old "make and break" engine with a big heavy flywheel and after I settled myself in the bows, he crouched down and primed the engine of the fly wheel and she "popped" into life and we started out. The noise of motorboat engines became something that I learned to understand. Without getting out of bed, I could almost tell the type of day it was by the noise or absence of noise. On good days, I heard the boats leaving at dawn carrying fishermen, but if a storm was up or the fish were gone they stayed in bed and the silence of the night continued into the early hours of day. None of the boat engines had a continuous rhythm. It was an interrupted popping sound and it is the sort of noise that one will remember all one's life. People by the sea grow up with it. Sometimes I couldn't hear it because I was so used to it, but if it isn't there or if a different sound comes I was suddenly aware of the change.

And so it was as I sat this morning in the bow of this man's boat and listened to the irregular rhythm of the popping. I thought of the endless trips that no doubt would be ahead of me in all kinds of weather and to all kinds of places, and I made up my mind that I would enjoy the trips and getting to know the men who sailed these boats and the difficulties they had. After about a mile the engine sputtered and stopped, and the man changed from his position at the tiller in the stern of the boat where he had been facing me, and he moved around the engine house and crouched down and looked through the little hatch and fiddled with the engine. He seemed to be a long time poking and fiddling with it. I don't know how or why but I was ready for him when he turned around and looked at me and asked, "Doc, have you got a bit of wire in your pocket?"

I almost laughed out loud. I certainly chuckled and he couldn't understand why. I said, "I'm sorry I haven't got any wire on me. I didn't know you were going to need any or I would have brought some." He ignored this and asked me, "Have you got a bit of line in your pocket?" I searched in my pocket and there was nothing there, and I said, "No I don't have anything." And then I remembered my medical bag. I opened this and I found that one of the packages of dressings had been tied up with a piece of string; I held it up and asked, "would this help?" and he looked at it and said, "well I'll try it." So I undid it and passed it over to him and in a matter of minutes we were on our way again. I made sure from then on that I had certain things in my bag. A piece of wire, some line, a couple of bobby pins, a couple of nails, and two or three broken springs. All these items have been used at various times by ingenious fishermen to effect sometimes temporary and often permanent repairs to their engines. Many the time these little bits that I carried in my bag managed to get us out of trouble. In fact I don't ever remember breaking down to the point that we weren't able to reach our destination because always these engines were somehow coaxed back to life again and saw us to our journey's end.

However, within a month of starting practice in Bonne Bay two things became apparent as regards travelling to visit patients by water. Firstly, since travel had to be done in all weather and by day and by night, it would be nice to have some kind of shelter in which to travel. I was thinking of a boat with a cabin. Secondly, by having a boat available, the doctor had the opportunity to pick his own time and make his call when it was convenient to the general operations at the hospital so that everybody got dealt with. At the end of a month I made the journey to Corner Brook to visit my friend, Dr. Bob Dove, and discuss with him the possibility of buying some kind of boat which would be suitable for the work in Bonne Bay and on the Coast.

Bob was most helpful and told me that, strangely enough, I had come at a time when there was a boat available and in fact it was his boat which he had bought and used in Bonne Bay. He had no use for it now in Corner Brook and would be glad to sell it. This boat turned out to be a cabin cruiser approximately 35 feet in length. It had been built in Bonne Bay of local wood for a man who had sold it within a year or so, and Bob Dove had bought it and used it in his work in the practice in the Bonne Bay area. When he transferred to Corner Brook in mid-1944 he had taken this boat with him. She had then been commandeered and used by the Bay of Islands Navy, which was the Naval Auxiliary put together during the war. They welcomed the additional strength Bob's boat gave them. I'm not sure whether perhaps she was the flag ship representing the entire fleet or whether she was one of a number of boats stationed here at the time. However, the war was now approaching its end. She could serve a more useful purpose by going back to Bonne Bay. So it was that I bought the boat. However, I didn't really know what to do to get her home.

I brought with me the Hospital Engineer, Martin Bugden. His knowledge of engines and seamanship proved invaluable and he assured me that this was a good buy. She was a good seaworthy boat, she had a reliable engine, which I remember was a Universal 25, and she would serve me well and serve the people well. The question still remained to be answered as to my ability to navigate or pilot a boat. Up to this time I had literally no experience, but I was willing to learn. Bob Dove told me that luckily the one man who could teach me, in no time at all, was in Corner Brook. Captain Geary, who was the Bowater Harbour Master, was a man of great experience and skill, and he agreed to undertake my training without delay.

It was approximately 6 p.m. I had dinner and then went to Captain Geary's house where I was given a course in navigation and pilotage. The Captain finished the course by midnight. I was then presented with Captain Geary's own parallel rule, which I never ceased to treasure and which accompanied me on all my journeys, a set of charts of Bay of Islands and Bonne Bay, and some advice. I thought I understood how to lay a course, how to read a compass, and generally how to navigate and control a boat, and was prepared to leave at 6 a.m. in the morning to take the boat to Bonne Bay.

I remember asking Captain Geary about the hazards of navigation such as rocks, and I well remember his answer. "You know," he said, "I know the location of every rock in the Bay of Islands." I was staggered at the thought that this man would have such tremendous knowledge of the Bay, which is vast. And then I said, "Then I suppose you must have studied your charts well." His reply flattened me, "Not a bit of it my boy," he said, "I've run up on every single one of them, and that's how I know where they are." I've never ceased to chuckle at his reply and recognise the wisdom, for the rocks that I know best are the ones that I nearly ran on, although I must admit that over the years I was fortunate.

The next morning at dawn, we set sail from Corner Brook, Martin and I. I was full of enthusiasm and excitement in charge of my own boat and heading out into the Gulf of St. Lawrence through Bay of Islands, which I had never travelled before, and up the coast. I had been warned it was a rough and tough coast to sail on but I had to do it to bring my boat home. The journey was beautiful. There was a gentle swell, just enough to let you know that you were out in the ocean. Passing out through Bay of Islands through the outer Bay, Martin called my attention to some seals who were swimming along beside us, and this reminded me so much of the porpoises which often travelled hour after hour beside the ships as we went on the school boat backwards and forwards to Britain each year. And so it was in the early afternoon that we sailed into Bonne Bay. They knew we were coming because the lighthouse keeper had spotted us and he had phoned Norris Point to Bryant Harding who was out on the wharf to meet us as we came in. We made a good approach to the wharf and a large number of people came down to welcome us. I think the general feeling was one of pleasure that I was the type of person who enjoyed boats. Perhaps as well people felt a degree of pride that the Doctor would have a boat in which he could make calls around the Bay and to do it at the best time to be suitable to everyone. The boat was moored up and we made our way to the hospital. I went home to tell my wife, with great pride, that I had bought a boat and I wanted the family to see it. Later I said "come on, I'll take you out for a trip in our boat." We went down to the Point, climbed aboard the boat, and had a good look around. Edna never enjoyed boats but she was tremendously courageous. I know now that she wasn't particularly fussy about the new boat, but she certainly pretended to be enjoying every minute of it. And so we cast off and headed out for a little run around. It wasn't difficult to start the engine and steer the boat and go for a little ride. Then we headed back for the wharf. At that point, for the first time my total lack of seamanship and knowledge showed up. Instead of bringing the boat in to a nice gentle landing, I rammed her full speed into the side of the wharf. There was a horrible noise of crunching and the heads appeared around every building and every window to see what on earth the Doctor was up to. We salvaged our approach the second time, Bryant Harding came out to our rescue and helped us bring her in and moor her up again. We then went in to join Bryant and his wife Em for a cup of tea and a discussion of what had happened. My second lesson in management of boats came that afternoon as Bryant explained to me how to bring a boat in and how to manoeuver. He generally laid it on the line for me.

The lessons which I learned from Captain Geary, from Bryant Harding, and most of all from Martin Bugden, laid a foundation which I don't think will ever be lost. After a little practice over a week or ten days I had reached the point where I could handle my boat in almost any weather and single-handed, for this I insisted on doing, and I could both moor and unmoor the boat, take her out or bring her in, and generally handle myself as a boat owner should when taking his own boat around.

One of the first things that I had to do after acquiring my boat was to find a suitable name. I took my time over this. I wanted to pick a name that would be acceptable and at the same time would mean something. One of my favorite authors was James Barrie. I was always fascinated by Peter Pan, especially by the fairy who flitted from place to place. It seemed to me as I moved about the Bay that I too had a tendency to flit from place to place seeing a patient here and then a patient there. We seemed to be on the go morning, noon, and night, nearly every day, and it seemed most suitable that the boat should be called *Tinker Bell*. I discussed this with Edna and it was agreed that this was a very suitable name. In due course, the name plates were carved by a local artist and were affixed to the boat and she started a new lease of life as *Tinker Bell*. In fact, she retained this name for as long as I owned her, which turned out to be approximately twenty-five years.

She was a fine sea boat. I can't remember a better one for the sea. She stood up well to the weather and was a comfortable boat by the standards to which she had been built. However, she was the old-type cabin cruiser with a beautiful sea hull, but box-like cabins on top. The forward cabin was square, the wheel house in the middle was a square structure sticking up into the air, and then the after cabin was another square cabin with a small cockpit aft.

She was painted white and the superstructure was varnished brown. I had a mast made on which I always flew my house flag, and we always flew the Newfoundland Ensign on the cockpit staff. She was equipped with a Universal twenty-five horse power engine which was mounted amid ships. This gave her a speed of seven or eight knots which was too slow for my needs. That first winter I started planning how she could be rebuilt to better use the space and how she could be repowered to make her faster and more efficient. I spent hours working on the plans, which I drew myself, for the rebuilding of the boat and the re-powering. I found people very helpful with suggestions and I would take my problems to them, particularly Bryant. He was never-ending source of information and assistance. Gradually, the picture that I wanted began to develop.

Mick Organ, who had connections in the United States, told me that he could help me get a large marine engine. We settled on a Scripp 95 horse power gasoline engine with two to one reduction gears. It was estimated that this engine should give us about twelve knots. It was brought in from Detroit a couple of months later, but it was a proud day when it arrived. It was probably the most modern engine at that time that had come into the Bay.

I engaged two boat builders and we started work in the spring of 1948. We stripped out the cabins and the inside of the boat so that she was just a hull. We then raised the sides and built her with a much larger cockpit. This modification gave us the lines of modern cabin cruisers, gave us more head room, and made her a much better boat for the work that I was using her for along the Coast, when I would be gone for a week or ten days at a time.

There were now three cabins with accommodation for six people, toilet facilities, the galley, a convertible dinette, a modern cooker using kerosene under pressure, a control station with the ability to be operated easily with all the controls in the one place, including the pump, the engine controls, the clutch, the light switches and so on. The new engine was mounted under the floor in the wheel house. Two large tanks were installed capable of holding three drums of gasoline, and a water tank which held approximately twenty gallons of fresh water. Eventually she was self-contained for possibly as much as 200 miles cruising. On board, we had ten or twelve days supplies of food.

During the building a number of amusing incidents took place. It was my custom to go down in the morning before I started work to see the builders. I would see if they had any problems or explain any of the things that they weren't clear on and that I wanted done. I would try and get back at lunch time to see how things were going. In the evening I would try and get down again to see how they had made out for the day and set things up for the next day.

I must say they were extremely patient with me. I knew what I wanted and my explanations were not always perhaps as clear as they might have been. At the same time some of the things I felt should be done may well have been impossible and they had great patience with me. They listened and explained to me how things could or couldn't be done. However we agreed on most things and it was all done in the best possible way. The most efficient and speedy methods were used, and there was always a constant stream of interested spectators who came to see what was happening.

One day I came down around tea time and found the builders convulsed with laughter. I asked them to share the joke with me, and they were a little reluctant at first. Then one fellow said, "Well look, it's such a funny story that I'm sure you'll understand if we do explain it to you." So I said, "Please go right ahead because I'd love to hear it." And so he explained how a man had come aboard the boat and had poked his head into every part. The boat was now decked over and the internal construction was going on, and eventually he poked his head into the washroom. Here, to make the most use of the space I found it necessary to build a small platform for the toilet which put

Billy Major our guide, Noel, student Perry Ottenburg, Edwina, and Gerine resting on their climb up Gros Morne in 1953. A.B. Harding said he believed they were the first women to make the climb.

On the top of Gros Morne. Gerine, Noel, Perry Ottenburg, Billy Major, and Edwina.

Billy Major, Edna, and Gerine on top of Gros Morne overlooking Ten Mile Gulch.

Gerine, Billy, and Perry overlooking Ten Mile Pond.

The S.S. *Northern Ranger*. One of the two boats which served the St. Barbe Coast. The other was the S.S. *Clarenville*.

Western Brook Pond.

'The Arches.' St. Barbe Coast.

Gerine, Edwina, and Noel in front of hospital snowmobile, 1950.

The remains of the S.S. *Ethie* at Martin's Point, 1980. Photo taken as I travelled the coast in my boat *Tinker Bell*.

Molly (St. Bernard) pully the sleigh.

Noel at work in his Bonne Bay Cottage Hospital office.

Noel and his Jeep outside the Bonne Bay Cottage Hospital, Norris Point, 1947.

A.B. Harding and Noel Murphy. Norris Point, 1945.

Noel outside the Bonne Bay Cottage Hospital just after performing surgery.

Edna Murphy outside the Doctor's House, 1946.

The front door of the Doctor's House at Norris Point, May 1945, when we arrived. The inside was only partly finished.

One year thousands of Dogfish invaded Bonne Bay and Neddy's Harbour. Edna is holding up several. "They tasted like blotting paper but the hens and cats enjoyed them."

Tinker Bell at her mooring 1945.

At sea with the skipper (Noel) at the wheel 1945.

Family picnic.

Edna and Molly. Photo taken from Burnt Hill overlooking the 'Point' at Norris Point during the summer of 1948 looking at Gadds Harbour.

'Susie the Seal.' She was brought to the hospital by someone who found her on shore. We adopted her, but after ten days she made her way back to sea.

Preparing to cast off. Molly, Noel, and Martin Bugden July, 1946.

Tinker Bell at her mooring, Norris Point, 1948. Shag Cliff is in background.

Doctor Paul Shelton with Noel visiting on his yacht from New York.

The Murphy family on the step of the Doctor's House in Norris Point.

The girls — Gerine and Edwina — on their sleigh.

Noel and Molly with the jeep to the right outside the Doctor's House, Norris Point, 1947.

Noel, Molly, and the snowmobile outside the Doctor's House, Norris Point, Spring, 1950.

Noel and *Tinker Bell* before being rebuilt, 1946.

Noel and *Tinker Bell* after being rebuilt to Murphy's design, 1947.

Tinker Bell at anchor, Norris Point, 1945. Shag Cliff is to the right.

Tinker Bell tied up at Harbour Cove-North Arm, Bay of Islands.

it slightly up the side of the hull and gave a little more space, in that particular section of the boat. Therefore, they had built a small platform raised about ten inches off the floor and going into the side of the boat, where I planned the basin to be. I had built in my own house a mock up of the completed room. We had collected bits of equipment over the many months and I had taken the toilet and put this in position. I had rigged a section of my basement the same size as the head would be, the toilet had been raised up and put against a curved wall, the other walls and the door had been put into position. We didn't have a proper basin. We took an aluminum basin and we drilled it and put a sink fixture in the bottom, and then drilled the top around so that it would screw onto the top of the cupboard which we were making and in which we had made a hole.

At the time this visitor was poking around, the toilet was not in position but the platform was, the cupboard for the basin was in position and the round hole had been cut, but this was about thirty inches high, and on looking into the room the visitor was faced with a situation where there was a box thirty inches high with a round hole in the top and at the side of this a platform. He jumped to his own conclusions.

He then turned to the boat builders and said, "isn't it a bit high?" Quick as a flash one of men who had a great sense of humour called out, "It certainly is, but don't forget the Doctor is a tall man." Everyone was convulsed with laughter except the visitor who nodded his head wisely and said, "Yes, I hadn't thought of that," and making his way aft he climbed over the ladder and vanished. When he had gone the men really let go and laughed themselves silly and it was at this point that I arrived and was delighted to share in the joke.

On another occasion when the boat was just about completed and almost ready for launching, she was still up on her slipway. From the original shape, the raised sides and the new cabins made her look very high. I was on deck and was standing on the forward cabin which made me look even higher, when a man walked underneath and stood for a long time sizing up the boat. Looking at her shape and her height and the hull, he cast his eye forward and he cast it aft and finally he looked up and shouted, "Don't you think she's a bit top heavy." I called down, "What do you mean?" He came closer and shouted, "Aren't you afraid she'll turn bottom up?" "Oh no," I shouted back, "she's designed with very latest technology and if she does turn bottom up, she'll come right up the other side." His jaw dropped open and out came the one big word, "No!" I said, "Oh yes, you don't think I would go to sea in anything that wasn't sea worthy," and with a great deal of wonderment at the new design he turned and set off for home, no doubt to amaze his family with the story of the new invention.

The Doctor's boat was the last boat to be hauled out every year and the hauling usually took place on my birthday, December 21. Of course it depended on weather, but it was usually that day, and year after year there was a ceremony attached to the hauling out of the boat. We prepared for it several days in advance, getting ready with blocks and tackle and ropes and rounding up men, telling them what day we figured we would do the hauling up. There was always a willing crowd. The reason there was a willing crowd, of course, was the fact that there was a reward.

The cradle was floated off, the boat was turned bow in from her moorings, and the cradle was fed underneath until it was in position and then lashed up to the boat. She was guided on to the slipway so that the cradle was in position, blocks and tackle were set in position, and anything up to thirty men would take the line. Bryant always supervised and when all was ready he would give the word, the men would start singing a sea shanty and they would haul on the line at right angles to the slipway so that they went along the little street that went past Bryant's house and past the stores. *Tinker Bell* would come out of the water and move up the slipway until she was in position and then she was lashed there for the winter. The bungs were then taken out from the bilge so that she could drain freely, tarpaulins were put over the top after everything had been cleared out from inside, and she was winterized and ready for whatever might come. When all this was done, the men would then crowd into Bryant's house where each man would get a good tot of rum provided by myself.

On December 21, it was usually cold and there was usually snow on the ground. While there wasn't too much attached to the hauling up, everybody was happy to get a tot of rum. I always felt it was cheap at the price. However, it was an annual event that I looked forward to as a wonderful display of fellowship and willingness to help one another.

In the spring, of course, the winterizing was reversed, the tarpaulins were taken off, the hull which had always been scrubbed when she was hauled up was now touched up, repairs if necessary were done, and she was painted before she was put off. She was always one of the first boats in the water, which made me mobile and available as much as any other boat in the Bay with the exception of the ferry.

In the early days I had lots to learn, and I also had a great deal of false pride in not wanting to admit my ignorance too much. In fact, looking back now, it probably was the best thing that ever happened to me that I insisted on doing things by myself, and a good example is a little story which I remember about a time that I got called to Woody Point one night. I went over one evening and tied my boat to the Government Wharf to do a house call. However, the house call turned out to be a maternity case which in turn was slow and dragged on through the night. It happened that the night was a Saturday night so it was Sunday morning before my work was finished. It must have been about 11 or 12 midday before I got back to my boat. During the night the wind had been just sufficient that she had been tugging on her forward line all night. I was tired after my night on this case and when I climbed aboard, put my bag in the cabin, and went up on the bow to undo the lines, I found a crowd of men sitting and standing on the wharf watching.

I didn't mind. On a Sunday they put on their Sunday clothes and went to church services and there wasn't much else to do. There were no roads through the country, so there were no cars, no visitors. If the coastal boat wasn't in, then it was just a question of who happened to come by. This particular morning it was the Doctor and his boat. I was worth watching for what I was worth, but in fact when I bent down to untie the line I realised at a glance that during the night *Tinker Bell* had tightened the knot so much that there was no way that I could loosen it up.

I fought that knot. That's the only way I can explain it. I fought that knot, I kicked it, I pushed it, I pulled it, I wiggled it, I did everything I knew and it wouldn't move. Not a man would hurt my efforts by suggesting that they come aboard. I knew and all of them knew that I only had to shout up and ask someone to come down and half a dozen men would have come, but having once started there was no way I would give up. I suppose I fought that thing for half an hour before eventually I managed to break the knot and untie the line. Long before I got it untied I was ready to cut it. Certainly I said a lot of things to it that they never heard, but I'm sure many people can guess. However, eventually it came clear. I started my boat and headed for home. I was a great deal more tired after my fight with the knot than I had been after a night out on a case.

I cheered up considerably a little later when I was tied up at a wharf and the next morning came on deck. I found that somebody had tied his dory so tight that when the tide went out the dory was hung now from its forward line, suspended above the water, and the poor man had no way of getting it undone. He had to take a knife and cut the line. At least that didn't happen to me.

Chapter 14

TIDE RIP IN THE STRAITS

On an occasion when I was making a trip on the Coast, the family were anxious to come along. We decided that it would be nice, after we finished working up the coast at Port Saunders, to go on up to the Flower's Cove area and across to Labrador which Edna and the children had never seen.

I had previously been to Labrador on a trip when I went north at the end of one of my tours to meet Dr. Curtis from the Grenfell Mission in St. Anthony. He had agreed to meet me at Flower's Cove as our territories met at the top of St. John's Bay. There were a number of mutual problems which we wanted to discuss so that we wouldn't be crossing wires and we would be making the best use of our medical facilities and personnel. I intended to cover the same ground with Edna and the girls, and then head across the Straits of Belle Isle. We left Port Saunders and carried on up to Flower's Cove, spent a little time there, and then moved across the Straits to Forteau and from there up to Red Bay.

Labrador is a delightful, rugged land. The people are hard-working and isolated most of the year and welcome the arrival of the infrequent visitors they receive. We enjoyed our stay in Red Bay, which only lasted a day, just long enough for Edna and the girls to see the area. The Organs from Norris Point had a store there and welcomed us. We enjoyed talking with the people. One of the first things that one learns is that in Labrador the permanent residences are called Liveyeres–people who live here–and they refer to the people from the island as Newfoundlanders. The first time I ever heard this usage, I was astonished that even though I was in a part of Newfoundland, I would be referred to as a Newfoundlander as if I were an outsider. It took me some time to accept that it was logical for a person living in

Labrador to refer to an islander as a Newfoundlander because so many from the island came to Labrador to fish for the summer and went back to Newfoundland to live for the rest of the year. They referred to themselves not as Labradorians, but as Liveyeres to stress their residency.

Came the day when we had to return and looking at the chart it seemed to me that the quickest and easiest way was to set a course to run across from Red Bay to Flower's Cove. This course would take us diagonally across the Straits and might be interesting as we might very well pass some ocean going liners as we went.

The liveyeres suggested to me that what we should do was follow the Labrador Coast down to Forteau and then cross over as we had done on our earlier crossing. However, on looking at my chart, I felt that the course I was going to chart would save time and mileage. Without asking why I should follow the Labrador Coast, we set off and I headed out into the Straits.

In that part of the Straits one can see the Newfoundland Coast and one has a feeling always of safety. When you can see land that you are heading for or when you are close to the shore everything seems secure. We were full of enthusiasm for what appeared to be plain sailing ahead of us. The weather was clear, we had the whole day ahead of us, and we anticipated a pleasant and uneventful trip.

All went well until we were half way across, when for no reason that I could see, the seas themselves became disturbed. The direction of the sea became difficult to follow. It seemed to move in all directions. At one minute it was coming at us one way, and another minute the next way. It didn't appear to have anything to do with the light wind that was blowing and generally I found it extremely difficult to control the boat. This sensation of rough water got worse and worse, and the boat became more and more difficult to control. We realised that what we were in was a tide rip, the point at which the tides of the opposing shores meet, and I suddenly understood that I had been warned. It is not easy to cross the Straits at this point in a small boat since you might face this type of hazard. However, we were in the midst now of the tide rip and had no alternative but to carry on.

The next hour was a nightmare. Everybody got sick and retired to bunks wherever they could crawl. Martin stayed with me in the wheelhouse and we fought the sea second by second, full speed ahead to climb over one large swell, and then throttle back to prevent breaching as we slid down from the other side. Then full speed ahead again to prevent a sea breaking in over our stern, all the time swinging the wheel as she started to turn one way or the other. It lasted for about an hour. It was not only frightening but extremely tiring. Then, as quickly as it had begun, it ended. Once we were out of the tide rip, we met calm waters all the way to the other side. For those who had never experienced a tide rip I can only hope you never do. Those who have experienced it in the open sea in a small boat will understand that it is one of the most frightening experiences I've ever been through.

In the course of making many, many trips on the coast in all kinds of weather we inevitably had a variety of experiences and some of these things still stick in my mind. I remember answering a call one day which was going to take us to Rocky Harbour. As we made our way out of Bonne Bay on a really stormy day, and knowing that we only had to go out the mouth of the Bay and turn into Rocky Harbour, we passed a coastal boat coming in. The coastal boat was bouncing around in the heavy seas and having a rough time. Of course, we were having an equally rough time as we butted out into an onshore wind. As we passed the coastal boat I had a feeling that the skipper figured we were crazy to be going to sea. We certainly lost some crockery and took a bit of a beating as we bounced along crashing down into the troughs with spray flying up over the top of us as we went through each successive wave. We had the satisfaction of knowing that we were in a good solid sea boat. We made our journey to Rocky Harbour and returned without any undue difficulties. After hauling into my berth at Norris Point and mooring up, as was my custom, I dropped aboard the coastal boat to say hello to the captain and he told me he couldn't believe his eyes when he saw us going out. He said, "Everything else, I know, was coming in, so the trip must have been urgent." I assured him that it was an urgent call, and that we didn't feel the weather was so bad that we couldn't make it to Rocky Harbour. He was not convinced.

I often had to make decisions as to whether it was too bad to go and we tried to give the patient the benefit by making the journey whenever possible, but of course there were occasions when it was too bad and we were unable to move. One of these occasions there was a big storm on the coast and we got a request for assistance from one of the nursing stations. We set out in the boat and battled for some hours to get out of the bay, but by the time we reached the mouth of Bonne Bay we had taken such a beating and it looked so much worse outside, that we had to turn back.

On arriving back at Norris Point all I could do was wire the nurse and tell her that I had made the effort but the weather was too bad and we had to turn back. If the situation was unchanged when the weather abated I would certainly try again. In this particular case, after forty-eight hours the nurse managed to take care of the problem and my services were no longer needed. I do recollect that this was the exception and there were not many times we were unable to get through. I had the greatest confidence in *Tinker Bell* and must say she never let me down.

At Port Saunders there is a rock known to every mariner that must be avoided. On one occasion when I was in that vicinity I was giving the rock a wide berth when approaching us came the coastal boat. It was my custom to exchange greetings with the coastal boat always, and so I edged a little closer, forgetting that I was trying to give this particular rock a wide margin.

The coastal boat appeared to be full of very friendly people because an awful lot of them were on the deck apparently waving cheerfully. Martin and I followed suit and waved back. As we did, we hit a long swell and the boat seemed to coast down the swell forever. The colour of sea changed suddenly from a dark green to a very light pale green. At this point, Martin went pale and shouted, "Look out, we're on the rock!" As I looked over the side, I realised that we were going to crash right into it. However our Guardian Angel must have been with us. We slid on across the top of the rock. I doubt that we had more than an inch of water under us but we made it over.

I realised then that the people on the coastal boat were not waving friendly greetings, but were frantically trying to signal us. Being higher up than we were, they could see our position in relation to the rock and they were trying to warn us off. We must have looked like fools, quite happily waving back as we headed for the rock. It was an act of providence that *Tinker Bell* didn't end her days, and perhaps ours too, on that rock.

Only once did *Tinker Bell* go aground, and that was at a time when it should never have happened. Visiting Bonne Bay at that time, as they did nearly every year, were Dr. Paul Sheldon and his wife, Carol, on the *Sea Crest* out of New York. Of all the visitors to Western Newfoundland and Labrador, Paul Sheldon had a greater knowledge of our coastline than anyone else I knew. He came nearly every year and brought with him friends who acted as crew. This particular year he had a famous American surgeon, Dr. Larry Sloane, with him. We always made our house available to Paul and his crew for changing purposes, for laundry and bathing, and so on, and they were free to come and go as they liked. We in turn were always invited to go aboard the *Sea Crest* and partake of meals with them and enjoy their company.

On this particular day it was agreed that we would go up the Main Arm to fish for trout and that we would go in my boat. So we climbed aboard and headed for Mill Cove where there was a little stream which always produced some trout. As we came into the cove I asked Paul and Larry if they would keep an eye on the bottom, and warned them to let me know when it started to shoal up so that we could stop and anchor and then go ashore in the dinghy.

We were coasting in quite slowly because I knew she would start to shoal soon and I waited and waited and still nobody signaled me. I kept asking, "Are you watching?" "Oh yes," they assured me. They would let me know in good time. However, when they did let me know it was too late and we grounded, quite gently but definitely firmly. I berated them for not keeping a close watch and letting me know soon enough. I told them that never before had I put my boat aground. I was horrified to think that experienced sailors like this would put me in such a position. The response was a chuckle. It was suggested gently to me that I was no kind of sailor if I hadn't been aground as many times as every other sailor had been.

Well, when I looked at it, it didn't seem a desperate situation. It is a soft bottom and wouldn't do the boat any harm. No doubt she would float off in due course, so the party took to the dinghy and went trout fishing. I elected to stay with the boat and keep an eye on it. All my efforts to take her off failed. I was firmly on and would stay on until high tide. The tide was presently half down and falling, so I knew that I had about seven hours before I could expect to get the boat clear again. This didn't bother me too much because we'd gone for a day's trout fishing, and I settled down to wait it out. What I didn't expect was that *Tinker Bell* would not stay upright. As the tide fell *Tinker Bell* started to go on her side and so at the end of three hours I was sitting on the edge of *Tinker Bell*, which was now at a 45 degree angle, a very sorry sight for my beautiful boat. When the visitors returned, they thought this was uproariously funny. They came back to the boat chuckling. They were gleeful as well with the trout they had caught, which we then proceeded to cook and eat. Dinner helped, a little bit, to mend my hurt feelings. Sure enough, as the water rose so *Tinker Bell* righted herself and at the correct moment floated clear and we made our way home. I never forgave them for putting me aground like this and while I didn't have any part in it, the tables were turned shortly afterwards when Paul Sheldon himself went aground and it fell to me to help him off. But that's another story.

On the coast, there was a great rivalry amongst the various boats. The rebuilding and repowering of *Tinker Bell* put us in a class where I now had a fast, good sea boat, and the other boats of similar type that were built over the years always came to race against us. Sandy Parsons of Rocky Harbour built a fine boat for the tourist trade and on several occasions Sandy and I raced to see which was the faster boat. His boat never beat *Tinker Bell*. Stewart Blanchard built a new ferry boat and I don't remember him ever outdoing me either. One or two other boats equally made their bid but the *Tinker Bell* was the queen of the coast.

Outboard motors were not used on the coast before my time and I considered that a small outboard motor would be most useful for my dinghy for getting ashore. I ordered my first motor in 1946, a three horse power Johnson, which incidentally I still have and which is still operable. When it arrived we reviewed it with a great deal of pleasure and set about preparing to try it out.

Nobody, least of all I, had the faintest idea of what it would do in the way of powering a small dinghy. The dinghy was a fairly heavy boat which I had built. It was about twelve feet long and made of heavy planking. I was assured by some of the fishermen that this motor would drive it clean out of the water and to be careful. A crowd gathered on the day we installed the outboard on the back of the dinghy, filled the motor with gasoline, and primed it. As I pulled the cord, she fired into life. I nearly fell overboard laughing because with full throttle she chugged along at a good five knots. To everybody's amusement, instead of flying out of the water as had been suggested, she just pushed the dinghy along at what I considered was probably the proper speed, not too fast and not too slow. It turned out that this little outboard, which was light and easy to handle, was ideal for this type of dinghy and served me well over the years.

It was approximately 1954 before the outboards caught on and became a recognised form of power for dories. The word outboard was changed by the local people into "outport" over the years, and the motors became known as "outport motors." It was customary for the fishermen to saw off one end of their dories and to put a square stern across. Bringing in outboards with extra long shafts and with ever more powerful motors, they adapted their dories to go ever faster. Today such speed dories are the common means of transportation all around this area. For safety sake the fishing boat with an inboard engine is a durable, seaworthy boat. A speed dory would never compare to the safety of the heavier, proper fishing boats. However, the speed dory is a boat which does exactly what its name says, it provides speed. It is ideal for certain types of fishing inshore and is being used extensively.

Chapter 15

HURRICANE

It was my custom each year to make at least one, and if possible, two trips along the coast covering the territory served by the Cottage Hospital, calling in at all the settlements and holding clinics and generally doing what I could to bring medicine to the people in their own homes or at least in their own settlements. Of course, I went in *Tinker Bell* and Martin always accompanied me. We both realized that we were doing something important for the people in the District, even though the trips were sometimes trying. We also knew the importance of not being away longer than necessary. It was usual then to make the trip in as few days as possible, somewhere in the region of six to seven days.

The first trip was usually made in June, and if another one could be worked in towards the early part of August this was done. However, this second trip depended on the amount of work which was going on at the Hospital, the amount of surgery slated for me to perform, and various other duties. The first three years I had to make sure that gas was available at Port Saunders, the most northern of the Nursing Stations, because the boat couldn't carry sufficient for the trip there and back. Later, with rebuilding and remodelling, larger tanks were installed to permit us to make the trip there and back without refueling. Always we sent ahead of us one or two casks of gas which were waiting at the Nursing Station. Incidentally, I was permitted to operate using fishermen's gas, which meant a considerable saving as the fishermen were given a special duty free gas. This helped them tremendously in their efforts to make a living and saved me money as well.

Edna had heard me talk so much about the Coast and the people in the various settlements that even though she was unhappy about being on the sea, being unfortunately a poor sailor, she, this particular year, expressed a desire to accompany me on the journey. It was agreed that in the August trip she and the girls would come along. We couldn't imagine going without Molly, our St. Bernard, and so when we set off there was myself, Edna, Martin Bugden, the two girls, and Molly.

All went well as we worked our way along the Coast stopping in at various ports. I would go about my medical duties and hold a clinic and visit patients, and Edna and the girls would explore and meet people. The general reaction to Molly, a very large dog by Newfoundland standards, was mixed. Some expressed great fears; others were sure that a dog that big had to be "saucy." All gave her a wide berth and yet she was a gentle, friendly dog who was slow and waddling but always inquisitive. I remember well Edna coming back chuckling after a visit to a store where, without thinking, she opened the door and entered with Molly on a lead. The reaction inside the store was instant and decisive. Everybody in the middle of the store promptly jumped over the counters so that storekeeper, attendants, and customers were on the inside of the counters looking out. Edna assured me they were served very quickly and on their way before anything terrible happened.

We arrived at Port Saunders, did our work, and were preparing to leave when I heard on the radio the news of a hurricane which was coming up from the south. It was expected to go along the south coast of Newfoundland and across the Avalon Peninsula. In port was the coastal steamer and, feeling it would be wise to seek expert advice, I went on board to see the Captain. The Captain was most pleasant and when I asked him what he thought about the hurricane, he took me into the wheelhouse and we looked at the barometer which appeared to be steady at around 29.90. We looked outside where it was a calm, clear, sunny day with very little wind. There was no sea running and generally it couldn't have appeared more of an innocent day. The Captain assured me that he didn't foresee any problems, and undoubtedly one should believe the radio forecast that in fact the hurricane would be going off to the east. Reassured, I bade him farewell, returned to *Tinker Bell,* and we cast off for the journey home.

We left Port Saunders at around midday expecting to make the straight run home in about ten hours, hoping that perhaps we would pick up a little time and might do it a little quicker, but happy that we would be home before it got completely dark. By the time we reached Belburns the wind was picking up; it was an offshore wind and the sea was beginning to get a bit ruffled. We were beginning to feel the fact that something was happening. The barometer was beginning to drop. It had now reached 29.5. Martin and I quietly discussed our options, but we were reassured by the Captain of the coastal boat and the radio broadcasts. I decided we'd carry on and if necessary put in somewhere along the coast.

The northwest coast is a hard coast in any kind of weather because between Bonne Bay and Port Saunders there is really no protected harbour which can be entered in all weathers. Certainly one could get into Parson's Pond, which is a small landlocked harbour, providing the tide is high to get up the river, but only if the weather is right. One could get into Portland Creek, again into the mouth of the river, if conditions were correct. Daniel's Harbour was nothing more than a sheltered pool behind a large rock which would take very skillful navigation to reach in any kind of storm.

The wind had really made up by the time we reached Daniel's Harbour, and it was obvious now from the fact that the barometer had dropped back to 29.2, that the hurricane had changed course and we were getting into the thick of it. The wind had picked up tremendously and heavy seas were making up across our course which made sailing difficult. I began to notice that the following seas were now in danger of crashing down on our stern and swamping us.

It was impossible now to turn back, and it was equally impossible to get into Daniel's Harbour because of the seas that were running as we went by. However, I decided that we had to take the chance to try and get into Portland Creek, and this we did. Our progress had slowed considerably, and it had taken us approximately four and one half hours to do a trip that normally would take two or two and one half hours. I had to work the throttle with one eye on the seas ahead and one eye on the following seas to make sure that we neither swamped or capsized. As we turned into Portland Creek, I looked at the row of houses. There are about five or six houses which lay to the south of the river. I wondered how we could attract their attention and get someone to come and perhaps pilot us into the river.

Martin and I had been in the mouth of the river on a couple of occasions before, but we knew, as well as anyone, that the entrance tended to change, that there were a number of rocks in the run, and that also we couldn't afford to fool around with weather like this. We blew our horn hoping to attract attention and Martin went on deck and waved a flag. Nobody appeared. The wind was now coming straight down the river at us, and was doing approximately sixty miles per hour. The sea behind us was now whipped into a fury, and we were pitching and tossing, nosing our way slowly towards where we thought the mouth of the river lay.

It was quite evident that to get into the mouth of the river where I knew there was water deep enough to float us, we were going to have to take some considerable chances and be quite firm in making a decision and charting a course. We agreed that it appeared no one was going to come out to guide us or help us in any way and we would have to go it alone.

Edna and the girls stayed in the cabin to give us freedom to move around as best we could and I started the engines and we headed up the channel. It was extremely difficult to see where we were going because with the wind was now coming heavy rain. The tremendous wind made it difficult to control the boat without increasing power to the point which was almost dangerous. However, having made up my mind there seemed only one thing to do and that was to run her in as fast as possible and pray that we wouldn't strike a hidden rock.

Martin perched on the bow to signal me as best he could if he saw any under water obstruction and we started. Half speed didn't seem to move her, three quarter speed only barely moved her, so that within a minute I had my throttle full out and she was beginning to pick up and move up the river against the wind and rain. We were halfway in to the mouth of the river when, without any warning, she shuddered and ran onto a sandbank. My heart sank because I realised that if we remained stuck on the bank we had no hope, and so ramming her into reverse gear, and with full throttle she hauled herself off slowly and after what seemed an interminable wait Martin was signalling me hard to starboard. Taking my courage into both hands I put her into forward gear, pulled the throttle full out, and turned to starboard. I moved out now into what appeared to be a channel and at full speed ahead we moved into the mouth of the river without striking anything else.

When we arrived in the mouth of the river we found ourselves in familiar territory, insofar as we'd been here before. In fact, it was a deep gut with fast flowing water, sixty mile an hour wind coming down the river at us, rain lashing the boat, and sandbanks on either side. Now we had the problem of putting out our moorings. We decided quickly that we had to put out four lines, two on the port side and two on the starboard side, one each over the bow, and one each over the stern, and they had to be made fast. So I ran *Tinker Bell* ahead and to starboard until I thought I could see the riverbed coming up rapidly and then we threw out a Navy Anchor and fell backwards to let the line stay out. Then I ran up again until we were almost on the sandy beach and threw out a second Navy Anchor on the port side over the bow, and then fell back again holding on these two lines with our nose into the wind. Then I cut the engines. We now launched our small dinghy, and went ashore on both sides of the stern carrying heavy lines, and two more anchors, until we had made our boat fast in the middle of the run. We were satisfied that she was safe and snug for the night.

It was now dark and the whistling of the wind and the lashing of the rain was a hard sound but we had the satisfaction of knowing that we had made it to safety anyway. We were soaked to the skin, for working against rain and against odds we gave no thought to our comfort, and were more concerned with saving the boat and protecting our passengers.

When all was finished we dried as best we could, and then discovered that every scrap of clothes on board was soaking wet as well. Everything was wet. The inside of the boat in the heavy rain was wet because it had leaked wherever it could leak. Still, we were happier. We cooked up a hot meal and settled down for an uneasy night, getting up every half hour or so, or at any untoward sound, to go out and have a look and make sure that our lines were holding. The gale continued all night, and we kept watch as the tide fell and we bumped on the bottom at very low tide.

In the morning when daylight came we were astonished at what we saw around us. When we entered the river the previous night the gently undulating sandbanks on either side were a familiar sight. They had always been like this and it was a typical beach as is seen in many parts of the world. By morning, however, the picture had changed. Now the heavy seas rolling in had eaten away the edges of the sandbanks and on both sides the river had cut sharply through so that we were now lying in a channel with perpendicular edges extending approximately six feet into the air. The sand had been washed clear by great waves washing in and the waters rushing down the river. The river was swollen considerably by the heavy rains and now the wind had shifted and was coming in from the sea driving the seas in before it and we were trapped in the mouth of the river. When the tide fell we had relative peace and quiet but as the tide rose the big seas drove in and up the river, and we found ourselves tossed around helplessly though our moorings held secure throughout.

I was sure that by the end of that day the wind would drop and we would be able to get out and continue our journey home. The radio forecast assured us that the hurricane had veered north instead of going along the South coast and into the Atlantic and had caused considerable damage in Western Newfoundland. It was presently blowing itself out in the Gulf of St. Lawrence. We didn't need the radio to tell us about this. It was blowing itself on us. There was no indication as to how long the blowing out process would last.

We took it in good part the first day and tried to dry out our clothes and sleeping bags and the boat generally. We didn't have too much food aboard as we were heading home. With five of us and a hungry dog on board, we didn't have much left by the first night. However, we had enough for the day and the seas were still sufficient to make it not too alluring to get into our dinghy and head for shore. We went through that day and headed into another night.

The wind didn't change. It still came on shore. The second low tide was a very low tide which grounded us. We started to turn on our side. Luckily the low tide had left a barrier of sand out beyond us and it was on this barrier that the seas broke. Although we were grounded, we were steady and there was no damage done by the heavy seas which couldn't reach us. As the tide rose we floated clear, and by the time the heavy seas again reached us we had plenty of water under our keel and I don't remember her grounding once in the heavy seas.

The very low water gave us an opportunity also to see the run that we'd come up, and I was horrified to see how many boulders lay strewn through the shore. There was no doubt in my mind that there was only one time to enter Portland Creek and that was at high water when one would go over the top of most of them.

The second night was another night of wind and heavy seas pounding us, and another sleepless night as we kept watch to make sure that our moorings held and that we didn't drag an anchor and lose our boat. By the second day we were running short of food, so we put a party ashore who returned in an hour or two with some home-made bread and canned foods. These would do us for another couple of days. We also received a visit from the local people asking if there was anything they could do and apart from the bit of food which we bought there was really nothing. We just had to sit out the weather until we could head for home.

The morning of the second day dawned and again the sand dunes around us had changed with the heavy seas breaking in during the night. Now on our starboard side was an interesting sight. Sitting, looking at us in the edge of the sand dune were two large vertebrae from a whale. We were extremely interested in this and when the tide fell we launched our dinghy and went ashore to have a closer look. Obviously a large whale many years before had driven in on shore. No doubt, if we had dug we would have come up with more vertebra but we were quite satisfied to take these two. We loaded them in the dinghy and brought them aboard the boat and kept them as souvenirs. They decorate our garden to this day. A heavy sea was still running outside making it impossible for us to move out, and the girls were getting a little bit impatient. They went ashore and Martin regaled us with stories of ghosts and hidden treasures and this fired the imagination of the girls. Aided by Edna they set off on a treasure hunt.

It was surprising what they managed to dig up, or perhaps it was the storm and the seas which dug things up, but they came back after two or three hours combing the sands with all kinds of odds and ends including bits of broken crockery and other similar objects most of which were taken home and stories woven around each bit brought in fancy named pirates who might well have lived and worked on the Coast.

One of the delightful stories Martin told us concerned a pirate who is reported to have died in the Portland Creek area and was reputed to have been about eight feet tall and whose weapon was a sword almost as tall as he was. I only regretted that we couldn't find his burial place and his sword to authenticate the story. The legend of course said that the treasure was buried in a pond. We couldn't find the pond. All we could find were the marshes surrounding the area and they extended for miles and so it was anybody's guess as to whether the story was true. The coasts are bound with stories of this nature and there may well be some truth to some of them.

It was the fifth day before the wind fell and we were able to move out and continue along the coast to Bonne Bay. Each night was still a night of vigil for the wind was still onshore. The seas were still pounding in and while we had relative peace when the tide was out, we had to watch our lines when the tide was high and the seas were coming in and reaching us. When we did haul off we did so at the earliest moment as the wind dropped and the seas started to fall away. We had a rough voyage home with a cross wind, but we pushed on knowing how important it was to get back, having been out of touch for five days. The hospital knew, of course, where we were and what was holding us up. We had been through some considerable discomfort, and had had quite an experience.

It was common knowledge on the Coast that from about August 20 onwards was a bad time to be travelling, for this was the time of year when the high winds always struck in following the approach of hurricanes from the south. It was the only time during my stay on the coast that a full scale hurricane ever reached the West Coast and, shortly after returning to Bonne Bay, I had to make the journey through to Deer Lake. I was amazed as we went through the country to see the destruction in the forest. The hurricane had cut a path through the country, looked as if it had been cut over by woodsmen, but in fact the trees were still there lying on the ground, uprooted where they lay.

There were many stories that reached us of experiences during the hurricane, but to my knowledge no one suffered anything except damage to roofs, or boats that broke loose from their moorings, and fishing gear that was lost. There was no loss of life on our part of the coast. Knowing the likelihood of bad weather, it had always been my plan to be off the coast by August 20, and each year I made sure that I was back to base before that date. Each year I noted that approximately on that date the weather would change and the storms would start. From that time on, I planned for an earlier date. If I had to go later it had to be done depending on weather. I had trouble reconciling this necessity with the fact that illness doesn't wait for suitable weather.

Chapter 16

THE YACHTSMEN

One afternoon in July 1947, I received a message from the Point telling me that a yacht had just entered the bay, had gone past Norris Point and entered Neddy's Harbour, and was anchored there. I was extremely interested in this news and as soon as I could get clear, Edna and I made for the Point. Taking *Tinker Bell* we headed around into Neddy's Harbour, and sure enough there was a beautiful yacht of about twenty-five feet. She lay gleaming in the sunshine, a brilliant white on the blue water, her name clearly visible, *Sea Crest*. We came alongside, stopped a couple of feet away, and looked at the people who were in the stern cockpit preparing to have a meal. I called out to them, "Welcome to Bonne Bay. Can we do anything for you?"

The skipper came to the rail and said he was delighted that we had come out to greet them. They were quite self-contained and didn't really need very much but would be grateful if there was some way that they could get some laundry done and all have a bath. I suggested that as soon as they were finished their meal they might come ashore and come up to the hospital if they could find their way. It wasn't far and we would look after them. He expressed his surprise that there was a hospital there. He seemed very pleased to find that not only was there a hospital but that I was the doctor. He said they would be along shortly.

When they appeared later, they introduced themselves. It turned out that this was Dr. Paul Sheldon and his wife, Carol, from New York City. Crewing with them was George Campbell, a teacher. We were delighted to have a medical man and a boating enthusiast at the same time to stay in the area. They remained for three days. We offered them our home as headquarters for baths, laundry, mail and when they returned, in later years, crew changes. We found that as we got to know Paul and Carol, they were most enthusiastic about cruising, that Paul had spent the past few years in the United States Army in Europe, that his great love was the sea and yachting, and his dearest possession was *Sea Crest*. He was an internist in practice in New York City and his objective was to take two months holiday every year and take off in the *Sea Crest*.

Our meeting was the beginning of a lifelong friendship during which time we offered them our home for themselves and their friends and crews. In return, on several occasions we visited New York and were always their guests. It was a wonderful friendship and opened many doors for us in New York and elsewhere.

On my first trip to New York in 1950, I took Edna and the girls for our first holiday. In the course of staying with the Sheldons, Paul took me to the New York Yacht Club on a couple of occasions. I was introduced to the editor of *Yachting Magazine*, Charles Rimmington, and lunched with him. I met Carleton Mitchell, famous yachtsman, photographer, and author. I attended with Paul the first lecture given in the United States by Jacques Cousteau, the famous French under-water explorer, later to become world famous with his televised underwater adventures. I accompanied Paul to the Corinthian Yacht Club meetings on several occasions and found that Paul was recognised by his fellow yachtsmen as an authority on the Newfoundland and Labrador coastal area. Paul received many awards for his skill and seamanship and it was a great honour to enjoy the friendship of this outstanding physician and yachtsman. Through my friendship with Paul, I met many other people including Dr. Larry Sloane, famed New York thyroid surgeon, and Dr. Cushman Hagenson, outstanding world authority on breast cancer who was Paul's brother-in-law. In fact, I was Dr. Hagenson's guest for a day at the Presbyterian Cancer Division in New York where I was brought up to date on the latest developments in cancer research and treatment.

Carol's sister, Dr. Jeannette Munro of Princeton, the sister of Dana Munro, United States Diplomat, had a pediatric practice in Princeton. She often accompanied Paul and Carol on their trips North. In due course we were invited to visit Princeton. It was on a visit to Princeton, while we stayed with Jeannette Munro, that we attended the Princeton-Rutgers football game, an annual event with a great deal of interest as they were great rivals. This was our first experience of live American football and we were quite fascinated. I was, however, greatly bothered by the fact that nobody stayed sitting down or standing up. It was a constant movement up and down, up and down, up and down all the time and I found it very disconcerting. However, the colourful display by the cheerleaders and bands in the intervals made it a lively piece of entertainment for the girls and I found the techniques of the plays extremely interesting although I myself was a rugby football fan. At that time didn't quite understand American football.

Paul came back nearly every year to visit us. Sometimes we were the end of the line. Sometimes we were visited on the way North, and he would go right up the Labrador Coast and then perhaps back as far as St. Anthony and leave *Sea Crest* there for the winter returning direct to New York. He would pick up the boat again the next year and then come South visiting us as he went back. Sometimes he did a trans-insular trip so that we got visited on the way.

Always they used our home as a crew change point. Since they could never be sure of their timing precisely, we often found crew members arriving and spending two or three days with us and crew members leaving and spending two or three days at our home before they started the journey back to the United States. We had crew members arrive from Europe and leave on their way back working as Paul's crew as part of their holiday. In this manner we met all types of wonderful people, all sharing one thing in common, their great love of the sea. Among the crew members were Paul's son, Dana, who graduated in medicine and later entered Psychiatry, his daughter, Cynthia, who was probably no more than fourteen or fifteen when we first knew her, Mrs. Kitty Thomas, and many others whom we only saw once and never again.

It was the custom for Paul to have an annual reunion of the crew members, and on one occasion when I attended this, Larry Sloane and George Campbell showed movies that they had taken and to which they had added a sound track. Although they were amateurs it was a very professional job. The soundtrack included Newfoundland folk songs and verses composed by themselves, one of which stands out clearly in my mind and concerns episodes that took place on the Labrador Coast when they were caught by a bad storm in a very unhappy harbour. The clock on the *Sea Crest* was acting up and, superstitious as sailors are, somebody felt the attempts to repair the clock had disturbed the elements and that somehow the soul of a puffin had got caught up in the clockworks. The storm was the result of the anger of the gods. It was a most delightful piece of light-hearted poetry and I only hope that somewhere it still exists today for somebody to enjoy.

Even after we left Bonne Bay, our friendship with Paul and Carol Sheldon continued. They still visited us when we moved to Corner Brook, and they still used our home as a crew change point, as a place to do laundry, and have baths. We enjoyed their friendship until Paul retired and no longer sailed *Sea Crest* to Newfoundland.

There were of course other visitors who came by boat but none who came as frequently and steadily and with whom we had developed such a great friendship as the Sheldons. Amongst the other yachts that came was John Cooley, also from the United States. It was his habit to bring aboard with him three or four students. The purpose of the cruise was to give them training in seamanship on board a yacht, and to this end he had no motor or power of any kind. His crews were utterly and completely dependent on the use of the winds. His outlook was that these young men had to learn to make do. During the voyage, they had to learn how to sail and they had to learn how to look after themselves. They made their own way catching fish, salmon, trout, and buying vegetables and other foods as they needed them wherever they touched in. I found this rather frightening, for there were times when it seemed all important to have some power on a small vessel of this type so that at least one could get into shelter out of the weather. John Cooley didn't share this opinion, and certainly never seemed to come to any harm because of his attitude.

Another visitor was George Whiteley Jr., a marine biologist who worked in Philadelphia, aboard a small vessel *The Seal*. This was a yacht of about thirty feet. George's father, the late Captain George Whiteley, was the Member of the House of Assembly for the St. Barbe District in 1932 when he was elected to represent the district for the Conservative Party. While Captain George Whiteley returned to the public scene in 1949 with Confederation, he did not get elect-ed again because of the people's feeling that "Tory times were hard times." George Jr. was not a politician, but he did circumnavigate Newfoundland six times during his sailing career. He stopped in Bonne Bay on many of his trips.

One of the most interesting experiences concerning visiting yachts occurred one day when I spotted a sizable vessel making its way up the Main Arm. I stopped the car and watched this vessel as it went by and said bluntly that I had never seen a vessel of this type in our waters before. I felt that she looked like a Norwegian trawler. Whatever information I had in the back of my mind I had gleaned from a number of magazines to which I had subscribed, amongst these yachting and boating magazines. She fitted the picture of such a vessel. Later that day she made her way down the Main Arm and into Neddy's Harbour where she anchored. It was too much for me to see this beautiful vessel there and not know more about it.

She was well over 100 feet in length. From the shore, she appeared to have every conceivable navigational aid on board. I could see the radar equipment and not only lifeboats power equipped but a fast motor boat on her deck. She was obviously a trawler of some kind, because she had the forward hold. However, she appeared to be converted into some kind of a private luxury yacht. I wasted no time. I went aboard *Tinker Bell* and headed into Neddy's Harbour to learn more about the visitor.

As I came up alongside, three crew members rushed to the side of the ship and fended me off with boat hooks and suggested that they didn't want me to come near. It now appeared that she was extremely well kept, the varnish and brass was evident in abundance and the crew were all wearing soft rubber shoes so that there would be no marks on the boat anywhere. I inquired if I could pay my respects to the owner and was informed that he was having dinner and could not be disturbed. I then suggested if there was anything we could do we would be very pleased and that if the owner would like to come ashore we would be glad to entertain him. I told them that I was the doctor, that the hospital was just a little bit up the road, and that they would be very welcome. At that, we left.

Later in the evening two men came to the hospital and introduced themselves. One man's name I didn't catch, but the other man, being a doctor, I made a point of getting to know. He was Doctor Mueller from New York and he told me that he was travelling on this yacht as the physician to the owner who was on board. The man with him was the owner's brother. He kept referring to this man simply as "The General," and while he must have introduced him at the beginning I had missed the name. All I knew then was that he was "The General." They were extremely interested in the hospital and asked if they could see over it. Of course, I was delighted to take the opportunity to show them around. We did a complete tour of the hospital, but the place that interested them most was the operating room. They spent a lot of time in the operating room asking me what kind of materials I used. The catgut I assured them was the finest that I could find–Davis and Geck. The Plaster of Paris again I assured them was the finest that I could find–Smith and Nephew plaster. And so we went to item after item and I was surprised at their interest.

Dr. Mueller told me that on board they had a good supply of all the latest antibiotics. They were fully equipped to carry out any surgery. The purpose of their voyage was to bring a supply of clothes up the Labrador Coast, and then continue on their way to Greenland for a cruise. Following our visit around the hospital they came up to our home for tea and spent some time with us. The General was very happy to talk to and play with the girls, and the time passed very quickly while I discussed various medical matters with Dr. Mueller, including answering many questions as to the extent of our operations. When they left, they extended an invitation for us to go to dinner with them the following evening, which we were pleased to accept.

The next evening the weather was fine. We dressed up suitably, boarded *Tinker Bell,* and headed for the visiting yacht. This time our reception was very different and the crew was ready to haul us alongside, make us fast, and welcome us aboard. We had been warned to put on soft shoes so that we wouldn't mar the deck and this we had done. Dr. Mueller and the General were on hand to meet us and the owner, a tall man who was most charming, immediately took us on tour of the boat. As I had suspected, the boat was a converted Norwegian trawler and it must have cost a million dollars to convert it. It was equipped with every navigational aid, such as radar, Loran, depth sounders, and ship to shore radios, all of which in those days were relatively new to this type of vessel.

We ended up in a sumptuous dining room sitting at two tables. Dr. Mueller, Edna, and I were at one table, and the girls, the General, and the owner were at another table on the other side of the dining room. I will never forget when the door from the kitchen opened and the waiter appeared with a silver platter on which were fresh lamb chops, meat which we hadn't seen for several months, done to perfection with fresh vegetables. The meal turned out to be a magnificent repast. In the course of the meal and the conversation, Dr. Mueller looked at me with a peculiar look and said, "I presume you do know who your hosts are." I admitted to him that I had missed the name and didn't really know who they were, at which point he turned sideways and looked across the room said, "Well, there are Johnson and Johnson." I was ready for the floor to open up and swallow me as I realised that the famous surgical and medical firm of Johnson and Johnson got its name from the two brothers who were sitting there entertaining the girls and ourselves.

Dr. Mueller realised my thoughts at once and hastened to assure me that they weren't that kind of people, that they were deeply impressed with my insistence on only the best for the hospital, and although none of it was Johnson and Johnson material, there were no bad feelings. They would just have to do better to insure that I in due course would see fit to put some of their supplies into my hospital. He will never know how grateful I was to him because I was feeling completely miserable at the way I had presented the hospital the previous day to the General. We spent a wonderful evening on board the ship. They were wonderful hosts and we will never forget the visit that was made to Bonne Bay by Johnson and Johnson.

When they left we know they went up the Labrador Coast into Greenland. They were loaded with clothes which they were taking to give to the less fortunate people who lived on the coast. They showed us the loads of drugs and antibiotics and equipment that they possessed and I felt sure that before their journey was over they would have given this out and helped many people who would not have received help in any other way. Over the years I watched with interest for news of Johnson and Johnson and it was with sorrow that I read a few years later of the death of the General. He got his nickname from the rank he held during the war.

Chapter 17

VISITING AND VISITORS

Over the years we had many visitors from outside the Bonne Bay area and we found ourselves always extremely happy to see people who brought a change of pace, change of outlook, and news from the great outside world. As well, when we had the opportunity, we made a point of visiting the surrounding area. I found it extremely easy to become very small-minded, but it wasn't easy to recognise this. One became somewhat petty and overpowered by local problems to which one gave more attention than they deserved. It was apparent to me and Edna that this could be seen more clearly if one got away for even two or three days. Then one could see the problems in perspective and realise what was happening. The problem is the common condition for isolated communities known as being "bushed," whereby one becomes secretive, introspective, and suspicious of everybody and everything. One resents suggestions from outsiders, and can make life unbearable for everybody around.

Therefore, approximately twice a year we endeavoured to slip away to Corner Brook for a few days. Such a trip was necessary anyway because there was always a certain amount of shopping to be done, not only for food but for clothing as well, and for the odd piece of furniture or furnishing or equipment for the house. These visits to Corner Brook gave me the opportunity to mix with my fellow doctors, and their friendliness and hospitality always overwhelmed us. They were extremely busy and worked day and night, but always found time to extend a hand of friendship to make the hospital, its cases, and their knowledge freely available to me. They welcomed me to their rounds and their staff lunches and took us into their homes during what free time they had to entertain us. Over the years, particularly Dr. Dove and Dr. Monaghan went out of their way with kindness and consideration and did so much to make everything pleasant for us.

Buying goods was always important and must have caused some raised eyebrows as we gave our orders. One of the most amusing was ordering dog biscuits and dog food, for having from two to six St. Bernards, we didn't order by the bag. We ordered by the half ton or ton and sometimes the food was just not available in this quantity and had to be especially ordered for us. Particularly in winter time we had to make sure that we got our order well in advance for it had to be shipped by boat to reach us in time. One funny instance which I recall happened when a shipment of dog food arrived and one of the 100 pound cartons broke open on the wharf, and out rolled dog biscuits. The locals couldn't understand what on earth we needed this stuff for. I doubt if they had ever seen this particular type of food stuff and they weren't sure what it was. Somebody asked me what it was intended for and I assured him very seriously that this was my breakfast cereal. I told him I couldn't consider starting my day without a goodly supply of breakfast. I invited him to try it, and those of us who knew what it was watched with amusement as he nibbled at a dog biscuit and tried to make out that it was pleasant. In fact, it was obvious that he couldn't stand the taste of it and as he walked around the corner he kept it in his pocket and no doubt quickly disposed of it at the first opportunity.

As soon as we were settled in we looked forward to visitors as we realised that it would not be easy for people to reach us. Over the years we did meet a considerable number of people who made the trip by coastal boat from Corner Brook as an interesting tour. It was much sought after not only by tourists from outside Newfoundland, but by Newfoundlanders themselves enjoying our own country. Often we knew in advance that friends would be travelling on the coastal boat, particularly the *Northern Ranger*, and we would make a point of going down to meet the boat. Perhaps if there was a fair amount of freight on board we would take them up to the house for a cup of tea. However, often the boat arrived in the middle of the night and it was impossible to enjoy a visit at that hour.

One of the first visitors in the summer of 1945 was Ken Goodyear from Grand Falls who made the journey from Grand Falls to Norris

Point especially to visit me and learn what he could about his son Denny, who was also in the R.A.F. and was serving with the 125 (Newfoundland) Squadron. It should be pointed out that there was no telephone in those days. If he had not visited, it would have been necessary to write but he wanted to get news of his son directly from me. I was very impressed that Ken Goodyear had gone to such trouble to visit me to get information about his son. Not only was I delighted to meet him, but I told him all I could. Denny was an observer on the Squadron. He had been with us for some time, was a very outgoing type of individual, and always ready for a party and full of jokes. At the same time, he was a hard working officer. His job as an observer was to sit alongside his pilot in the Mosquito Night Fighters that we operated and take care of the radar equipment, guide his pilot, and be the other half of a team. A pilot and observer was a specially skilled unit for night fighting. I was able to assure his father that when I had left the Squadron, he was in good health and, hopefully, now that the war was over would soon return home. We discussed the fact that the war in the Far East was still very much active and that possibly personnel would be transferred out there to hasten the end. We agreed that more than likely the Newfoundlanders would now be demobilised and returned home. From this first visit, Ken Goodyear of Grand Falls became a good friend of mine.

On our way out of Bonne Bay in May of 1945, during our stopover in Corner Brook, we also looked up Albert and Peg Martin. I was related to Peg. My grandmother and Peg's grandmother were sisters, which made us second cousins. Albert was now Assistant Woods Manager to Bowaters Paper Company and he introduced me to H.M.S. Lewin, the President and General Manager of Bowaters in Corner Brook. Albert and Peg were always very hospitable and went out of their way to help us in every manner possible. The first summer, Albert, in the course of his work, visited me at Norris Point. He brought two things which pleased us immensely; first, the local newspaper two or three days ahead of the time when we would expect to get it by mail; and, secondly, a large piece of fresh meat which was not too easy to come by. He made many visits over the years by road, by boat, and later by plane, and never failed to bring something which we valued immensely when he came. The only thing that we could do in return would be to entertain him to a meal and try and glean news from the outside world before we got it in other ways several days later.

Over the years, H.M.S. Lewin also made a number of visits and I enjoyed developing a friendship with him which continued when we later moved to Corner Brook. Even many years after his retirement, when he lived in Bermuda, it was my good fortune to visit there and I paid a visit to see him at that time. One of the most interesting of Mr. Lewin's visits was a forced visit with Albert Martin one year when they were going in the company motor cruiser, the *Porpoise,* from Corner Brook to Hawke's Bay to visit their operation there. They left Corner Brook late in the evening and planned to travel all night arriving at Hawke's Bay early in the morning. When it came time to retire, they all settled into their various bunks and a crew member stayed at the wheel to guide the boat. However, during the night, when they were off Cow Head, he noticed Mr. Lewin go out into the cockpit and stagger and nearly fall overboard. The crewman immediately went out to see what was wrong and found Mr. Lewin on the point of collapse. He, too, when he went into the cockpit and the fresh air, realised that something was very wrong. He guessed that they had a leak and carbon monoxide was filling the interior of the boat. He immediately switched off the engine, roused the other members of the party, and got them out into the cockpit. It was evident that they had all begun to suffer the effects of carbon monoxide poisoning. Cow Head lies some thirty miles from the mouth of Bonne Bay and they promptly turned around and made their way back to Norris Point. I was summoned and came to look at my patients who were feeling pretty miserable and sitting on the wharf at Norris Point. I made a diagnosis of carbon monoxide poisoning, which wasn't very difficult. One only had to look at them to realise what had happened, and I suggested that without delay they return by road to Corner Brook but in the meantime get some rest and fresh air, which would take care of their condition in time. They took my advice and made the journey by car back to Corner Brook. Of the party, Mr. Lewin was the one most affected, but he was an extremely strong individual and in twenty-four hours he was back to normal again. This was an extremely nasty experience for the group and a very fortunate ending to what might have been a complete disaster.

During 1947, Sir Eric Bowater, the President and Chairman of Bowaters International, on one of his visits to Newfoundland, brought with him a medical doctor from England, Dr. Neville Whitehurst. Whitehurst was the family physician to the Bowater family. During the war he was a ferry pilot flying Air Force planes from factory to airfield. Bowater had brought Dr. Whitehurst with him for business reasons. Sir Eric's idea was to introduce into Newfoundland and the Bowaters operation a flying medical service which would supply medical attention to the many operations which Bowaters carried out and for which they were responsible.

In those days the Bowaters Woods Camps were directly a part of the Bowater operation and the provision of medical services was the responsibility if possible of the company. However, it was extremely difficult to provide medical services to isolated camps. If planes were used for medical deliveries the workers would enjoy much better service. Dr. Whitehurst, who was a good pilot in his own right, was therefore brought in to become the "Flying Doctor" for Bowaters. He and Mr. Lewin had flown to Norris Point to talk to me.

As usual we were delighted to see visitors, particularly Mr. Lewin. Although I hadn't met Dr. Whitehurst before, we were pleased to entertain both of them. I noticed that Mr. Lewin was busily engaged talking to my wife in one corner of the lounge and Neville Whitehurst was edging me into another corner and finally he brought us the point of his visit. Having gone through the idea of the Flying Doctor Service and how it might be operated in Newfoundland, he asked me if it was true that I had served in the R.A.F. during the war. When I replied that this in fact was so, he then asked me if I would consider joining Bowaters and becoming the Flying Doctor. At that point the intention was that he would return to Britain and I would take over, travelling the country providing medical services as and when needed. Being perfectly happy where we were and settled in my work, I told him that there was no way that I could give up what I was doing to join Bowaters. Both Dr. Whitehurst and Mr. Lewin made strenuous efforts to get me to change my mind, but I was quite firm about it. I preferred to stay where I was. They left with no hard feelings, and Dr. Whitehurst himself stayed on to become the Flying Doctor. Later, he played an important role in the Bowater operation as he took over many of the subsidiary companies which Bowaters owned in Corner Brook and operated them for the main company.

The first official visit from the Department of Health was a visit from the Commissioner of the Department of Health and Welfare, Sir John Puddester, accompanied by his wife, Lady Puddester. We were notified by telegram that Sir John and Lady Puddester would be visiting us. We prepared to receive them, show them around the hospital, and tell them about the work that was going on.

News of their impending arrival threw us into a bit of a turmoil. The arrival of such a distinguished personage, and particularly the Head of the Department for which I worked, was going to be a big day. We prepared ourselves, the house and the hospital, and arranged that when they arrived at Norris Point, Martin Bugden would take the hospital truck and go down to meet them and bring them up to our house where we could entertain them.

I was advised by phone when the party arrived at Norris Point, and the truck set off to meet them. Eventually the party arrived at the front door of the house and I opened it to greet Sir John and Lady Puddester, and my wife stood slightly behind me so that I could present her also. Sir John Puddester stepped in through the door and shook my hand and then turning towards his wife he said, "Meet my woman." I was taken aback by his use of this expression, having heard it used around the district but not expecting it from a personage like Sir John. I quickly recovered and greeted Lady Puddester, but when I turned around to introduce them to Edna, the look of amazement and dismay was still on her face and she wasn't quite sure what to make of it. It was quite obvious that Sir John and Lady Puddester were perfectly normal and natural people. Sir John was using an expression which he heard throughout Newfoundland when a man referred to his wife, although we were unused to it. The Puddesters spend some time at the house. After we had a meal, they toured the hospital, and spent some time talking with the patients. Then we accompanied them back to the Point where we said our farewells as they set off for Corner Brook and St. John's.

Sir John seemed to have a good understanding of many of the difficulties facing a doctor working in isolation and assured me that any assistance I needed within reason would be available. Certainly my requests to the Department were dealt with in a practical and understanding way from that time on.

The other important personage who paid us a visit within the first two or three years was the Governor of Newfoundland, Sir Gordon MacDonald, and his wife and son who visited one summer. We had ample warning of the visit as it was a recognised practice for Government House to set it up well in advance. They made sure that the proper arrangements were made in every part of the country where the Governor would go so he would be received with the proper respect for his Office. A committee was organized in Bonne Bay for the Governor's visit, and an itinerary was worked out so that he would be seen by and meet as many people as possible. It was agreed that he would be taken from Lomond to Woody Point where there would be an official reception. Then he would go to Norris Point for another reception, he would visit the hospital, he would have a meal at the Doctor's house, and then would be returned to Lomond.

A delegation came to see me and asked if I would make my boat, the *Tinker Bell*, available for the occasion as it was the best, most comfortable and fastest boat in the Bay. I agreed to this immediately and then set about making the necessary arrangements. It was agreed that there would be two crewmen. Martin Bugden would be one and Jim Snow would be the other. Both of them were well-acquainted with *Tinker Bell* and knew how to handle the ship and themselves. I was proud to have a crew like this, and I agreed to go with the boat to meet the Governor at Lomond.

It was my understanding that the Union Jack should be flown wherever the Governor was, and I discussed this at great length with Bryant Harding. We agreed that when the Governor stepped aboard the *Tinker Bell* a Union Jack would break out on the mast. The problem was to find a Union Jack of the right size, because the flags in Norris Point were either too small or too large. Eventually we found a suitable one. Then came the problem of how to rig it so that a tug of the line would release the flag. I spent hours working on this problem and eventually developed a technique whereby the flag was folded into a small packet and hoisted to the top of the mast. On signal, someone would tug at the line to release the flag, which would flutter out in the breeze. It worked beautifully at each rehearsal and on the great day was set in position for the moment when the Governor stepped aboard. At the same time I arranged for the Union Jack to fly from the hospital flag pole in exactly the same way so that when the Governor entered the hospital grounds the flag could be released to signal his arrival.

There was considerable excitement at Lomond when we arrived there. The Governor and his party were not due for half an hour or so. It was a beautiful day and every man, woman and child was on hand to see the Governor. The community consisted of about fifteen or eighteen homes, and there must have been all of 150 men, women, and children standing by. The *Tinker Bell* was tied up at the foot of the wharf's steps and I saw that one man was standing beside the line running up the mast to where the Jack was furled and all was in readiness.

In due course, the car arrived, the Governor and Lady MacDonald and their party alighted, and introductions were made. When it was time to move on after the Governor had a chance to meet the people of Lomond, as he stepped aboard the *Tinker Bell*, I saw the line yanked. Nothing happened. The crewman yanked the line again and again and nothing happened. Finally, with a sigh of disgust the crew member climbed on top of the cabin and yanked the flag out by hand and it fluttered in the breeze. I discovered later that in his excitement he had been hauling the wrong line. No wonder nothing happened. Nonetheless we set off for Woody Point and had an uneventful journey with an opportunity to talk with the Governor and Lady MacDonald as we plied waters. We were met about a mile from Woody Point by a large open fishing boat filled with men of Bonne Bay, a sailor wearing his uniform standing erect in the bow of the boat, and nearly every man with a loaded shotgun. They looked for all the world like a bunch of pirates bearing down on us. As the boat came abreast of us a volley of shots was fired. When it rounded up on the other side, another volley of shots was fired. This "attack," of course, was the traditional way that the people welcomed the Governor of Newfoundland to their settlements.

This salute prompted the Governor to tell me that the first time he had made a visit to a settlement outside St. John's was by car and entailed following the road down into the settlement through a forested road. Behind nearly every tree was hidden a man with a shotgun, and as the car went by the men fired their shotguns. The Governor hadn't been warned. He thought in the early moments that the people were taking potshots at him. He wasn't sure whether he should get on the floor of the car or go to his end as a man. Fortunately, it was explained to him before he lost face, and he learned to accept the salute as such.

The arrival at Woody Point was greeted again by more gunfire and the Governor went ashore for the official reception and met with the hundreds of people who turned out. The settlement and the waterfront area were gaily decorated with flags and bunting and it was a gala day for all concerned. After lunch the party moved again in the *Tinker Bell* from Woody Point to Norris Point accompanied by a number of other boats making a flotilla that moved across the water to Norris Point. On arrival in Norris Point, again, there was crowd present and the wharves were gaily decorated and everybody was in a cheerful holiday mood.

The hospital truck was backed up on the wharf and the best that we could do was to put an armchair in the back of the truck for the Governor to sit in so that not only would he see everybody, but everybody could see him as he travelled along. Lady MacDonald was put in the cab of the truck and when the moment came the party moved to the hospital in this manner. As we approached the hospital I noticed that the Union Jack was flying and obviously somebody had yanked on the line well in advance. No matter. Nobody noticed, but the Governor was pleased that his presence was recognised by the flying of the Union Jack. He and Lady MacDonald toured the hospital and spoke with the patients and staff, and eventually we arrived at "Treetops" for a meal before they left to return.

The excitement in the house was intense. Edwina and her friend Gerine were in the background but enjoying it all for this was a day to which everybody had looked forward. Finally the moment came for the party to leave and as we walked down the front steps of the house I heard a loud but clear little voice from inside. It said, "His name shouldn't have been Sir Gordon MacDonald, it should have been MacDonald Duck!" It was impossible for the remark not to have been heard. It was quite obvious who said it. It was quite obvious that it was the genuine feeling of a child. While at first I was horror stricken, when I looked at the Governor and Lady MacDonald, I noticed their smiles. They understood the situation and took it at face value. The party then boarded the truck and again we made our way to Norris Point. Then the *Tinker Bell* took us to Lomond where I bade them farewell.

This was the only time that the Governor visited Bonne Bay during my stay and, of course, in 1949 with Confederation, Sir Gordon MacDonald returned to England and was replaced in Newfoundland by a Lieutenant Governor.

Every year we received visits from either the Deputy Minister, the Assistant Deputy Minister, or the Administrator of the Health Department, respectively Dr. Leonard Miller, Dr. James McGrath, and Mr. Dave Butler. These were business visits but they did bring news of what was going on in the Cottage Hospital system around the province, what other doctors were doing, which other doctors were employed in the system, and what sort of medical progress had generally been made. Our problems were aired and often solutions found on the spot. Other times they were taken into consideration for decisions to be made later in the department headquarters in St. John's. On the whole it was always a pleasant time to have a visit from somebody in authority, and to be able to show them one's work and one's accomplishments, looking for criticism, looking for suggestions. It was never easy being alone and responsible for so many patients, for the running of the medical side of the hospital, and for the multitude of other problems and decisions that had to be made. It was a twenty-four hour operation, 365 days of the year, and it always helped to know some support from the administration was available.

One of the most interesting visits was during one summer when Dr. McGrath brought the *Lady Anderson*, the Department Hospital ship which operated on the south coast, on a trip up the west coast to Port Saunders. This vessel, which was a luxury yacht designed for inland river work and bought in the 1930s from the States, had a reputation for being a very poor sea boat. When I was advised that Dr.

McGrath was coming and would like me to accompany him to Port Saunders on the *Lady Anderson*, I responded by saying that I would be glad to go but would prefer to accompany them in my own boat, *Tinker Bell*.

Dr. McGrath had no objection to this. I pointed out that while we would make the run up to Port Saunders in a day, I would then take the opportunity to stay on, do some work there, and work my way back down the coast visiting the settlements as I did. This was agreed and we set off.

I was delighted to discover that my boat was faster than the *Lady Anderson*, and felt good having the throttle back so that we would keep abreast of Dr. McGrath's boat. However, I was overwhelmed when it came lunch time and the *Lady Anderson* signalled me to come alongside and they passed over dinners for Martin and myself which were a great deal better than we could have produced. They had the advantage of having a full crew aboard whereas Martin and I were used to looking after ourselves. It was the only time in my years on the coast that anybody ever gave me a meal over the rail at sea.

When we arrived at Port Saunders the *Lady Anderson* went alongside the Government Wharf and we came up on the outside and tied on. We noticed that lying in the Port Saunders Inner harbour was a Canadian mine sweeper. This was unexpected but not unusual because during the summer months quite often the Canadian Navy sent vessels on training cruisers and they used the West Coast quite frequently. We had seen them in Bonne Bay and therefore were not surprised to find a vessel in Port Saunders.

However, shortly after going ashore to the Nursing Station with Dr. McGrath so he could conduct his inspection, a message arrived that the Canadian Warship requested the service of a doctor. They didn't realise there were two doctors in port and since Dr. McGrath was the senior doctor, I suggested that he was the one they should have aboard. He retaliated by saying that since it was my district it was obviously my responsibility. We settled this by agreeing that we would both go aboard. We agreed at a certain hour they could send their launch for us.

We were ready that afternoon at about four p.m. when the launch came alongside. To my horror the sailors then proceeded to slam their boat hooks into my deck which was canvassed and carefully painted to make it waterproof. I certainly "went aboard" that launch and let them know in no uncertain terms what I thought of their ability and understanding of boats. Following my dressing down and their apologies, which incidentally didn't repair the holes in my deck, they then made the most awful display of seamanship that I'd ever seen trying to bring their launch up alongside the gangplank of the mine sweeper. We made two or three unsuccessful attempts to come alongside before they finally did. I was appalled at their apparent lack of understanding and their unnecessary chains of command which were so slow in giving orders that they missed the moment of timing every time. I learned later that they were all young Canadians training under the University's Program and, in most cases, this was their first time at sea. They were only trying to put into practise what they had been taught by some instructor probably 1,000 miles from the sea.

However, we did get aboard in one piece and eventually were greeted by the second in Command. The Captain had gone ashore fishing, so the second took us to the wardroom. It then became apparent that they had a patient aboard in need. Dr. McGrath and I went to the sick bay to see the patient. In charge was the Pharmacist who was acting as medical attendant. He explained that the patient in the bed was having trouble seeing. His vision was blurred and they were very concerned about him. Dr. McGrath examined the patient at my suggestion and I busied myself at the desk looking at the drugs, and looking at the notes made by the pharmacist's mate. I had a suspicion of what we might be facing before Dr. McGrath returned. He admitted that he was a bit baffled by this. He couldn't find too much wrong although there appeared to be some unexplained dilation of the patient's pupils.

I asked him if I could just talk with the patient and he was only too willing to let me do whatever I could. My questions were quite simple. With Dr. McGrath and the Pharmacist busy talking in the other side of the room, I asked the patient how long he had been in the Navy. He told me this was his first time at sea, and they had left Halifax about ten days previously. I asked him if he was enjoying it or whether he got very sea sick. He replied that he had been extremely sea sick and really didn't know how he could manage to last out the rest of the trip. I then asked him how often he was helping himself to the sea sick pills and with a sheepish smile he told me that as often as the pharmacist's mate was out of the sick bay he would help himself. This was probably five or six times a day.

My diagnosis was made. The sea sick pills contained Scopolamine, which affected the pupils so that his vision got blurred. The more sea sick he got, the more pills he took. The more pills he took, the sicker he got. It was a vicious circle. Obviously, he would be cured if we could stop him taking the pills. I told Dr. McGrath what I had found, and he agreed this was the answer. We then told the pharmacist he was to give the patient no more sea sick pills but to put them away under lock and key. Since there were no other cases, we repaired to the wardroom. We were invited to stay for dinner and had a very enjoyable evening. Later we returned to our own quarters. It's interesting to note that amongst the officers was a Lieutenant Commander who told me that although he had been in the Navy for some ten years or more, that this in fact was the first time he had ever been to sea. I realised that it wasn't only the ratings who were new but apparently some of the officers were as well. The next day I checked with the ship and found that twenty-four hours abstinence from sea sick pills had brought our patient back to normal. I felt happy in the assurance I gave the patient that he would have no further trouble if he would take no further pills.

Following Confederation one visitor that we were looking forward to immensely was the Minister of Highways. By now not only was there a hospital truck but I had a jeep, the only one in the district, which I used to take us around and for house calls on the limited roads that were available. Norris Point still only had one road and it was in bad shape. It was agreed that the Minister, the Hon. E. S. Spencer, would be hosted by me. I assured everybody that given the chance I would see that he saw every pothole, and would feel each one too. After his arrival at Norris Point, I picked him up in my jeep and made sure that I put my wheels into every pothole as we went along the road. I took him out to Rocky Harbour over the rutted road so that he got a first hand impression of our difficulties. As we drove, I waved to the children, as was my custom. They always waved back. In fact, it had become such a custom that usually the children waved to me before I even waved to them. As we drove along the children were waving at the Jeep and the Minister got the impression that they were waving to him. I didn't say anything and let him enjoy his apparent popularity. It was back at our house over a meal that he told me that he was going to be the guest speaker at the Newfoundland Medical Association banquet the following week. While I was hoping to get there, it seemed doubtful because there was so much work in the hospital. All I could do was tell him that I hoped to be there, but somehow doubted that I would make it. Later, I took him back to the Point to catch his boat to the other side of the Bay, and through to Corner Brook and St. John's. I hoped that I had accomplished my objective of showing the Minister the difficulties of our roads.

Two weeks later I was told how the Minister, before he left, had been talking to some of the local men who remarked on the way the children waved to me all the time, and the Minister learned how he had been mistaken in thinking that they were waving to him. In fact I doubt if the children realised that he was the Minister of Highways. But I also learned to my embarrassment that he had told this story to the Medical Association banquet and I realised then that he had taken it in good sport and enjoyed telling the story on himself. It wasn't long before a crew was at work improving the road, and we were grateful indeed that his visit had been fruitful for us anyway.

Another interesting visitor was Captain Ambrose Shea, the grandson of Sir Ambrose Shea, the leader of the first Confederation movement in the 1860s. Captain Shea visited the coast on a number of occasions in his capacity as Ranger Officer. The Canadian Forces set up a Ranger Force which was equivalent to a local defence force. On the coastline of Newfoundland and Labrador, Captain Shea's responsibility was to tour around and visit his forces in the various parts of the province and make sure that their arms and ammunition were in good shape and that they knew their duties.

I had met Captain Shea many years before, and we had a common bond. He had been at Ampleforth College in York, England, and was at the top of the school when I entered the school at the bottom. As a good Newfoundlander he was pleased that another

Newfoundlander had come to the school and went out of his way to visit this little boy who was only too pleased to have any visitors even though it was from the top of the school. He was most helpful to me while he was still at Ampleforth and later we became good friends. Ambrose always stayed with us on his visits and we looked forward tremendously to having him. He was most entertaining, not only for his stories of his trips on the coast dealing with the Ranger Force, but also because he was able to bring us news from St. John's of our families and friends. He always spent hours at our insistence telling us stories of his adventures. They were so interesting and such fun that I've always hoped that he would find time to sit down and write them so that everybody could enjoy.

In the early days Magistrate Tim Wade was the visiting magistrate, and before Confederation he took the responsibility during his visit to Bonne Bay to always pay a visit to the hospital and spend some time with me in the hospital. He also visited us in our home and carried back with him a report on our activities.

Later a full time magistrate, Leonard Walsh, was appointed to Bonne Bay, but his health didn't stand up and within a year or so he resigned and returned to St. John's. He was succeeded by other magistrates over the years but they all lived at Woody Point and the possibility of any social activity was minimal because of the distance. However, there were times when the Magistrate and I would find ourselves either going in the same direction or visiting the same settlement and while there was no close association there was a close liaison with the magistrate in Bonne Bay.

At intervals the Roman Catholic priest would visit, the parish being supplied by Deer Lake or by Corner Brook. The priest would come through four or five times a year. The Anglican Church at Woody Point had a permanent resident minister, and the United Church and the Salvation Army, which was strong in Rocky Harbour, had a resident officer in that settlement.

One most interesting incident happened one afternoon when without any warning the *Porpoise*, Bowaters cabin cruiser, arrived at Norris Point with Mr. H.M.S. Lewin and the British High Commissioner and their party. They had come directly from Bay of Islands at top speed. They arrived at about 2 p.m., visited with us for a couple of hours and had tea, and then boarded their boat again at about 6 p.m. and hoped to make it back to Corner Brook by about midnight. It was one of those unexpected visits. We had no time for preparation. We told them they would have to make do with whatever we had, and we found a very pleasant light atmosphere as they relaxed and there was nothing formal about the visit. It stands out in my memory as extremely interesting because one of the members was the man who helped to deal with my passport and transportation arrangements when the Newfoundland Government in 1945 requested my release from the Air Force and my return to Newfoundland. He had shown me at that time a picture of Bonne Bay and now was able to stand in the actual spot itself and reminisce about the time we discussed how I would get home and get to Bonne Bay.

One of the most interesting of our visitors was a man who appeared unexpectedly and literally in the middle of the night. It was my custom to arrive at the hospital if I was operating just before 8 a.m. and we got our morning started. On this particular morning as I approached the hospital I was amazed to see a tent pitched on the land just outside the hospital. I was not only surprised to see it in this position but was aware, since I was late leaving the hospital the previous night, that it hadn't been there at that time. It was therefore obvious it had appeared sometime during the night.

When I arrived in the hospital the first thing I did was to inquire as to whether anybody knew anything about it. Martin Bugden told me that it belonged to a man who had come late at night. Martin had nowhere for him to stay, but having his own camping equipment with him on his back, he had simply set it up and settled down for the night. I asked him if he would make contact with the owner and invite him to come in and have coffee and talk with us later in the morning. And so it was when we finished in the operating room, this man appeared at the hospital and introduced himself. His name was Elmer Harp and he told me he was an archeologist from Dartmouth College in the United States. He was spending some time this particular summer on the Northwest Coast looking for any signs of Eskimo and Indians, and would be grateful for any information we could give. He was very hopeful of finding traces of some earlier cultures.

We were delighted to have him with us and immediately invited him to strike his tent and transfer himself to our home. He did this willingly, although he kept saying he didn't want to put us to any inconvenience. His description of the work he had been doing and what he hoped to accomplish, we found quite fascinating. I was able to put him in touch with several people who knew something of the stories and legends that abounded on the coast which were in any way connected with the Indians. One of the first people I introduced him to of course was Bryant Harding, for Bryant had often told me of the tours which brought tourists from the Mainland before the war on a ship known as the *North Star*. These tourists were sold arrowheads which the local people had found and dug up in the area of Norris Point. Elmer Harp was very interested in this and wished to pursue an investigation in this area. Bryant was able to put him into the right places without delay.

I was also able to introduce him to William Prebble, the Hospital Secretary, who had told me on many occasions that as a boy he remembered the Micmac Indians coming out in Bonne Bay, usually at the head of the South West Arm at Glenburnie. His description always interested me because he would say that the Indians would suddenly appear there one morning. They might stay for several days or even weeks and trade with the local people the skins and the things they had made for tools and food and clothing. Then suddenly one morning they would no longer be there. They would have vanished during the night and they might not be seen for another full year when they would appear as suddenly as they had disappeared. Bill Prebble told me they were Micmac Indians and he was talking of a period around the 1880s.

Elmer Harp left us after a day or two to go North but not before he took us out onto the cliffs overlooking the Bay. As we walked along, he told us that this looked like the sort of place the Indians would make camp and watch out over the Bay and possibly make arrows and other tools. He showed us how to "dig" and under his supervision we did dig. Sure enough, only a few inches down we uncovered several good examples of arrowheads, particularly broken parts of arrowheads which Elmer told us indicated this in fact had been a spot where they would sit and work and naturally had their failures as well as their successes. We were very pleased with our finds and have kept them through the years.

Elmer was back in about six weeks having not only travelled the coast as far as Flower's Cove, but having got across to the Labrador Coast and travelled some of that. It was an exciting evening when on his return he laid out on the carpet in our lounge his finds. We had cleared all the furniture back to make room and he laid out on the floor in various categories approximately 1,000 items which he had discovered and brought back with him. These included arrowheads, bone instruments, small toys and ornaments, and many other artifacts which were to form the basis of his collection on the North West Coast.

I had been able to tell Elmer before he left about the "stepping stones" on Keppel Island of Port Saunders. I had never seen them myself, but I had been told that the large flat stones were placed at regular intervals and were some kind of a game played either by the Beothuk Indians or the Eskimo many years before. The actual stones themselves had been buried in a storm when a lot of sand and gravel washed up onto Keppel Island, and they hadn't been seen for many years. Elmer told us that he had looked for these stepping stones and had confirmed the story I had told him insofar as the older inhabitants of the area had reaffirmed the story. However, there was no time to start digging to unearth them. He was quite happy to believe that they were there and they fitted in with similar games which were played by inhabitants of Iceland and Greenland. It was his opinion at that time they belonged to the Dorset Eskimo culture.

Elmer also told us how on the Labrador Coast he had found layers of beach rising some thirty or forty feet from the sea representing different levels over hundreds and hundreds and perhaps thousands of years. It would appear that the land was rising out of the sea for each of these beach levels had produced evidence of campsites and confirmed they had in fact at one time been at sea level. I was able to tell him of Cannon Richards' account of Flower's Cove and what was happening there. Cannon Richards was stationed at Flower's Cove for some forty years and had kept careful notes. In his notes he had pointed out that when he first went there the ledges of Flower's Cove were never awash, but at the end of forty years when he left they certainly were washing which suggested that in that short period of time a considerable change had taken place. Flower's Cove is situated opposite the part of the Labrador Coast which Elmer had described to us and which I remembered having seen. I did not realise the significance of the beach levels then and just felt it was some peculiar kind of formation that I was looking at.

Elmer Harp returned to Dartmouth College a very happy man with his finds and assured us that he would return as soon as he could arrange the proper expedition. In fact, Elmer Harp returned twice more during our stay, once with a group of students and once with his wife and family. Each time they produced some remarkable evidence, the most remarkable of which was their find in Port au Choix where they discovered a complete campsite area which they began excavating very carefully. We kept up with Elmer for a number of years and on one occasion when we were in Boston we made contact and had a very pleasant visit with Elmer and his wife and family.

Over the years we had many visitors and we looked forward to their coming, mostly of course during the summer months. The numbers increased as the communications and service improved, such as the road being put through to Woody Point, the improvement of the ferry service across the bay, and the advent of Confederation which brought Federal involvement and many people coming from the Mainland.

Chapter 18

GET OFF MY ICE PAN!

Certain times of year presented special hazards when it came to crossing the Bay. Apart from stormy weather which often made it difficult though rarely impossible to get across from one side to the other, the most hazardous times were when the ice was forming in the Bay and before it was solid enough to cross on foot or horse and sleigh. Later, when the ice was breaking up for a short period it was often suggested that one should forget trying to cross. The yard stick was the mailman, in those days Steve Pike of Woody Point, whose job it was to get the mail across from the Woody Point side to the Norris Point side. He was usually the first man across and took what seemed often to be unnecessary risks as he carried the mail across the Bay.

I had been brought up with a clear understanding that one had the greatest respect for ice. From the earliest times I could remember one was always being warned about skating on pond ice and the dangers of doing so until the ice was thick enough to bear weight. This principle was borne out by the annual crop of tragedies of people who lost their lives through the ice. The many stories in every Newfoundland family about "going to the ice" carried with them always clear warning that one should know how to handle oneself.

And so it was that first winter that my first experience of tackling the ice came upon me without warning and frankly without any thought in my mind as to what I was facing. It was early winter. The ice was forming in the Bay. It was difficult to cross. The ferry was making one trip a day, and if there wasn't sufficient reason, it might not make that trip. The usual custom was that the ferry would take aboard a number of men and would make its way across the Bay through the pans of ice, the numbers on board being able to help fend off the ice pans and gradually the boat would work its way through the ice heading for open patches wherever they could be seen. They hoped they would not get carried out to sea in the ice should the ferry become trapped. It was still loose ice and was still moving with the tide so the tendency was as the tide went out for a trapped boat to be carried out to sea. Certainly there were a number of occasions when the ferry appeared to be in real difficulties, but never in my experience did it get carried out to sea, although the threat always remained there.

On this particular day I simply got a call at the hospital that there was a patient across the Bay who required my attention and the ferry had come across to get me and was waiting at the Point. I gathered my equipment, which I had now put into an army type haversack for ease of carrying in winter. I found that carrying a medical bag was too much of an encumbrance when one is clambering around in the snow and over snow drifts and fences and generally through the difficult winter conditions. Therefore, I had packed the necessities of a house visit into a haversack which I could sling over my shoulder and which I could carry much more easily. So taking my medical haversack, I arrived at the Point and found the ferry was not in at the Government Wharf where it usually came. In fact, it was off-shore, by the Point itself.

The Point was a rocky outcropping pointing directly out from Norris Point over towards the Woody Point area. It presented a navigation hazard to those weary mariners who did not look at their way and stand well clear trying to round the Point to get into Norris Point. At the same time, it helped to break up any heavy seas that were coming in from the outer Bay and gave added protection to the Point itself. A crowd had collected on the shore of Norris Point idly watching the ferry and wondering how matters would proceed. No doubt many of the people watching were aware that this was going to be my first experience. Although at that time I was still unaware of it, they had gathered to see how I fared. Bryant Harding met me and accompanied me to the shoreline where Stewart Blanchard, the ferry owner and operator, was standing talking to a group of men and awaiting my arrival. Bryant was anxious that I get across the Bay and back as quickly as possible, being concerned that I not be trapped on the far side and unable to get back perhaps for some days, which would leave the hospital without a medical officer. He was anxious to do anything which would speed the trip across and back.

Stewart Blanchard asked me if I was ready to leave, and when I assured him that I was, as a sort of an afterthought, he said, "Have you ever been on the ice before, Doctor?"

"No," I replied, "this is my first time and you will have to tell me what to do and how to do it."

The reply came quickly, "Stick close to me, and do exactly what I do."

I assured him that I would stick very close to him and my mind flashed back to pictures of the men on the ice at the seal hunt. As I looked at the ferry boat, which was about 400 feet offshore, it was a completely different picture that I saw in front of me. Between the shore and the ferry boat was a gently modulating floor of ice pans, varying in size, but probably averaging about five feet square. It was across this that we had to go to get to the ferry. It looked simple, but Bryant turned to me and said, "Stick tight to Stewart. There's a trick to this and if you've never done it before you'd better learn it quickly. Don't fool around on the ice. When you start moving, keep going."

"Alright," said Stewart, "let's go, Doc, and remember what I said."

I hooked my medical haversack round to my back, made sure that my coat buttons were all fastened, put on my gloves, and moved to the edge of the ice. The wind was cutting across the Bay through the undulating pans of ice. Stewart led the way. He jumped onto the first pan and before he was off it I had jumped on as well. As he jumped from pan to pan I was right close to him and on the same pan before he could get off, which produced a howl from Stewart. As the ice pans gradually sank under our combined weight, we both drove on faster. After we'd gone about fifty feet, and still running fast, he shouted over his shoulder at me, "Get of my ice pan. These pans aren't big enough to hold two of us at the same time."

"But you told me to stick tight to you," I shouted, "and that's all I'm doing. So get a move on." Stewart sped on his way to the ferry boat trying to get onto the next pan before I could get onto his pan, trying to choose pans which would be safe to hold us, and trying to get to the boat as quickly as possible. The faster he flew across the ice, the faster I followed him, and any sense of fear that I may have had at the start was gone in the excitement of the mad race across these small pans of ice to reach the boat.

Stewart got there first and willing hands reached over and grabbed him and hauled him up. As I came alongside the boat I too was grabbed by strong arms and hauled aboard the ferry boat. Out of breath and flushed with the excitement of a new experience, I took off my bag and joined the others in the wheelhouse for the trip across the Bay. It was my first experience of this form of travel through the ice and knowing that the ferry boat was wooden, I asked what damage the ice would do as it forced its way through. "Don't worry, Doc," Stewart assured me, "sheathed in green hart and that will take care of the ice." Green Hart, of course, I knew was an extremely hard wood which is used to sheath boats which are to be used in ice. I had learned from bitter experience with my own boat that an unsheathed boat suffers badly.

Before the freeze up had come I had answered a call in my own boat on an early morning when there was a dead calm through the night with very low temperatures resulting in a skin of ice up the Main Arm where I had had to go. As we cut through the ice it was almost like going through a series of sharp knives and in no time at all I was able to lean over the bough and see the wood being cut out in long slivers. To rectify this problem, we hung a rubber tire, which we carried as a bumper to protect us from wharves, over the bow and lashed it in position so as we cut through the ice this took most of the wear and tear and broke up the ice and protected the boat. Even so, quite a lot of damage was caused to my boat before we completed our journey and I was very leery of going out without adequate protection from then on.

We set about then crossing the Bay. The additional hands onboard used long poles to help push the ice away from the side of the boat. Stewart himself took the wheel and headed on every occasion for open water whenever we would see any. The journey, which normally took about twenty minutes to accomplish, took about an hour and a half which was actually very fast considering conditions. On arriving at Woody Point we were able to get into the Government Wharf, and Stewart assured me that if I was not too long and the ice conditions didn't change, he would be able to get me back.

Meanwhile our progress had been watched through the ice from both sides of the Bay. Bryant had his binoculars out and was watching from Norris Point to make sure if in fact we got stuck or into difficulties of any kind attempts to free us would be made. The men on the Woody Point side were watching anxiously for the return of the ferry bringing the doctor to deal with medical cases. I set about my work and wasted little time knowing how important it was to get back to the hospital and not be isolated for perhaps days at Woody Point to the detriment of the hospital.

The return journey in fact was made even more easily as the tide had carried some of the ice out of the Bay and there was a large stretch of open water on the eastern side which allowed us to return much more rapidly and to get into the wharf at Norris Point. I can only marvel at the ability of the ferry man and his brother and the other men who went along to help. Everyone pitched in to help in time of necessity and against the difficulties of winter living in an isolated area such as that. I enjoyed the journey in both directions because this was the appropriate time to ask for information and be told stories of boats that got caught in the ice, of difficult crossings that were made, of the mailman and his crossing of the ice with his dogs and the mail, of people falling in, of near drownings, and of rescues that had taken place over the years. My admiration for the men increased enormously that day, but was to grow even more as the years went on, and I saw them take so many things like this as a matter of fact. Such trials were dealt with in the course of the day's work. Never for a moment did any man refuse to help his fellow man in time of need and particularly in time of illness.

I shall never forget my first trip on the ice pans chasing after Stewart. We both might have got a good ducking or even drowned through my not understanding that the weight of two of us could not be held by a single pan. We laughed about it afterwards, as did everybody who watched it, for the spectacle of Stewart flying across the ice hotly pursued by me wasn't understood until later when people heard that I had been told to stick close to Stewart and this I was endeavouring to do. I had learned my lesson and from then on I made sure that I never got on anybody else's pan. I understood clearly the meaning of "Get Off My Ice Pan!"

Chapter 19

NIGHT CALL TO LOMOND

It had been a cold hard winter and presently we were experiencing very low temperatures in the sub zero range, but the weather was beginning to settle a bit and with the settled weather due usually to the ice in the Bay and in the Gulf the temperatures would drop even lower.It was night time and it was a clear night with the stars shining brightly and a gentle off shore wind of about ten to fifteen miles per hour.

About ten o'clock came a call from the hospital to say that a man had arrived from Lomond and wanted me to make a house call to see a patient who needed help.

Lomond is a small settlement of about twenty families, approximately five miles from the hospital straight up the main Arm of Bonne Bay.The Arm was frozen solid and the ice was anything from a foot to a foot and a half thick, and should quite safe at this time.

I agreed that I would get myself ready and knowing how cold it was I dressed warmly and left my house, the Doctor's residence, and walked down to the hospital to collect my medical bag. As an after thought before I left the hospital I decided to take with me a couple of hospital blankets in case it got cold on the way.

There were two men, one of whom was the man who had come to fetch the Doctor and his friend with a large horse and a flat sleigh, the type used for hauling logs in the woods.This is not a particularly comfortable type of sleigh to ride on, but they had thoughtfully put a box on board and so I sat on the sleigh with my bag beside me and because there was a cold wind blowing I put the blankets loosely around me and figured that my parka and its hood would keep me warm for the journey.So we set off, the two men rolled on the sleigh and we bounced down the road at a slight angle for roads always seem to develop an angle as the winters go on and we bumped our way along to Yes-Mam's and eventually reached Neddy's Harbour

I had been watching the sky. Once we cleared Neddy's Harbour, suddenly it was no longer visible. Instead there was a mild dusting of snow being swept off the surface of the ice and scattered over us as we drove along. I felt that the wind was probably rising and this was whipping up the light snow into a mild blizzard. However, shortly afterwards, I sat upright and to my surprise I found that my head came out of this blizzard and it was now back in a clear atmosphere with all the stars distinctly visible. I could see the heads of the two men and the top of the horse clearly. When I leaned back, I found myself once again in the blizzard. I realised then that the wind was just picking up enough snow to raise it to sleigh height, approximately two feet or so, off the ice. Once my head came through the surface of this level, then the clear sky was there for me to see.

I was getting colder and colder as we rode along. The horse had set a steady pace and the men said little and we made our way gradually up the Main Arm. It took the best part of an hour to reach Lomond and by the time I had arrived at the house I was as much in need of the doctor as the patient. I was completely frozen, stiff, and must have looked pretty cold because the mother of the patient insisted that before we did anything I thaw out. I was given a cup of tea and began to rub my hands, get the circulation back in my face, and generally revive.

It took fifteen or twenty minutes. While I had revived myself, I was still very aware that I was extremely cold. However, I set about dealing with the patient and in due course my visit was finished. Then came the question of returning to the hospital.

At this point it was quite obvious that my hosts were expressing some concern about my welfare. The good lady of the house insisted that I warm up with another cup of tea and something to eat. I was advised that the temperature was twenty-seven degrees below zero. If I had known this before I left I would have brought many more blankets and endeavoured to protect myself from the intense cold. Not walking but riding on a sleigh one tends to get colder because of not using one's extremities and the sheer movement of walking or running alongside the horse would keep one from freezing. I felt that perhaps on the return journey I should be free to get out and run but it was now about 1 a.m. I was very tired after the day's work and the journey and the cold. I doubted that I really had the energy to run alongside. If I did try to run alongside for a while then when I sat on the sleigh I wouldn't be wrapped up. I foresaw getting even colder in this temperature. Now that I knew it was twenty-seven degrees below zero, I would feel twenty seven times as cold as I had coming up. And so it was that the lady of the house now insisted on putting on her outdoor clothes and coming out to supervise and participate in getting me on the sleigh and wrapping me up.

I made myself as comfortable as I could on the sleigh with my bag beside me. I was wrapped around in layers of blankets and I seem to remember that they added a couple of blankets from the house. Finally I was wrapped up like an Egyptian mummy. My hands were across my chest so that I could just open the blankets, which were now tightly across my face with a slit vertically up and down, enough to see out. This wrapping I was assured would give me the best protection and keep me warm and safe on the journey back to the hospital. Who was I to doubt anybody's word? And so we set off for the return journey. We backed down the road, down the slope, onto the ice, and set off up the Main Arm.

In about half a mile we were off the point on which the flashing beacon was mounted. I sensed that something was happening. I could hear the sounds of crushing ice, and it seemed to me that the horse was breaking through the ice, and this thought disturbed me to the point that I realized suddenly I was somewhat helpless being wrapped up so tightly on the sleigh. At this time I heard the two men jump off the sleigh and while I couldn't hear quite what they were shouting, one was shouting at the other, and one voice seemed to be going off on one side of me and the other voice seemed to be going on the opposite side. I could hear the horse breaking through the ice more and more.

I still could not move, could not free myself, and I had a picture of the horse going through the ice and dragging the sleigh right through after it with me helplessly bundled on the back with not a hope of helping myself and just sinking slowly to the bottom. That would be the end of that. I could hear the men on either side, now at some considerable distance shouting to one another. The horse appeared to be floundering more than before, movement had slowed considerably, and in fact I didn't know if we were moving at all. The horse was thrashing around and apparently breaking through the ice. I couldn't understand why we hadn't gone completely through, and I expected the water to hit me at any moment. Just as I was beginning to really get very anxious I heard the footsteps running back towards the sleigh on each side and the men shouting and then the horse seemed to be on firmer ice, and I no longer heard the breaking of the ice and the floundering and crunching going on. The sleigh was moving now and the men were running and guiding it and they seemed to be back now beside the horse and encouraging it on. We seemed to be safely on solid ice again and moving up the Bay.

I didn't say anything. There didn't seem to be anything to say. The horse continued on the way hauling the sleigh, and the men now got back on the sleigh and we proceeded with our journey. I wondered how long before the same type of thing happened again. As I lay there now beginning to get colder I began to wonder about my predicament and what would happen if in fact we went through the ice again, but this time completely through. I also wondered why, with a temperature of twenty-seven degrees below zero, we had found a soft spot somewhere in the ice and gone through. It was approximately one hour later we arrived at the hospital, now my turn to be the host and I invited the men in to warm up with a cup of tea before they went back. Now they would be making the journey for the fourth time that night. I took the opportunity of joining them for a cup of tea and asking them some questions.

I was surprised at the answers I got. Did we start to go through the ice? Yes, the horse certainly did start to go through the ice. Well, how was it that we didn't go completely through? Well apparently there was a pool of water which had formed on top of the ice and frozen over the top and it was the top layer of thin ice that the horse had gone through, but underneath several inches of water, there was solid ice probably a foot and a half thick. Even the men admitted they hadn't realized at first that this is what we were going through until everyone remembered that the heat of the sun the previous day and some rain the day before would cause water to settle on the ice in pools and then catch over. When the men ran off from each side of the sleigh, in fact they weren't sure whether we were going through or not, but they ran out to see if there was solid ice which would be the best way to take the horse and sleigh. They realized that in fact we were still on safe ice with a pool of water on top.

I expressed myself as delighted with our safe journey and told them how frightened I had been; wrapped up like a mummy I would have gone through with the sleigh and that would have been the end of me. In fact, they assured me that they wouldn't have left me and I am convinced they would have made quite sure that I would have been hauled to safety if something like this had happened. I have always felt that any of the men, be it by dog team, by horse and sleigh, by boat or by any other form of transportation, have always had a great concern over the doctors or nurses that they've carried over the years. That was the coldest day that was recorded during my stay on the Coast, and I was told that it was the coldest night that had been recorded for many, many years. It certainly was a memorable night.

Lomond, even though it was small, was quite a historical settlement. It had been of considerable importance in the 1930s during which time a Scotsman named Simpson had come out to take care of the wood cutting and saw mill operations that were going on there. He had built a beautiful home at Lomond and had equipped it with one of the earliest electric generators, a thirty-two volt mixer, a polisher, a washer, and various other electrical equipment. When I arrived I was fortunate to be able to buy and use it in the course of my stay. The same thirty-two volt generator and battery type equipment was installed in the Doctor's house. Many stories were told about Simpson and the things that he did and said. Bearing in mind the experience I had on that very cold night going up over the ice to Lomond, I should recount a story that is told about him which also concerned the ice.

It appears that a tractor was being used during one winter on the ice hauling materials. It was common for wood that was cut to be hauled across the ice with horse and sleigh, but in this instance, I suppose they felt that the ice was thick enough to warrant putting a tractor on the ice. So here was the tractor coming across the ice with its driver. When it reached a certain point, the ice proved incapable of carrying it and broke. The tractor vanished in deep water and the driver vanished with it. Simpson himself was on the spot, and he and the other men who were around waited and waited and waited. Apart from a few bubbles there was no sign of the driver and as the seconds ticked by everyone began to get very agitated and worried. They wondered whether in fact as the tractor went down somehow the man had been caught up or entangled in it and possibly they would never see him again. However, when it seemed almost too long a time had passed and the driver would never be seen again, suddenly he surfaced in the hole caused by the tractor. Instead of a great gasp of delight, Simpon's first words to the man were, "What kept you?"

The very wet and very cold man was hauled out on the ice and he stood up and looked at Simpson and said, "I went down with her to take her out of gear and see where she'd go too so we can get her later." In fact, he did know exactly where she was, and when the ice went out and conditions were suitable they were able to put equipment over the tractor, hook on to her, and haul her out for further use.

Chapter 20

THE BREAK-UP RESCUE

It was an early March morning, clear and sunny, the sun having just come over the hills. As I stood by the window dressing and looking across the Bay, I was startled to see what appeared to be the commencement of the breakup of the ice in the Bay. Everybody had expected the ice to breakup and go out. Often it happened during the night that one went to bed with the Bay full of solid ice and woke in the morning to find only scattered pans left in the Bay. It was somewhat unusual to me to witness the breakup of the ice and be able to watch it actually happen.

There was no doubt the cracks were appearing in the ice, and they did seem to be widening. As I continued dressing I would, every few minutes, watch out the window, and yes, there was no doubt, the cracks were getting bigger. And then suddenly I saw a small figure moving across the ice from Wild Cove, which lay beneath the bedroom window, towards the Curzon Village side. The figure was quite oblivious of the fact that ahead lay a number of cracks which were widening every minute. A look at the figure through my binoculars showed me that it wasn't just the figure of a man. It was a man and a horse and sleigh, and I watched with a great deal of apprehension wondering whether he was going to be faced with difficulties when he got further out in the middle of the Bay. What might he find if the ice continued to break up and his return route was cut off from our side of the shore?

Knowing enough about the dangers of such happenings I picked up my phone and rang the Point and got hold of Bryant Harding. I asked him whether he was aware there was a man on the ice, and he replied that he was aware. The man had been watched by the men from Norris Point, he had been advised not to go, and he now was being watched by the men from the Woody Point side who had been alerted to the fact that he was now on the ice and the ice was breaking up. Bryant also told me that a phone call to the lighthouse at Rocky Harbour had confirmed the fact that the ice was breaking up and moving out the Bay. From the lighthouse at Rocky Harbour, the keeper had a good view of the outer reaches of the Bay. While he couldn't see the man on the ice, he certainly knew the state of the breaking up of the ice.

I asked if there was anything I could do. Bryant replied that there was nothing anybody could do but wait and see what happened and take action as necessary at that time. He added that it was possible that the man would make it safely across the Bay and that would be the end of that episode. I thanked him, assured him that I would resume my watching, would keep him informed of any development, and we hung up.

By this time the cracks in the ice were quite wide. I would estimate from looking at them from the distance, it must have been a mile or a mile and a half from the centre of the Bay, but the cracks would now be two or three feet wide. It was quite evident, I would have thought, that the man on the ice could see the difficulties ahead of him. However, one forgets that at ice level he might not have been able to see clearly the widths of the cracks, and by this time he had reached about the midpoint in the Bay. The ice was breaking up behind him, and while the pans were very large, at the same time I didn't know how long they would stay that big or whether with the movement of the sea these pans in turn would break up and the more movement there was the more they would break up and the smaller they would get.

By the time the man reached the center of the Bay it was obvious from his movements he realized now he was cut off. Sure enough, in front and behind him there were cracks in the ice which made it extremely hazardous to proceed any further. He did probably the only thing that he could at that point. He stopped and had a look in all directions.

He accomplished this by leaving the horse and sleigh on the pan that it was on, and running rapidly from pan to pan jumping across the gaps and trying to find an area where the ice had not yet broken or at least hadn't moved enough to make it hazardous. Apparently in his mind there was no such route, so he went back to his horse and sleigh and appeared to be resigning himself to just staying with his horse.

At this point I was aware suddenly of a movement from the Curzon Village side. A group of about six men appeared jogging across the ice in line ahead and heading for the man marooned on the ice. Looking at it from a distance, it seemed that there was no hope that they would reach him in time for the cracks were widening and the ice moving all the time with the tide. This gentle jogging–it was neither a fast run nor a fast walk, it was in fact jogging–brought them with great speed to the middle of the Bay. At this point things happened almost too rapidly. Before I even realized the full extent of their plan, the men were in action. They had decided what they would do, how they would do it, and who would do each particular job. The final executed movement turned out to be similar to a football play; it was carried out with precision and speed.

As the six men reached the pan on which the man and his horse and sleigh were marooned, one after the other jumped across the gap which now must have been fully three feet wide. Without discussion they went about their tasks. Two of the men immediately unhitched the horse, one took the halter and the other gave the horse a hard slap on the rump and the horse immediately jumped the gap and accompanied by the two men headed at full speed for the shore. The remaining four men with the owner of the horse and the sleigh immediately grasped the shafts of the sleigh, and also without any delay headed across the gap pulling the sleigh with them.

In a matter of seconds the ice pan was cleared of horse and sleigh and owner, and all hands were on their way across to the Woody Point side. The same jogging movements carried them swiftly ashore across the various gaps which had opened. Almost as fast as it is possible to read the account, they were all on safe ice across the Bay. At the same time that they reached safety on the south side of the Bay, the gap in the ice reached a point where doubtless it would have been impossible to affect the rescue. I was quickly on the telephone and in touch with Bryant to give him the good news, but he only chuckled and said, "Yes, we watched it all from here and as soon as I saw that all was well I went in to get my breakfast."

When I discussed the episode later with him, he told me that had it not been possible to effect the rescue on the ice at that point an effort would have been made at least to get a dory from Rocky Harbour and get out and reach him. The horse and sleigh would probably have been lost because, with the ice in, no boats were available of a size large enough to take the horse and sleigh. However, I doubted this belief for, knowing the ingenuity of the men, I could forsee three or four dories going out and two or three lashed together, and the horse having the fore legs in one and the hind legs in another being brought safely in and with the sleigh being put across another dory and being brought safely in also.

While on the subject of ice rescues, a word about horses is important. Amongst the most important positions of families living on the coast would be their horse and dogs. Not always did a family have both, but the possessor of a horse had a machine that had to be well looked after all year round to get the use out of it that was required. The summertime was simple because the horse was turned loose to graze where it felt like grazing and sometimes it would wander several miles in company with other horses looking for good pasture land. Other times it would stay close to home and was easily caught and brought in for work. However, during the winter the horse was most valuable for working in the woods, and for hauling wood to keep the house warm. It was quite common for a man to go into the woods with his horse and haul out loads of logs which were then sawed up and put in stacks by the door or under the house to be used through the winter as needed.

Horses were also used for woods work in the woods camps for hauling logs both for the paper company and to the saw mills for producing lumber. Owing to the lack of roads it was quite common in winter for horses to go across the ice hauling their loads, and it was equally important for travel purposes to cross the Bay and ponds for traveling. Occasionally an incident would occur where a horse would go through the ice. When one considers that the weight of a horse comes down on four hooves, a 1,000 pound horse would therefore spread its weight over four points representing 250 pounds on each point. With the basic thought that very often a horse's hoof is about the same size or slightly bigger than a man's hand, it can be seen that the ice has to be fairly strong to take the weight of a hoof coming down on it. At times, on poor or deteriorating ice, especially when it doesn't seem apparent, or where a stream cuts into the ice and softens it, a horse would go through. When a horse went through the ice it was a major disaster and had to be dealt with very quickly to save the horse.

While I never witnessed a horse being rescued from the ice, I talked with enough people who took part or who had managed to save their horses that went through to realize that there was a great deal of sense to the methods used to save them. It is quite obvious that with a horse through the ice, while the horse may be able to swim, being surrounded by ice at a lower level in the water, it would be impossible for the horse to crawl out. Equally it would be impossible to put a line about and haul a horse out because of the weight and the legs being tangled. The solution to this problem is so simple, if it works, as to make it worth telling.

The owner immediately seeks help because he needs strong hands to help him. Often there would be other woodsmen around who could come to his assistance. He then throws a line around the horse's neck and he pulls it tight to the point of strangulation. The horse can get a breath in but tends not to be able to get it out again. As it thrashes madly around and is starting to suffocate it is taking more and more air into its lungs tending to inflate them more. It then becomes more buoyant. At the point that it is about ready to die, it rolls on its side and all hands get lines around the horse and can haul it to safety. The rope around its neck is then cut and with luck cut in time for the horse to make a recovery and be saved. This is a drastic and dramatic method of rescuing a horse, but all that the owner asks is that he get his horse back again.

The ice was not always a potential hazard. Every settlement had its young people, and some not so young, who used to enjoy skating on the Bay. One saw a variety of skates. Homemade skates made of hoop barrel sections hammered and filed and set in wooden bases were used. The wooden bases were strapped on the feet of the owners. As well, some people had proper imported skates fixed to shoes or, for those who were luckier, proper skates fitted to boots.

Once on the ice, the boys would engage in a game of ice hockey. It was amazing how, without television or other sources to show them the technique and the plays, they managed to have a good game and spend endless hours enjoying themselves. Others would simply skate for pleasure, some would practice figure skating, but all had a good time.

Some people tended to experiment in ice play. Over the years people had experimented with sails which they strapped to themselves on small masts which were carried in a holster, and Bryant Harding told me that he himself had traveled at over sixty miles an hour across the ice using one of these sails. It was exhilarating but a somewhat dangerous method of amusement. The other activity which was tried was ice boat sailing, but a fair amount of time had to be spent building an ice boat and acquiring the materials for the sails and making them work. For the short time that it could be used, it seemed a great deal of work, and while even I toyed with the idea of building one, I never got around to it in all my years. I don't remember seeing another machine in the course of those years although many people talked about building them. The powered ice boats which were starting to appear on the mainland, basically a punt with a flat bottom with an airplane engine and propeller mounted in the rear, was something that I was anxious to build. While I acquired the plans and was always about to do it, again we never found time to do it, and I've always regretted that I never put aside the time for this purpose. Largely the need for this type of transportation was unnecessary because it was suppressed by the arrival of the snowmobile and later the skidoo which are much superior in every way.

Chapter 21

HUNTING SEALS

In the spring of the year the people on the Northwest Coast always looked hopefully to the possibility of catching a few seals. Not only did they enjoy flippers and sometimes seal meat, but they looked to the skins that were used for various purposes including skin boots that were commonly worn by the people in that area. The seal skins themselves would often bring many extra dollars which were welcome to the families who prosecuted the hunt. Unfortunately, every year saw a few casualties of men who went looking for seals and never returned. Often when the men launched their boats and tried to reach for the seals out on the ice, they would either become trapped on the ice and carried out to sea, or their boats would be crushed by the ice and they would perish by drowning. Over our entire stay of ten years I only remember one spring when the seals came in any quantity in the Bonne Bay area and the men turned out to take advantage of this opportunity.

However, there were other opportunities to see seals, and occasionally in the spring and often throughout the summer traveling in *Tinker Bell*, we would spot a seal sunning on the rocks or even traveling along close to the boat. One year while doing my tour on the coast Martin and I decided to put into St. Paul's Inlet for the night. We had finished work at about 4 p.m. and we left Cow Head and headed for the inlet at St. Paul's, knowing that the tide was high and we would be able to run in without much trouble. The entrance is very shallow and even at high water Martin warned me that there were many rocks in the run. He stationed himself on the bow and in the still water and against the current running out of St. Paul's we groped our way in. The narrows at St. Paul's were quite commanding, with a cliff on each side and deep water in the middle. This water led through then to the inlet which is several miles deep running back to the Long Range Mountains. We cruised in for two or three miles until we came to a nice brook running out. We decided that this would be a good spot to put out our anchor and after tea I would be able to do a little trout fishing. While we were preparing tea, I spotted a seal about 100 yards from the stern of the boat and pointed it out to Martin. He told me this was the home of many seals and we were quite close to a number of large rocks which he said the seals used for sunning themselves.

Martin also told me that seals in many ways are almost human in the way they behave and apparently think. He suggested that I watch the seal which had appeared, for it would station itself about 100yards stern of us and appear at regular intervals and keep an eye on us to see what we were doing. I must admit that I doubted what he was saying at first, but as time went by he proved to be quite correct. The seal did appear at intervals and was obviously watching closely to see what we were doing. Martin then told me it was very difficult to catch a seal but that the fishermen used a method involving a gly which we decided to try. This consisted of a float made by taking a small junk of wood from which was suspended a hook wrapped inside a trout and placed approximately three or four feet from the float. I immediately took off for the shore where in a short space of time I had caught a number of trout which would do nicely for our next meal and provide bait for the gly. Martin then cut one of the trout down the length of its body and inserted the hook which was one part of a cod jigger. He then lashed the whole thing together using cod jigger line, set it three or four feet from the float, and cast it adrift behind out boat. We let it float out toward where the seal was stationed. While we were working and making the gly, the seal would appear at intervals and appeared to be watching me closely. When we launched the gly again the seal watched closely and Martin warned me that he felt we would have no success because the seal knew what we were doing. This sounded ridiculous, but I stationed myself in the cockpit determined to see if I couldn't catch a seal. By this time I really didn't want to catch the seal because I had become attached to this particular one and felt it would be unfortunate if he took the bait. However, the seal was much too clever. When the gly reached the position where the seal was stationed I made it fast and sat waiting. Shortly thereafter the seal came up a few feet from the float and examined it closely, disappeared for a few moments, returned and examined it again, had a good look at us, and then stationed himself in a new spot well removed from the gly. Martin chuckled and said that he thought our friend the seal now knew exactly what we were doing, had inspected the bait, and would have no part of it but would continue to keep an eye on us. The seal kept watch on us for the rest of the day, and early in the morning we slipped out of St. Paul's Inlet on the high tide and continued on our way. At least I had seen for myself the interesting behavior of this particular seal and taken part in the construction of a gly. I enjoyed the experience. I was in fact relieved at our failure to catch the seal.

Martin and Bryant Harding both told me another story about the seals in St. Paul's Inlet of how the local men were able to catch them during the summer months. As previously mentioned, there are a number of rocks in the area where the seals sun themselves. Two men would take a dory and a gun and row to the rocks. As the dory approached the rocks, they would spot a seal on one of the rocks sunning itself. The seal watched their approach very carefully and when the dory was about 100 yards from the rock the one with the gun got into the bottom of the boat so that it appeared to the seal as if there was only one man in the dory. The dory then rowed to the rocks but when about halfway there the seal realized that the dory was going to affect a landing and it dove into the water and headed south past the dory. The man in the dory then rowed as hard as he could to the rock. The men waited until they were sure that the seal was still submerged and the man hiding in the bottom then climbed out and hid behind the rock. When the seal now surfaced it looked carefully and saw that the dory still had the man in it, who was now rowing away from the rock. When the dory got far enough away the rock still being watched by the seal, the seal would dive, heading obviously for the rock again. At this point the man with the gun came out of hiding and prepared himself for the arrival of the seal. The seal, thinking that all was safe, now appeared at the rock and found himself face to face with the hunter and his rifle. I have been told that there was a look of total dismay on the face of the seal as he realized he had been tricked at the very moment before he was shot. Having watched the seals both in St. Paul's Inlet and other parts of the coast I am now firmly convinced that in fact they have a large degree of understanding. I can readily believe that a seal tricked into a position like this can be truly horror stricken in his last moments.

One year the hospital snowmobile had to make a trip up the Coast to fetch a patient and as they passed along the shoreline they saw a whitecoat, which is a baby seal, on the shore. Temptation was too great and they quickly captured it and decided to bring it back to the hospital. We were delighted at this prize and spent considerable time with a large crowd of local residents watching it and examining it on the hospital lawn. The girls were very excited and felt we should keep it as a pet. We agreed and said we were willing to try. We carried the baby seal off to the house and decided we would put it in a little pond which we had constructed and which was now frozen over but through which running water passed. It wasn't too difficult to break a hole in the ice and we put the seal in. Many visits were made each day to the seal who had now been named "Susie." The main problem now became one of feeding the seal and we aquired herring and other fish, but Susie was not in the mood to eat. We began to worry about this and eventually I hit on the idea of a bottle of milk. We tried to feed the seal using a baby's bottle and rubber teat. Strangely enough, this worked and if one could coax Susie onto the ice and get the bottle in her mouth she would take it. Gradually she began to take bits of food from us and it looked very encouraging. We thought that we had reached the point where she would in fact become a pet.

However, the call of the sea was strong and after about ten days we discovered one morning that she had disappeared. Her tracks were visible in the snow going from the pond down through the woods towards the sea. Edna found her in the woods, put her on a sleigh, and hauled her back to the pond but within a day or two she had gone again. This time the tracks led to the water's edge. We had lost our pet. For several years every time we saw a seal we wondered whether it was Susie and whether she would recognize us and come to us, but none ever did.

The white coat of the seal, of course, is the white fur which leaves within the first few weeks. In fact, during the period that Susie was with us she began to lose the white fur. When this first began happening it looked as if she was sick or had developed some skin condition but in fact close examination revealed that she was simply losing her baby fur. The white fur soon rubs off and seals then assume the normal appearance of a grayish black fine short hair, the seal common to our waters.

Another interesting story told me by Bryant Harding concerned the duck hunt in the St. Paul's area. St. Paul's Inlet abounded in birds. There was a great deal of game to be had at the turn of the century on the whole coast. However, Bryant made it a practice each year to go on a hunting trip in the fall and one of the spots he always aimed for was St. Paul's Inlet where he would hope to bag some ducks. The procedure consisted of setting out decoys which would attract the ducks who would then land alongside the decoys. The hunters who were hiding in the nearby grass or bushes would then have the ducks within range and would be able to shoot them.

Bryant used a more lively method than the majority of people by bringing with him live ducks as decoys. These were set out in the water with a line around one leg attached to a stone which was put in the water and served as an anchor. The resulting picture was of several ducks sitting on the water and apparently resting or feeding. Any other ducks flying over would see them and, considering that they were enjoying life, would not hesitate to join them.

On one such occasion, as Bryant and a companion lay hidden in the long grass perhaps 100 yards back from the shore line waiting for the ducks to arrive, they spotted a covey of ducks come over. With the usual hunters expectation and excitement, they waited for them to come in and land by the decoys. This they did. Just as Bryant was preparing to fire, a shot rang out from behind him and went directly over his head as someone who had come up from the rear saw the ducks and fired at them.

Bryant immediately jumped to his feet and turned around to see who the intruder was, angry at the fact that a stranger was taking advantage of their efforts and their decoys. This new hunter was acting in a very dangerous manner, for he might well have killed one or both of them. The man who fired was astonished to see a figure leap out of the grass in front of him. He not only got a terrible fright, but thought from the way the figure acted that he had shot a man. He promptly fainted. Bryant realized what had happened and he and his companion had their hands full then bringing the man around and reassuring him that they were alright. Bryant realized that anyone could come along and see the decoys and consider them wild ducks resting and feeding and take a shot at them. It was another part of the risk during the hunting season.

The risks which one faces during hunting seasons still exist today and every year there are fatalities as hunters mistake noises or shadows for game and kill fellow hunters in the excitement of the chase. Bryant told the story often and used it as an example of how careful one must always be. Still, he never ceased to chuckle at the terrible fright the other hunter got when he thought that he had killed a man.

In the early 1950s St. Paul's Inlet was also to be the sight of great possibilities and great expectations as the American financier, John Fox of Boston, invested funds in drilling for oil in this region. It had been known for many years that oil existed on the coast in uncertain quantities. Back as far as 1910 a well was put down at Parson's Pond and for many years produced crude oil at the rate of two or three barrels a day. While it was never used commercially it was certainly used by the local fishermen and residents. Many are the stories told of the use of this crude oil in the motorboats. Since it was not refined, it burned in the engines so vigorously that the engines themselves would get unbearably hot. Often, they would continue to fire on even though the ignition was turned off. I was told stories of boats that were run ashore and fired on until the engines ran out of oil. I can't believe that the local oil ever did the engines any good, but certainly during the hard times it was a cheap form of power and heat.

On another part of the coast near Sally's Cove apparently there is one area where the oil can be seen through the rocks. It is possible to pick up a rock and strike a match and set it on fire. It will burn as long as the oil in the rock lasts. Assessing these stories and the geological formations, John Fox sent a crew into the St. Paul's area. There was great excitement on the Coast as their equipment was brought through the country and hauled over land to St. Paul's. Daily reports were sought as to the progress being made, how far down the drill had gone, what if anything they had found. I believe a number of holes were sunk but I don't think oil was ever struck. If it was, the company never admitted it. Most of the work took place through a one year period and at the end of that time the crew and rig was taken out and the excitement subsided.

I was gravely concerned at the time of the drilling as to what effect it would have on that section of the coast if in fact oil should be struck in any quantity. None of the communities were organized in any way as local councils and municipal governments were concerned. I feared that a sudden influx of people would cause great problems in future years if no control was exercised. The plan as outlined to us was that oil would be brought overland from oil wells by pipelines to the Eastern Arm of Bonne Bay where it would flow into great tanks which in turn would be used to load oil tankers coming to take it away. It promised to be a major industry for Newfoundland. When I talked to the various leaders of communities in the area, I found that they were reluctant to move in the direction of local government until it was absolutely necessary. While the industry never materialized, the majority of the communities saw the wisdom of organizing to help themselves and are today taking part in the benefits which come to all communities from the recognition by provincial governments of municipal organizations. John Fox himself never visited the area although it was reported that he had flown over in his aircraft. Years later, it was reported that he had got into financial difficulties. Certainly, after the initial excitement of the early 1950s, we heard no more of him.

Chapter 22

GROS MORNE

When asked, "Why do you want to climb it?" who was it that replied, "Because it is there"? Was it Sir Edmund Hilary or one of the thousands of other mountain climbers who throughout the world are challenging the mountains and high peaks that await to be scaled?

Frankly, I have never been too anxious to climb a mountain, but when I lived in an area which boasts the highest mountain in the country then there were days when I wondered at what point I would tackle it. And so it was with Gros Morne. We lived in the shadow of Newfoundland's highest mountain. Or so we thought. In the late 1950s, somebody scaled a hill south of Bay of Islands in the Lewis Range and announced that it was approximately six feet higher!

Gros Morne, officially listed at 2,666 feet, lies just northeast of the Eastern Arm in Bonne Bay. We had been told that a few people had reached the summit, but that the going was very difficult as there was no trail and the journey through the forest to the foot of the mountain was a long and difficult one. The challenge was there daily, but it was five years before we decided that we would attempt the climb. We made our plans carefully for we needed a full day of good weather and as much daylight as possible. Our expedition would include Edna, myself, Edwina, Gerine, a guide, and one of our friends. Although the climb is not extraordinarily difficult, it is long. Accordingly on July 15, 1951, we left our house early in the morning, boarded *Tinker Bell* and went up the Eastern Arm. We moored the boat as close to the mountain as we could, went ashore, and set out on our climb. It is fitting that I should let Edwina tell the story, since she wrote an account when she got back from the trip, which was published in *The Log,* the official organ of the Newfoundland Lumbermen's Association, in 1952.

A TRIP UP GROS MORNE
BY EDWINA MURPHY, NORRIS POINT, AGED TEN

My friend and I were the first little girls to climb Gros Morne. On the morning of July 15, 1951, we left our house in our jeep. Mommy, my little friend Gerine, Daddy and I went on the trip. We stopped at the hospital and picked up our guide, Billy Major, and a friend, Dr. Perry Ottenburg. Then we went on to the point. We got in *Tinker Bell* and went up the Eastern Arm (or Deer Arm). When we reached there we went ashore in the dinghy "Twinkle." Daddy and Uncle Perry rowed in the dinghy while Billy, Mommy, Gerine and I walked to the point. We covered ourselves in fly-oil and we needed it too!

On the way to Gros Morne, there were lots of slippery stones, holes, sticks and roots you could trip up in and other things. We saw flowers, trees, grass and lots of moss. We followed the small sort-of-path which no strangers could see or find. We passed lots of fresh water streams and rivers where we had drinks but those flies were some thick. There were so many flies we could hardly see one another.

The way was quite long, but we stopped only once, going until we reached the foot of Gros Morne. There were lots of low bushes and quite a few lakes. We could see from the foot of Gros Morne, the rocks called Crow Cliff and we heard crows, too.

After we had something to eat we packed some food to take with us on the climb. First Gerine and Uncle Perry started going up, then Mommy and Billy. Daddy and I did not know if we could make it, so we went last. We climbed and we climbed. After a while Daddy and I could not see Gerine, Uncle Perry, Mommy or Billy. After climbing a long time we reached the top and we walked around the top till until we met the others. Daddy took lots of movies. Gros Morne is Newfoundland's highest mountain, but it is not nearly as high as Mount Everest. From the top we could see all around. From up there the Eastern Arm looked like the head of a duck.

We went over and saw the place where the geographical survey had been made. On the cement was June 10, and in the circle was printed "Geographical Survey." We left a bottle there with our names in it.

Then we turned back. We went down to the brook where uncle Perry and Gerine were. After having some tea we left. On the way back the tide had come up so we had to go in a garden so as not to get too wet. It took us all day from the time we began until we ended and we did not see a moose, caribou or a bear, but we did have a lovely time!

How well Edwina wrote her account of an exciting adventure, for it was exciting in many ways. First of all, we were told that Edna was the first woman to climb Gros Morne, and certainly no girls of Edwina's and Gerine's ages had ever climbed it. Secondly, it was a demanding journey that took us all day to get to the top over very difficult terrain. The hike in to the mountain was tiring enough, as it went along a trail that increased in elevation as we covered the two kilometres to the foot of Gros Morne proper. Up the face of the mountain, there were rocks of all sizes which were quite loose underfoot. They made climbing extremely difficult as we went up through the gully made by rocks that had been blasted into a sort of chute to give access to the top of the mountain.

Edwina and I, as she said in her account, didn't know if we could make it to the top because we were really very tired by the time we reached the foot of the hill. However, after a lunch and a rest, and while we watched the others set off up to the top, we gathered enough strength to go a little way, and then a little way further, and then still another bit, and finally to our surprise we found ourselves in gentle stages on top of Gros Morne. It was a clear, sunny, but hazy day. The view from the summit was quite breath-taking for we could see north as far as Cow Head and to the south the entire Bay was laid out before us. We could see over the top of Table Mountain towards Trout River and well to the east towards the White Hills.

Walking to the north side of the mountain we found ourselves looking straight down, an almost sheer drop into Ten Mile pond from the gulch. The abrupt drop was quite unexpected and most startling. The last ice age had torn a fjord in amongst the mountains with a cliff approximately 2,500 feet high. One could look over the cliff into the water so far below and then follow the fjords to east and west through deep gullies that mark many routes through the mountains in this part of the country. On the mountain facing Gros Morne across the fjord we could see waterfalls cascading down from ponds at the top of the flat lands emptying themselves into the water below.

At some time a geological survey had reached the summit and set up their marker, with a brass plate advising of the purpose. As Edwina mentions, we took this opportunity to leave a bottle with a piece of paper and a note advising anyone who might find it that we had visited there. We believe this was the accepted procedure for adventurers and mountain climbers.

There was no evidence of any wild life on the rough terrain at the top of Gros Morne, although Billy, our guide, told us that it was not uncommon to see an occasional black bear in the woods around the foot of the hill. He said as well that in spring the snowshoe hare and the ptarmigan can be seen by the quick eye in the brush and tamarack of the flat lands. Across to the southeast, Billy pointed out the high cliff known as Crow Cliff, the noisy residence of many crows. This area is the home of a pair of eagles as well, but we saw no sign of them on this trip. I had taken my movie camera with me and took photographs along the way. They came out very successfully but the view from the summit could not be captured on film in its true glory because of the haze.

After a good rest and having fully explored the top of Gros Morne, we then started the descent, which was done in fast time. We made our way back through the forest to where we had left our boat in Eastern Arm. It was dusk by the time we got back to the boat. We had spent some sixteen hours on the trip from the time we left the shore at Eastern Arm until the time we got back. It was a very satisfactory experience and we have all been proud over the years to be able to say that we climbed Gros Morne, but I think proudest were the girls who were able to say that they were the first women to climb Gros Morne.

Although Table Mountain lay facing us across the Bay for all the years that we lived in Bonne Bay, knowing that it was only about 1,600 to 1,800 feet high it didn't offer the same challenge, and at no time did we attempt to climb to the top of Table Mountain. The barren appearance of Table Mountain suggested that it would not be of a great deal of interest to us. Certainly it presented the same difficulties of having a long trip through the forest to get to the foot of the hills and then to climb to the top. I doubt if the view would have been as grand and we left it for others to do.

However we did explore every part of Bonne Bay. Eventually we knew every little cove and beach, we had visited them all. I think I knew where every rock lay in the bay, and we knew the good spots for swimming. The water was always very cold in Bonne Bay, but over the years we did have two or three good summers when swimming was a joy. During our time there was no such word as pollution and I doubt that the waters on the Bay were polluted in any way. I learned the likely places for trout fishing, which I enjoyed, but for which I had little time because I was always kept busy. The Lomond River was famous throughout Newfoundland for salmon fishing and during our time was not difficult to reach, yet never once did I manage to find time or the inclination to go salmon fishing either there or anywhere else on the coast. I restricted myself to trout fishing which I could do at the drop of a hat and was quite happy to spend an hour at. Even if it was unproductive, it gave me an opportunity to unwind and relax. The flies of course, were always troublesome but in those days I smoked and used to set up a smoke screen and smother myself in fly dope to help protect myself.

One of our favorite sports was jigging for cod and other fish from the stern of our boat. We learned not only where the good spots were, but also where we might be likely to land a good big flatfish of which we were very fond. The local residents ate mainly cod and had no use for this type of fish, always throwing them back, as they did throughout Newfoundland, but we went out of our way to try and provide ourselves with a varied diet. We were prepared to eat any fish that we could lay our hands on. At one time when Bonne Bay was invaded by dogfish, just out of interest, we caught some, skinned them and ate them. We proved that they were edible, which the local folk had doubted. In Britain, dogfish are sold in the fish and chip shops as "Rock Salmon." Frankly they taste rather like blotting paper, but at least they contain some protein. We found that we could give them to our pets, the dogs and the cats, and even the hens were given boiled dogfish to eat.

The fish population included cod, herring, mackerel, salmon, trout, flatfish, halibut, haddock, and caplin, all of which we enjoyed at the various times that they were available. We were particularly fond of roes, and I would walk ten miles anytime for a meal of cod tongues. While we were not fussy about seal flippers we loved seal liver and seal heart, and went out of our way to try and procure them to add to our diet. The local people were somewhat surprised at this, but I remembered my grandfather telling me how when he went to the ice they used to cut strips of seal heart and hang them on their belts and chew them as they went along. In my turn, while I didn't do this, I found that the seal heart was a very nutritious and tasty food. Even though I tried to encourage others to emulate us, I was never successful.

In fact, one family which tried to copy us sent for me and I found them all sick and extremely ill with gastroenteritis. When I sorted it out I found that they had blamed the seal liver which they had eaten and which they told me previously was not fit to eat. Further questioning elicited that they had found a seal dead on the beach which had probably been there for several days and taken the liver from that to eat. They were very sick for twenty four hours and then recovered. It was a miracle that their foolishness had not killed them all. This incident certainly didn't help my suggestion that seal liver and heart were good food and could be eaten by everyone at a time when the extra food supply would have been most helpful. I never pursued this subject again, and felt that I would let sleeping dogs lie.

Chapter 23

OBSTETRICS

From the beginning of human existence, women have had babies. Today, the medical profession, nursing profession, and mid-wives stand by to render what help and assistance they can. Many of our people in isolated parts of the province have gone through their labours and deliveries without any trained help for miles. Many died in childbirth and many newborn infants were lost because there was no one to provide help at the time it was needed. This chapter in our medical history has probably been the hardest for the people to bear and cemeteries throughout Newfoundland offer mute testimony as to the numbers of infants who died at the time of birth or shortly thereafter.

Every settlement had some women who even without training became accepted as the Midwife and who turned out when needed to give reassurance and help. Some of these midwives were fortunate in that they were trained in St. John's, but investigation showed that their training consisted usually of being allowed to watch a few deliveries and sort the linen. They could do little more than preside over the arrival of a newborn infant, cut the cord, and pray that the afterbirth would deliver itself and that the patient would not hemorrhage to death afterwards.

In the early days of the Cottage Hospitals, patients had to pay to be in hospitals. It was difficult for many families to find the money for what was after all a natural process of giving birth, so the majority stayed at home. The arrival of the doctor in the district meant that he could be present and take care of the home delivery, but it was extremely difficult to manage a hospital practice, a district practice, and home deliveries as well. Times change and education proves that things can be done better in other places and in new ways. Gradually the tendency was for the women to go to the hospital where they could get better attention and where there were better facilities.

We averaged 100 deliveries a year in the hospital and at home, and my mind was always so much at ease when I had my patient in hospital for I knew that I could do so much more there. My fear of finding myself with a complicated case some distance from the hospital, perhaps two or three hours to travel by boat or sleigh, was never a happy one. Of course, the trend toward hospital delivery in itself was a recognition of the fact that more could be done and more confidence built in the hospital itself. However, some of the early cases can never be forgotten and it's amazing what was accomplished with literally nothing.

I learned that the medical textbook is fine in its place, but that often one had to, so to speak, throw away the book and use one's common sense and local surroundings as best one could. I well remember being called to a house many miles from the hospital which took about two hours to reach by horse and sleigh. When I arrived I found the house was no bigger than an average garage, and consisted of three rooms. The kitchen was the living room and contained a stove, a table, a couple of chairs, a bench, and a wash basin. A cat and dog were among its inhabitants. The stove was set in the middle of the room and backed on to a wooden partition which divided the house into half, which in turn was divided into two parts making two small bedrooms. The girl I was attending was one of the bedrooms in a small bed wedged into the space which was only just big enough to take it, and surrounded by piles of clothing, bedding, boxes, and various collected items gathered over the years. There was just enough space to get a chair beside the bed on which I could put my bag and then prepare to deliver the patient.

To keep the house warm, for it was wintertime, the stove was being loaded up with wood and was almost red hot. The heat in the little room was tremendous. The delivery was coming along nicely and the patient, though frightened, was responding to my directions. As I manoeuvered myself in the cramped space and as the delivery was about to take place, I put a knee on the bed to steady myself. It collapsed. I fell through the lower end of the bed as the patient fell through the top end. I can't remember who as more surprised.

Luckily the delivery was effected immediately and I retrieved myself, the baby, and the new mother with the help of the young husband who was busy feeding the stove. It was the only time that I can remember falling through a bed while doing a delivery.

On another occasion, attempting to do a delivery in a home a long distance from the hospital, I was assisted by the local midwife. When it appeared that there were complications and there wouldn't be time to get the patient transferred to hospital, I decided that if I gave the patient an anesthetic I would be able to apply forceps and deliver the baby. When I asked the midwife if she had ever given an anesthetic, she assured me that she certainly had and it was no problem. She would be glad to do it again. I produced some Chloroform and the mask and told her that I would start the anesthetic and then pass it over to her. At this point she told me that she had misunderstood me and thought I asked her had she ever seen an anesthetic being given. However, it now appeared to her that I expected her to take part in the giving of an anesthetic and this she had never done and had no intention of doing now. In view of the circumstances, I talked her into watching what I was doing and assured her that from the minute she took over I would be watching her every move and would instruct her as exactly what to do. This is how the anesthetic was given. I put the patient to sleep and the midwife then carried on under my direct instructions while I carried out the delivery. It was a very shaken midwife who went home that night having given an anesthetic for the first time in her life. However, I am sure that she boasted about it many times in the years to come.

It was quite common for girls to be married when they were fifteen or sixteen, and it was quite common for them to get pregnant about the same age. The youngest maternity patient I ever had was thirteen years old. She appeared much older, was obviously much more mature than her years and, as I had expected, there was no trouble with the delivery. However, being pregnant at age thirteen was a criminal offence and no minister would marry her at that young age. It turned out that the father of her child was only a year older than she was, so it would obviously have served no purpose to take legal action. I understand that the authorities agreed. After all, quite a number of fourteen year old girls delivered, and the fifteen and sixteen year old girls were accepted as perfectly normal.

Every year there has always been a race across Canada to see who would have the first baby born after midnight on New Year's Day. I gave little thought to this until one year I found myself delivering a baby a few seconds after midnight. The post office was closed the next day, which of course was New Year's Day. If I remember correctly, the following day was Sunday when the post office was again closed. So it was approximately forty-eight hours before we were able to get word out. By that time the newsworthiness was lost and I don't believe that the baby and the mother received recognition to which they were entitled. However, I felt strongly about the baby being named in some fitting manner. I suggested to the mother that perhaps she would like to be a little different and might consider, since it was a girl child, using the first letter of the Greek alphabet, Alpha, as the child's name. The mother gave this some thought and talked it over with the father and they agreed that this was indeed fitting. The child was named Alpha, and the first baby born that year in Canada was born at the Bonne Bay Cottage Hospital.

On another occasion I received a telegram from the nurse at Parson's Pond advising that she was in the middle of a delivery, that the first baby had arrived and that the second, a twin, had not arrived and it appeared there was some complication. She would like me to come as quickly as possible. It was unfortunately extremely stormy at the time. It was quite impossible for *Tinker Bell* to tackle the trip, there were no other large vessels around, and there was apparently no hope of getting to the woman and children. The nurse was well aware of the storm conditions. I could only wire back that I would suggest she have patience and that I would be along as soon as the storm abated. For two days the storm raged and there was no hope of moving, and then suddenly there appeared on the scene Lee Wulff, the American sportsman who had a fishing camp at Portland Creek. He used to fly his sportsmen from Lomond to Portland Creek. Lee Wulff landed at Norris Point to pick up come supplies and Bryant Harding, knowing I was waiting to get to Parson's Pond, grabbed him and asked him if there was any way he could help me. Lee Wulff was only too willing to be of assistance and within the hour I was in his plane and bound for Parson's Pond. We were flying against a head wind and the journey of some forty-five miles took approximately two hours. Finally when we arrived at Parson's Pond to put me down in the settlement, Lee Wulff landed in the river. He did this by dropping over a small schooner which was moored in the little harbour and landing in a piece of water I swear was no more than 100 yards long. I am convinced to this day that the plane stopped before we crashed against the bank only because I had my feet straight out in front of me and was using them as landing brakes.

In a matter of minutes I was in the house and, believe it or not, as I walked in the twin appeared. I was able to effect the delivery without any difficulties in a matter of only a few minutes more. The community was convinced that by some marvelous means I had accomplished this delivery. There was no way I could tell them it would have happened anyway. It would have happened five minutes before I arrived if the wind had been a little stronger. The nurse was greatly relieved, the mother was delighted, and I felt I had not had a worthless trip. After staying long enough to see that all was well with the new mother and the twins, and checking one or two other patients in the settlement, Lee Wulff kindly flew me back to Norris Point. We arrived twenty minutes after take off because we now had the wind following us.

Lee Wulff carried out a number of Mercy Missions over the years on the coast, and was always ready and willing to respond to any emergency calls that we made to him. I made a number of trips with him up and down the Coast. On one occasion he flew me to Port Saunders and on my way back decided that he would drop in at his camp at Portland Creek for tea before proceeding to Norris Point. As we went over the fields between Daniel's Harbour and Portland Creek he spotted a man that he wanted to talk with, and so he swooped down, shut off his engine, opened the door of the aircraft and shouted down telling the fellow to come over to the camp where he wanted to see him. The man shouted back his understanding and agreement. Lee shut the door, started the engine and in a few minutes we landed on the lake. I had never seen this type of performance before and was not a little startled by it, but I enjoyed looking back on it as quite an experience.

Many are the stories that could be told of patients who had to be taken from their homes and carried on stretchers or doors or makeshift litters, on horse and cart, on horse and sleigh, in snowmobile, by boat, or any means possible, to the hospital when complications interrupted a delivery. But the majority of cases were quite straight forward, there was nothing to talk about, and whether they were delivered in their own homes or in the hospital there was no hitch. Beyond the population being increased there was little worth recording. Life was proceeding as it should. The practice of obstetrics is a most satisfying occupation. When complications occasionally arose, the pleasure that the newborn child brings to its parents is more than worth the anguish and suffering and long hours spent working on these cases.

Chapter 24

NUTS AND BOLTS

In the course of years of medical practice in small communities every doctor is faced with situations which, when they occur, may be startling, dramatic, acute emergencies, matters of life and death, all of which need quick decision making. Rarely at the time of happening are these problems amusing or humourous. The humour of any particular case or incident usually occurs at a later point when one can look back at what was seen, said, or done.

To be told that a female patient is ready for examination in the examining room and to walk in and find a young woman lying on top of the sheet without a stitch of clothing except her hat is startling to say the least. Normally a patient is at least covered by a sheet. Hats are optional. However, such occurences are no time to embarrass the patient by laughing at the situation nor to make any comment about it but to be about one's business as though it was a perfectly normal and everyday happening. The complete opposite of this incident is to be found in the case of the elderly lady who presents herself for medical attention, is only too willing to describe her symptoms, but when the moment for examination comes informs the nurse that there is no way that anyone, even the doctor, will ever see her body or examine it. I well recall a number of years ago some elderly patients who positively refused to undress and be examined, who refused even an examination fully dressed. On several occasions, I was told in no uncertain terms that no man, not even their husbands, had seen them and I certainly was not to be the first. While these may be amusing incidents to look back on they certainly are problems to be dealt with by the use of tact and understanding at the time of happening.

Patients are human beings. They have feelings and they have fears, especially fear of the unknown. A lot of the mystery of medicine has disappeared through education and understanding and because people today expect the doctor to explain fully the details of their condition and the treatment which is to be used. As ignorance and misunderstanding have disappeared, an even closer relationship is established between doctor and patient. The patient shares the difficulty of diagnosis and the sometimes trying period of treatment with the doctor.

Being isolated for so many years the people had developed a considerable knack of making a diagnosis. The most important part of these lay diagnoses was to be able to recognise the acute and severely ill patient and seek immediate medical attention. The people's ability to make a correct diagnosis was also quite astonishing. I was always amazed when a patient was brought in labelled as a case of meningitis and in fact turned out to be just that.

With a fair amount of tuberculosis rampant there was a recognition of this disease, but a reluctance to use the word or admit that it existed in one's family. In the same way there was often a reluctance by some patients to submit to x-ray, for there was a clear cut feeling that an x-ray might show something which the patient didn't wish to be seen. Some people thought that refusal to have an x-ray would hide any condition which would therefore probably take care of itself. It took many years to get rid of this feeling and implant the idea that early diagnosis and early treatment was the way, in most cases, to a quick and sure cure. Certainly the chances of successful treatment depended in many cases on an early diagnosis. As the word spread and understanding came, so the volume of diagnostic work increased and the wisdom of this line was accepted throughout the district.

The other side of reluctance to have an x-ray was the idea that an x-ray in itself was a form of treatment. It was not uncommon in the early days for patients to demand an x-ray and, while the plate was being developed and read, the patient would disappear. It might be several days, weeks, or even months before the patient was located and informed of the result of the x-ray. Strangely, in nearly all of these cases one was informed that the x-ray had been truly "wonderful" and the patient had immediately felt a great deal better. If ever one wanted an example of the effect of placebos, surely this was it.

However, there wasn't much time for work in this field, although I did on occasion have an opportunity to use straight-forward techniques. One of the most interesting cases concerned a woman who had been married for many years but had no children. She had a long history of abdominal symptoms and had been a patient in another hospital where a laporatomy had been performed. My request for information from the other hospital elicited the fact that at laporotomy (the opening of the abdomen) they had discovered that the patient had tuberculous peritonitis. In those days there were no specific drugs for the treatment of tuberculoses but in the case of tuberculous peritonitis in most cases the laporotomy which allowed air to enter the abdomen seemed to cure the condition. Coincidentally, of course, there was always a long period of prolonged convalescence, and the rest and careful attention to dieting also helped the patient to combat the condition.

There was a possibility that the woman's condition had caused her sterility and her anxiety about her inability to get pregnant could be explained by this. There was little that could be done for her and I was therefore extremely surprised when she visited one day and announced that she wanted an anti-natal examination as she was pregnant. Examination revealed that she appeared to be about seven months pregnant from the size of her abdomen but also revealed that no fetal parts could be felt, nor could a fetal heart be heard. I was concerned about this case and, because she resisted examination which made it difficult to be sure, at the same time I did not wish to submit her to an x-ray because of the possible danger to the baby.

I decided that the best way of dealing with the situation was to give her a gentle anaesthetic and I would be able to complete my examination in this manner. Accordingly, I gave her a small dose of intravenous Pentothal which induced sleep and relaxation. When the patient was settled, the nurse pulled back the sheet to reveal a perfectly flat abdomen and no sign of the pregnancy. The diagnosis was made immediately. It was a straight-forward case of Pseudo-Cyesis (phantom pregnancy). This is a condition where the patient for one reason or another firmly believes that she is pregnant and to produce the physical appearance of pregnancy induces some disten-sion of the abdomen using a contraction of the diaphragm and spasm of the abdominal muscles to produce the desired affect. It is usually a hysterical manifestation although the patient of course shows no sign of what is commonly expected from the word hysteria. In fact, she is cool, calm, and collected and quite confident that she is pregnant. She receives from her family and friends the comfort and encourage-ment due to all who are pregnant.

Once I verified that this in fact was a case of Pseudo-Cyesis through further examination, the patient was then returned to bed and I went about my business. Later I checked in to talk to the patient and make sure everything was well. To my astonishment, I discovered that the condition had returned and that I now had a patient who believed she was still pregnant and was quite unable to accept any other diagnosis. I realised that the situation had to be resolved quickly and firmly, but I knew as well that the patient's well-being needed to be considered. I explained that we were unable to complete the procedure due to some technical hitch and that it would be repeated the next day. The next day the patient was again given an anaesthetic, the same sequence of events took place, the pregnancy disappeared instantly, but this time I had only given enough intravenous Pentothal to induce a state of "twilight sleep." At this point it is possible often to catch a patient before they lose total consciousness and, by the use of the right line of questioning, elicit information which is really being held in the subconscious mind.

In the darkened room and in response to my questions she poured out the whole story: her desire to have at least one child, the approach of the menopause and the urgency of getting pregnant before it was too late, her desperate attempts at getting pregnant, and finally after so much illness and so much determination, her triumph. She was now able to show her family and friends that in fact she was pregnant. I realised then that to allow her to continue in her belief would have destroyed her, for of course the day would come when she would have had to admit that her pregnancy was all imagination. I had learned from her all there was to learn. My course of action was clear.

When she awoke in her bed, I was sitting as I had been for some time beside her waiting for her to return to consciousness. I was ready to greet her with the unwelcome news. Her previous illness made it impossible for her to have a child, and therefore it had had to be removed. There was an obvious reaction of disappointment, yet satisfaction, disappointment that she would not have her child, yet satisfaction that her problem–for she knew it herself to be a problem–had been solved for her and she could face her family and friends with a clear explanation. The pregnancy did not recur and in a short while she was able to go home. She had no further abdominal symptom or pregnancies.

This form of treatment was going through a phase of popularity. Patients in a state of twilight sleep would respond to questioning and would release feelings hidden in their subconscious minds. Suggestions made to them while they were in this state could often solve their problems.

In a similar vein, I was baffled by a big strong woodsman who kept coming to see me with a variety of symptoms which didn't ever seem to make a great deal of sense. I could never find any physical signs to help me make a diagnosis. I was greatly concerned about the man, for obviously something was driving him continuously to come out of the woods and seek medical attention. I was either missing the diagnosis or failing because of a deeper problem that had not yet been revealed. I decided that this might be a good case on which to try the "twilight sleep" technique and accordingly I arranged to give him some intravenous Pentothal and see if I could learn more from him. For about an hour I balanced him on the edge of consciousness while I tried to elicit information, but the man was slightly deaf, and I had to shout my questions at him and every question was answered by the same word, "Huh?"

The first half hour nearly finished the whole attempt to find out what was causing this man's symptoms for every time I asked a question and got the same answer "Huh?" I was on the point of breaking up. However, it was no laughing matter, and I persisted and eventually was able to elicit from him the information that he was suspicious about his wife's fidelity and felt it wise to come out of the woods and spend more time at home. However, to protect himself and his job and not make her suspicious he produced symptoms which necessitated many visits to the doctor.

Later, when he recovered consciousness, I was able to sit down with him and have a long talk. I explained what I had learned about his problems. I was able to reassure him that he was perfectly fit, for he had got to the point that he had begun to believe his own story and was beginning to feel sick. Of course, some of the illness which he was developing was due to worry about his family affairs. He had begun to "worry himself sick." Not all cases where there was a difficulty in diagnosis were suitable candidates for this type of approach. In fact, quite the opposite is probably true, and it is the isolated case only which might be helped in this manner.

I remember well a young woman from the Coast who presented herself with a bizarre set of symptoms and who obviously was very sick. She appeared to be between thirty-five and forty years of age but in actual fact was twenty-six years old. She had been married for eight or nine years and had already seven children. Like others in her situation, she had aged beyond her years. Such women had little chance to recover after one pregnancy before they became pregnant again. On top of pregnancies, they had growing numbers of children all aged closely together and all young causing a great burden. Life was not easy. There was a lot of hard manual work to be done, water to be carried, wood to be cut for the stove, and so on.

This young woman, obviously showing the effects of a large number of children in a short period of time and the hard life she lived, was suffering from some condition which was causing her to lose weight and become totally apathetic. She didn't seem to hear too much or perhaps she didn't want to hear too much. She spent a lot of time just gazing into space and looking as if she hadn't a thought in her head. Physical examination and exhaustive diagnostic tests got me nowhere. The nursing staff had trouble coaxing food into her and she showed no interest. Although she responded somewhat, picked up a bit and put on a bit of weight, she still had no interest in life whatsoever. She never asked about her family or her children, and was too far away from her home to receive any visits. She was a very lonely and sick individual.

There was obviously something wrong but I couldn't make a diagnosis because I couldn't pin anything down specifically. I spent periods talking to her quietly in my office trying to obtain information or any clue which would help me in my quest for a diagnosis. I led her away from the ordinary type of questions and tried to get some background on her life and her general activities. Accidentally I stumbled across the answer to this peculiar case.

In the course of discussion about her everyday life and activities, I found that she quite often visited the woods. I nearly missed the point of these visits, taking it for granted that perhaps she just enjoyed walking through the woods until I realised that this was most abnormal for a woman who had a large family and household duties. I pursued this line of questioning and found that she had a purpose to her visits and it was to collect the bark of juniper trees. She had been told that by boiling the bark and drinking the fluid so obtained she would not get pregnant. Having already had seven children in such a short space of time and feeling that they were unable to look after any more she was desperate. And so she was continuously drinking juniper bark extract.

I could find nothing in my medical library about the action of juniper on the body. With further research, I found some information that suggested it would have an action on the central nervous system and would therefore produce the picture that this young woman presented. The treatment, of course, was the withdrawal of the offending agent. I forbade her to take any more for it was poisoning her. Over the course of a few weeks she picked up remarkably and this progress continued on her return home. Of course, it was important to discuss this whole matter with her husband, which I did before she was released from hospital. With his understanding of the situation and what she had been trying to do to help family affairs, I felt that they would work out the problem and live normal, happy lives from then on.

The whole question of psychology seemed so far removed from the type of practice one conceives of in an isolated part of the Coast that I doubted I would ever come across any cases. And yet every year a certain number of cases cropped up which, in spite of the fact that people were unaware of such conditions, presented themselves in clear-cut textbook fashion. I was always astonished at the appearance of a young girl who presented some condition which was obviously hysterical in origin and I never ceased to wonder at how these patients had produced these symptoms when they had never heard of such things. There was no television and few magazines or books that would give anybody the ideas that some of the patients produced. A typical example would be the patient who complained of sudden complete loss of sensation of an arm from the elbow down. It was usually a sudden onset and to prove how completely the sensation was lost the patient would never flinch when needles were driven through the skin and really put on a remarkable display. These cases usually responded to a careful history taking, the finding of the reason for the development of the symptoms, and then talking out the problem with a patient. Sometimes dramatic results could be obtained from treating a patient with placebos. The psychological effect on a patient who believes he or she is receiving a powerful and healing medication can work wonders.

Of course, the reaction of different patients to the same operation or similar conditions can often be vastly different. I well remember two men who each had a kidney removed but who had responded in totally different ways. One man was over-anxious to get back to work. The other man was convinced that he would never be able to work again and was so incapacitated that he had to go on welfare assistance as he was incapable of supporting himself and his family. The man who was anxious to return to work was a problem in one way because he was so convinced that the operation had cured all his problems he refused to be brought in for a check up each year. He considered it a total waste of time and had never felt better in his life.

The other man presented the opposite picture. He assured me that he lived in misery all the time and was quite incapable of doing anything. For the first two or three years I accepted his reaction as quite reasonable for some people do tend to respond in this manner. However, one year when he came in for his annual check up I questioned him more closely about what he was capable of doing. I wanted to find out for the records to what degree he was incapacitated. The answer to the straight-forward question, "Are you capable of working?" produced a prompt and firm negative. However, I suggested that perhaps he was able to bring in a bit of firewood, to which he replied that he managed somehow to bring in his firewood. I then suggested that perhaps he was able to jig an occasional cod and to this he agreed. I asked if he put out any lobster pots and he admitted that he managed to get a few in the water. I asked him if he managed to get some salmon in the course of the year or herring or mackeral, and he agreed that he was able to do this to the point of perhaps being able to provide the family with a variety of fish. I wondered whether he was able to grow any vegetables or potatoes, and he admitted that with a great deal of effort he did manage to get his gardens in and supply the house with vegetables. I found that he had a cow which he looked after, and they had the milk for their use. He had some sheep which they kept, and his wife used the wool to make garments. They either sold the sheep or killed one or two for their own use each winter. He kept a small horse which he used to help him get the firewood and generally move about in the winter time. He managed each year to go on a hunting expedition and to get a moose which helped see them through the winter. He took advantage of the birds and managed to bag a few to keep his pantry. If the seal struck in, he usually managed to get a few and was able to use the seal skins himself or dispose of them to the buyers who travelled the Coast.

By the time I had finished leading him along through the year-round activities, I found myself sitting across the desk from a man who was fully occupied through all seasons of the year, a man who was doing as well as any other man although he didn't actually go off and work in the woods as a woodsman or spend his entire time fishing. Still, he managed to provide for his family and they lived as good a standard as anybody else and enjoyed the additional benefits of welfare payments. On top of these benefits, he enjoyed "ill health."

Others were not so lucky. Inevitably accidents, those unforeseen circumstances that confront us all at one time or another, occured in the isolated communities. One of the main culprits was the power saw, especially in its early days. A man who was tired or who slipped would drop a saw onto his arm or leg and sustain a severe and often crippling injury. Men working in sawmills would find their clothing caught in the machinery or would slip and lose a finger or a hand or an arm. Trees would fall the wrong way and hit men as they fell. Boats would overturn and fishermen, who rarely knew how to swim, would drown. Legs would get tangled in mooring lines resulting in fractures or even loss of limbs. People would fall off houses building or repairing the roof, or off vessels they were building or repairing. They would suffer burns from the hot tar being used for caulking a vessel. Once the tar spilled on the deck and ran all over a man's head and face underneath. One could never tell what type of case would present next or what kind of accident might happen. The man out for a day hunting would have his rifle explode in his hands or would be kicked by his horse. Children sliding could suffer severe injuries when they ran into trees or sustain nasty injuries crossing fences.

I must admit, however, that I was considerably shaken one day when a man walked into the hospital with a bolt sticking out from his forehead. He was a big powerful man with a reputation as an outstanding woodsman capable of cutting with a bucksaw between four and five cords of wood a day and bringing home a pay packet each month ranging between $400 and $500. On this particular day he had been working with his father and brothers at a sawmill they owned. One of the bolts had come loose and got caught up in the machinery, which had flung it out and imbedded it in his head. It drove through the outer surface of his skull in the middle of his forehead fortunately in a place where there were two layers of bones separated by an air pocket. The force of the blow knocked him down and temporarily stunned him but did not knock him out. His brothers wanted to carry him to the hospital but he would have none of that and instead insisted on making his own way, accompanied by them, of course. Any other man might have been killed on the spot and certainly would have been knocked unconscious. I doubt that many men could have made their own way to seek medical attention.

However, at the hospital and using only a local anaesthetic, I removed the bolt and then removed the large number of splinters of bone and repaired the hole as best I could. I did all this with fear and tribulation, for I had no idea how deep the bolt went into the man's head. When I was fininshed, he sat up, refused my suggestion that he spend a few days in the hospital where we could keep an eye on him and make sure there was neither infection nor any other untoward complication, and left. He did reluctantly agree to return after four or five days for a dressing and to have the sutures removed. He didn't turn a hair from beginning to end. The wound healed without incident or infection, and he suffered no ill effects of his accident.

A similar type of accident occurred one morning when a man was starting his motor-boat engine. This task he accomplished in the fly wheel by spinning it; however, he got his face too close to the fly wheel, the machine backfired and the bolt flew around in the fly wheel and hit him in the face, breaking his jaw on both sides. He was brought to the hospital and x-ray showed the extent of the injury. The jaw required wiring in such a way that not only was the broken piece of the jaw wired to both sides, but the lower jaw is then wired to the upper jaw. This is accomplished by putting wire around each tooth and then lacing them up and down to form a sort of network. When the work was complete the man's jaws were tightly wired together. This wiring acts as a splint and allows the bone to heal. However it takes several weeks for this healing to take place and in the meantime he had to be fed by straws and lived mainly on liquids for he could not chew.

It was a very lengthy procedure to do this wiring and get it all firm and tight and in the proper position, but the man was most cooperative. When I went to look for the materials there was no wire of the type that I required in the hospital, but in hunting around I discovered a bell by the front door which was wired with exactly what I wanted, and so we dismantled the bell, took the wire, cleaned it, sterilized it, and used it. It worked beautifully. Tired after my exertions, for it was a slow, tedious, back-breaking business, I went home that evening. In the morning when I came to the hospital the first thing I did was to go and see my patient. He greeted me with his mouth wide open and no sign of a wire anywhere. He explained that he had been bothered by the wires and he spent the entire night removing them. I explained that his only hope of having the jaw heal up properly was to keep the wire there and I proceeded to rewire them. Again it was a long painstaking process and again I exhorted him to leave everything alone and give it a chance to heal. This time I took the precaution of warning the nurse and the staff to keep an eye on him. Sure enough the next day he had removed some of them but not enough to make a great deal of difference and I was quickly able to put them back again. He learned over a few days that we meant business and were determined to help his jaw heal. He was just as determined to remove the wires. Fortunately we won, and his jaw healed and he returned to his work in due course.

Another man was brought in one day having been struck on the head by a falling tree and complaining of inability to turn his head. X-ray revealed that he had fractured two vertebrae in the neck and was in fact fortunate that he hadn't been killed outright. He responded to treatment which necessitated a cast enclosing his head, neck, and shoulders, and when the healing had taken place he advised me that there was no way he would ever be able to work again. He now entered into a lengthy legal negotiation with the company for whom he had been working and finally received a settlement of total disability of several thousand dollars, which was a lot of money in those days. There followed a glorious period when the family had all it wanted, but soon the money was spent. The company refused to ever take him on again because they had agreed to a total disability award. Although I had advised him earlier that I was sure he would be able to work again, it now became apparent he would not be allowed to work with that company again. However, from the day he received his award he was suddenly able to walk properly, he regained full movement of his head, and never had another complaint. He sought work wherever he could get it and provided for his family until the day he died many years later of a completely unrelated condition.

Chapter 25

HAZARDS

Spinal anaesthesia was my choice of anaesthetic for a large number of surgical cases for two reasons. First, being alone, I could handle the application of the anaesthetic myself and it meant another pair of hands available amongst the small staff in the operating room. Secondly, it was a very pleasant form of anaesthesia for the patient, with very little, if any, side or after effects and it could be used for most abdominal and lower extremity surgery.

I became very skilled at giving spinal anaesthetics. It was possible to become very accurate in pre-determining the level of the anaesthesia. However, one had to be aware of certain dangers and staff had to be made aware of these as well. The patients had to be handled with care for they had no power of movement of the anaesthetized part of the body nor did they have any sensation.

In spite of every effort to watch each patient carefully and to watch the staff as well, the day finally arrived when we had our first casualty. While I worked away in the operating room on other cases a new nursing assistant responded to a patient who had been returned to bed and was complaining of feeling cold. Trying to be helpful, the girl bustled off to the kitchen and got some hot water bottles filled with boiling water which she then placed alongside the patient's legs. Although all staff were under strict instructions never to put hot water bottles directly against a patient's skin but always either to wrap them in some covering or place them on the outside of the blankets, in her anxiety to be of help she had placed the hot water bottles against the skin. The nurse came to me shortly afterwards in a great state of dismay and asked me to look at the patient. I was horrified when I saw what had happened for the patient had sustained severe burns to both thighs.

We commenced treatment immediately. I advised the Department of Health about the incident and also advised the husband who was very upset. To make matters worse the patient was a young woman and it was inevitable that the result of this accident would be scars on both legs. The Department of Health advised that they would undertake the full cost of the treatment of the case, would make available any treatment which was considered necessary, and generally were prepared to do anything which would be of benefit in this case without charge to the patient. It was obviously going to be a long term case, as the healing process is always slow in burn cases, and the patient was suffering a great deal of pain and discomfort. We did everything we could for the patient and she responded in good spirit considering the circumstances. However, the husband lost no opportunity to criticise the hospital and our ability to treat patients. He let all and sundry know how he felt in no uncertain terms. We were all very upset over what had happened and his attitude only helped to make matters a great deal worse.

Shortly after this incident, and while the burn patient was still in hospital receiving treatment, a young girl was brought to the hospital complaining of abdominal pain. The diagnosis was not clear and I felt it wise to admit her for observation. I assured her parents that I would keep them fully informed of any developments, and would certainly advise them well in advance if undertaking any surgery if it proved necessary. Within forty-eight hours after admission she had settled down nicely, the pain had gone. I was content that it had probably been a severe case of abdominal colic; therefore, she would be ready to go home in another day or two. Suddenly her father dashed into the hospital, demanded to see me immediately and, since I was already in the hospital, this was arranged at once. He demanded to know why I hadn't advised him of the seriousness of his daughter's condition and why I would admit to everyone that the case was hopeless and that the girl was dying, and yet not tell her own parents. He was quite distraught and beside himself with a mixture of anger and despair, angry at me and despair at the thought of what was happening to his daughter.

It took some minutes to calm him down and assure him that his fears were groundless. It was obvious that the best way of doing this was to take him immediately to see his daughter. This I did and the sense of relief when he saw that his girl was well, that her condition appeared to be back to normal, and that his fears were groundless, was visibly evident. After he had realised that the situation was not as he had believed, and since he had come a long way and was still somewhat emotionally wound up, I invited him to have a cup of tea and sit down with me while we discussed the matter.

His story horrified me. It appeared that the husband of the woman who had suffered the burns to her legs had appeared at his house and, having visited the hospital to see his wife, had been aware that this man's daughter was also a patient. The father of the girl had not been home but the girl's mother was there when the man appeared. He told her bluntly that her daughter was dying, that the doctor had given up hope, and that the doctor himself had told him this. The girl's mother promptly fainted and the house and settlement were thrown into utter confusion. Under the circumstances, the girl's father set off for the hospital immediately, filled with despair for his daughter and anger at my having withheld this information from them.

He had now seen the girl for himself, and was satisfied the story was not true. I was able to tell him that it was my opinion this man was seeking to take revenge on myself and the hospital in this terrible way. He was trying in his simple way to ruin my reputation but without a thought as to the feelings of the people whom he was using as his instrument. I assured the girl's father that I had never gone back on my word to patients or their families and he realised he had been used. He set off to return home with my assurance that he could fetch his girl the next day, and with a determination to settle his score with the man who had caused them such suffering.

A few days later the woman's husband arrived at the hospital and asked to see me. He informed me that he had decided to take court action against me and would be suing for $10,000 damages, which was an enormous sum of money in those days. There was no point in discussing the matter with him for he had obviously made up his mind, but he still seemed reluctant to leave and I presume hoped that I would make a settlement on the spot. However, I had nothing to add and told him that I would be pleased to appear in court to answer to the charges. There was silence when he realised that I was going to say no more. He started to walk slowly through the door and as he did I said, "Well, I'll see you in court, and by the way I hope the court will be able to hear both the cases on the same day." He stopped and looked at me and asked, "What two cases?" "Oh didn't I tell you?" I replied, "I'm suing you for defamation of character, slander and other things, but I'm looking for $20,000." He immediately stood before my desk and wanted to know all the details. I refused to discuss it with him, only reminding him of his own actions and particularly his actions in regard to the parents of the girl who was in hospital. He left the hospital immediately and there was never another word heard from him about any legal action he might have contemplated. The burns healed in due course and the scars were not as severe as had been anticipated.

Every so often a dramatic and sometimes very urgent situation develops where it is felt wise that it be handled by a doctor. This was the situation one day when I was asked to go to a settlement to deal, if I could, with a young man who had barred himself in a house and was threatening to shoot anyone who came near him. The young man was deaf and dumb and had been the butt of the settlement all his life, considered by his contemporaries to be good for nothing but to be made fun of, and by everybody else as stupid and simple. Actually, he was a very intelligent young man who had, in spite of everything, developed an ability to communicate with those who had time to spend with him, and also an excellent ability to work with wood.

By day and by night he was taunted by anyone who came near him and finally his next door neighbour did something which had proved to be the last straw. He promptly got a rifle and took a shot at him across the field. Distraught at what he had done and afraid of reprisals he barred himself in his house where he lived alone, pulled all the curtains and blinds, and refused to come out. His parents were terribly upset, his father could get no response, and they appealed to me to sort out the situation.

I must admit I felt this was more of a job for the police, for the question of getting the young man to come out of his house and the dangers of him opening fire on anyone who might approach the building seemed all to great. However, the appearance of the police might well have precipitated another crisis. He did know me and he might allow me to get to him and talk him out of this situation. I agreed and proceeded to the settlement.

A fair size crowd had gathered to watch what they considered would be the fun, and I looked across the field to the house which was completely devoid of any life, no smoke coming from the chimney and all the windows barred and with blinds drawn. The obvious first thing was to get rid of the audience and this I proceeded to do explaining that it might only cause further upset and that anyhow it was really nobody's business except the parents and the doctor. The father explained that he had been around the house, he didn't know in which room the boy was, and since there was no sign or sound inside he didn't even know whether the boy had perhaps taken his own life.

I decided that perhaps I would go alone to the house and try and make my presence known. I think it was the longest walk that I have ever taken. To cross the field and walk directly up to the front door of the house knowing that inside was a young man with a rifle, who felt that the world was against him, who had already taken a shot at one man, and possibly was ready to do the same to anyone else who approached his house, was not a happy situation. I prayed that he would recognise me should he be watching, but as I walked towards the house there was no movement of the curtains and I had no idea as to whether he was watching or not.

I reached the front door and knocked hard. His father had told me that he could feel the knocking on the door where he wouldn't hear a voice. After I knocked hard on the door, I stood in front of the window hoping that he was either watching or would see me and recognise me. There was dead silence inside. I knocked again harder. Still no response. I pounded with my fists on the door and on the wall of the house wondering perhaps whether the young man was asleep. But still only silence. I walked around the house knocking on the windows and back door, but there was no response. His father, who had been watching now joined me and we discussed the possibility of the next step. The father thought that we should break in. I felt that any attempt like that might lead the young man to think some adversary was breaking in and he might well open fire.

I suggested that we have one more try, and that this time I would stand at the front door and knock and then move in front of the window while the father would go around and knock on the back door. This we did and for the first time I heard a responding noise somewhere inside the house. At least it appeared now that the young man was inside, was alive, and might now be induced out. His father continued to hammer on the door and I believe the young man recognised the fact that it was his father and eventually, after what seemed a lifetime of waiting, he unbarred the door and let us in.

The house, even though it was broad daylight, was completely darkened inside because all the windows were heavily curtained. It was cold for there was no fire in the stove, and the young man, who had been sleeping on a couch in the kitchen, appeared tired and hungry, looked sick and was obviously in need of food, warmth, and care. His rifle was propped against the table and there was a knife on the table as well. I examined the rifle and found that it was not loaded. I suggested then to the father that he take his son across to his own house where we could have a good look at him and see what we could do to help him. His mother was overjoyed when we arrived and I refused to allow any curious visitors to enter feeling that this would be better handled by the family. The boy was fed and warmed in his parents' kitchen and then put to bed and I talked with them about his case.

It was quite obvious from what they told me that he had been having a very rough time from a number of people who had no understanding at all of how difficult life was for him. It was also quite obvious that his neighbour had taunted him beyond the point of reason and that the boy had finally cracked enough to take a shot at him to show him that he resented it and would put up with no more of it. The neighbour, I think, had learned a lesson. The parents, at my suggestion, refused to allow him to move back into his house again, but kept him at home and helped him more perhaps than in the past. Strangely, this seemed to be a turning point and the young man devoted himself to his woodworking ability and became much sought after for the many things that he did make such as tables, chairs, and country sleighs.

Chapter 26

WARTS

E very doctor in his years of practice is exposed to a large number of conditions ranging over the entire medical field. Doctors develop great skill at the recognition of certain conditions and learn that certain problems are prevalent and should be thought of first. I have found over the years that I was able to expect certain conditions to turn up regularly. It is therefore permissible that I document and comment on some of these.

I think it is commonly accepted in the medical profession that warts are caused by a virus and that they are contagious. They are unsightly and a nuisance when they occur on the fingers, hands, or face. It always gives the impression of someone who is dirty, and patients are always seeking help to find a way to get rid of them.

Warts can be treated in a variety of ways. The usual treatment is to apply to each wart, carefully, a specially prepared solution (either Trichloracetic or Salicylic Acid) which has a destructive action. The surrounding area of course must be protected and it becomes a procedure which must be done with care. Probably the most effective way of dealing with warts is by burning them off (the use of Electro-Cautery). This is even more specialized and can only be done with the injection first of a local anesthetic, and then by a trained practitioner. Unfortunately, we had no such equipment at the Bonne Bay Cottage Hospital or I would have been very busy indeed, for I saw many, many cases of warts. The third form of treatment which was accepted by the local inhabitants was known as "charming." I had certainly heard stories of people's ability to charm warts, but I had never come in contact with it. A search of my medical library turned up the startling fact, which I had overlooked during my years of training, that "charming" was recognized and noted in text books. It was made quite plain that no explanation could be given as to how it worked, but a simple statement was made that it was recognized as being effective in many cases.

The application of wart removing material was often not successful and I often saw patients who told me that my treatment had failed, but they had then had their warts "charmed" off. I became very interested in this phenomenon and set out to learn what I could about it. I found that usually it was one of the older residents, always referred to as "uncle" or "aunt," who had the reputation for being able to "charm off warts." I also found that usually they were able to "charm" away a toothache.

Several times as a trial, when I first saw a case of warts, particularly on the face where scars might result from any application of material which had destructive properties, I suggested that they be taken to a "wart charmer." I always asked that they return a month later so that I could see what had happened and was astonished at the number of cases who in fact on their return showed no sign of a wart anywhere.

I talked to some of the "wart charmers" who were always reluctant to discuss their vocation, and while I was told how to do it I was never told what strange power one had to have before one proceeded with the directions. Obviously, one had to have tremendous confidence and belief in one's own ability to do any "wart charming." I never tried this method because I never felt I had this strange power. The instructions given by the "charmers" varied. Sometimes one had to take a rock, put a chalk mark on the inside of an oven, heat the rock, and then throw it away in the middle of the night. Sometimes a potato had to be cut into half and the two halves planted in widely separated places. Sometimes there were no instructions and the people were simply told to go home and the warts would disappear. I found it awfully difficult to believe that any of these procedures would be so effective, but I could never explain why in fact the warts did disappear.

Then came the day when to our horror we discovered that both the girls and boys of the community had developed warts around their faces, particularly around the mouths, and that our children were infected. I haven't got the heart to apply anything to their faces for fear of leaving scars. This had been my policy to all my patients. However, it so happened that at that time there was a woman, a patient in the hospital undergoing treatment, who had a reputation in her settlement as an outstanding "charmer of warts." I gave the matter grave consideration and discussed it with Edna. Being convinced that no harm could come of it, I took the girls with me one afternoon and we approached the lady in question as she lay in her bed in the ward.

I must admit I felt somewhat foolish, and very embarrassed, as I explained in full hearing of all the other patients that I would like her to "charm" off the warts from the girls' faces. She was most sympathetic and understanding, talked with the girls for a few minutes about trivialities, said nothing about the warts, and then after a few minutes while I shifted uneasily from foot to foot told me that we could now go home and all would be well.

As we left the ward I felt even more foolish for I had witnessed no activity on her part which in anyway would result in the removal or disappearance of the warts. As we walked home the girls of course wanted to know what had been done, how it had been done, how soon the warts would disappear, and a million other questions, none of which I could answer with any degree of confidence in myself. All I could tell them was that this woman had a great reputation as a "wart charmer." I said, "Forget everything, put it totally out of your minds, and we will all wait and see what happens." I was even less able to explain to Edna the procedure and I believe that she was as skeptical as I was although I tried to bolster the two of us with my experience with other cases and other "wart charmers."

About two weeks later, having neither thought about nor kept an eye on this aspect of the girls since the great day, we suddenly noticed that both girls had no sign of a wart anywhere on either side of their faces. We were astonished and none of us could recollect when we had last seen them, whether it had been the previous day or previous week. The fact remained that they had disappeared. How do you explain something like that? I can't understand it myself. My estimation of the power of "wart charmers" is unchanged but the fact remains that whatever the mechanics are it certainly works.

Chapter 27

SHIPWRECKS, PIRATES, AND GHOSTS

Many are the legends and stories abounding in Newfoundland about shipwrecks and pirates. The northwest coast of Newfoundland has its share of stories and also has the evidence to go with it. The north circle route from Britain to the Gulf of St. Lawrence and the river leading to Quebec City and Montreal uses the Straits of Belle Isle and for several centuries a mass of shipping sailed in this area. It was inevitable that there would be wrecks on the coast and particularly up around the Straits where fog is common and storms and tides harass the most expert of navigators and sailors. Throughout the world, an abandoned wreck is fair game for anyone who is interested in salvage. In Newfoundland, the most hazardous part of the coast, the Southern Shore, led many people to believe that men set lights purposely to guide passing ships onto the rocks so they would have a chance to salvage some of the cargo. Even without such enticements, the weather, the rugged seas, and the rocks made for many a wreck.

I suppose the three best known wrecks on the West Coast in the past fifty years were the S.S. *Ethie*, which ran on Martin's Point near Sally's Cove, H.M.S. *Raleigh*, a British light cruiser which ran ashore at Point Amour, Labrador, opposite Flower's Cove, and the *Orion*, a Greek tramp steamer, which was wrecked on Flower's Cove ledges. There were of course many other wrecks on the Coast but these three are of particular interest. The story of the *Ethie* is known to every Newfoundlander, and has been memorialised in song, plays, and books. Unlike so many shipwreck tales, the *Ethie*'s wreck in December of 1919 has a happy ending. All hands were saved even though it was a dreadfully stormy night. Seemingly miraculously, a baby on board was landed safely in a mail bag and didn't even get wet.

Of course, after the ship had been abandoned, the fittings and whatever could be salvaged was lifted by the local residents, and for many, many years afterwards she lay rusting and deteriorating.

H.M.S. *Raleigh*, a British light cruiser, was wrecked in August of 1922, was declared a total loss, and was abandoned accordingly. Of the 700 crewmembers on board, ten were lost. After the Navy declared the *Raleigh* a wright-off, the local people from both sides of the Straits looked upon it as a bonanza and salvaged anything which they could locate and move. Many homes for many years boasted fittings, equipment, and other material taken from the *Raleigh*. Cabin doors, portholes, brass tables, chairs, cutlery, crockery, silverware, bed linens, table linens, kitchen utensils, and many other objects rescued from the wreck found their way into people's homes. It was quite common to find these items in daily use when visiting on the Coast.

The wreck of the *Orion* occured in 1949 during my time at Bonne Bay. I happened to be in the Flower's Cove area in the summer of 1950, and had forgotten the news item of the previous year which had informed everyone that the *Orion* had run on the Flower's Cove ledges and been lost. As we approached Flower's Cove, I was astonished to see a ship apparently anchored just outside the entrance to the harbour. As we got closer it was apparent that she was at a peculiar angle. It could now be seen that her stern appeared to be underwater and the bow upon the ledges. The bridge was above water and so one had the appearance of a ship which was sinking by the stern. It was seemingly in perfect condition with the forward half out of the water. When we arrived, it was late evening and I was determined to pay a visit to the ship at the first opportunity. The next morning was a beautiful sunny day and we lost no time in going out to visit the *Orion*.

As we approached the ship I was amazed to find a large number of motorboats tied on the shore side of the vessel and we moored alongside and went aboard. There must have been twenty men at least working hard in the forward hold of the ship. As I walked across the deck I was aware that there were an equal number of boats moored on the Straits side of the *Orion* as well. From her deck one could clearly see Labrador which was ten miles away and it now became clear that the boats on the Flower's Cove side of the vessel were from Newfoundland and the boats on the Straits side were from

Labrador. All the men were seeking coal which was available to those who wanted to work for it.

I wandered around the deck, went into the forecastle and then walked back and through into the main saloon under the bridge, fully expecting the remainder of the ship to still be there. However, as I stepped into the saloon I found myself looking down into clear green water for the ship had broken in half and the after part had slid away into the depths leaving the forward half firmly gripped on the ledges. The lapping of the water against the twisted and buckled plates and the insides of the hollow broken ship was indeed an eerie sound, one which I will never forget. I made my way up the companion way to the bridge and was able to survey the forward part of the ship and the activity occuring on the deck below. The bridge was completely stripped. There was not a single fitting left which could have been moved. The port holes had all been removed. The glass was gone from the bridge windows and even the woodwork wherever it had been had been removed. In fact, I was standing in a skeleton and I even looked at the remaining mast and found that everything had been stripped from it except two extremely large pulleys which I presume the locals were unable to move. In the same way the crew quarters in the forecastle had also been stripped, the doors, the port holes, the bunks, the chairs and tables, everything was gone, even the toilet fittings had been removed and the only thing remaining was many tons of coal in the forward hold.

The ship was in the water to about four feet from the main deck. As I looked down into the hold I saw a hold full of water into which the men were dipping sticks some thirty to forty feet long on the end of which was a circular iron hoop and attached to which was a brim sack. From the lower part of the hoop a line went to a man on the opposite side of the hold. The operation of this mechanism is quite simple. One man drove the stick with the hoop and bag straight down into the hold and his partner opposite him, when the hoop reached the bottom where the coal was, hauled the line which drew the hoop and bag across toward him and scooped up coal. As it came to the surface it was dumped on deck and each group working had its own pile of coal. When they had enough they would shovel it into their boats and leave for their homes where they would unload it. It was a simple and clever method of acquiring coal for the coming winter. The coal was there for the asking, and getting it only necessitated some hard work. Every home in Flower's Cove had a pile of coal in its garden, and I am quite sure that coming winter was one of the warmest they had ever had to face.

I was interested to find out what else had been taken off the vessel and was perhaps available for sale in the settlement. I let it be known that I was interested in acquiring a full set of international signal flags which the vessel had undoubtedly carried but of which there was not a sign. Word filtered back to me that some of the flags might be available but that basically they were distributed throughout the village on the basis of more or less one to a home. It would be virtually impossible to acquire the entire set. However I was offered several compasses, although I doubt that the ship carried more than one main compass on the bridge and perhaps one spare in case she ever got into difficulties. I was also told that if there was anything else I wanted I should specify what it was and they might be able to get it for me. I decided it was too long and complicated a business and I would leave them with their spoils distributed wherever they may be.

In the late 1940s, a small schooner, the *Hawk,* was lost off Trout River with a crew of three onboard. It was a stormy night in the fall and she was making her way from Bay of Islands to Rocky Harbour when the light was seen as she passed Trout River, but she was never seen again. A search was instituted to look for her but the weather was too stormy and it was a couple of weeks before the *Hawk* was found floating off Bonne Bay. She was upside down and had obviously capsized. She was towed into Neddy's Harbour where a search was made of the vessel in case the crew was trapped below decks. However, nobody was found and she was left on the beach on her side to end her days. She had of course been stripped of everything worth moving and was just a wooden hulk.

I remember another vessel which struck on the rock at Western Head, which is the entrance to Bonne Bay. It was obvious she was sinking and the word flashed quickly around using the ancient telephone system. Since I had a fast boat, I was asked if I would be interested in going out to salvage anything but I was not particularly keen on doing this and turned down the offer. However, before the vessel sank, the boats were out from Rocky Harbour and it was my understanding that they had removed everything that could be moved in the perhaps hour or so before she sank. A valiant effort was made to remove the engine but it proved too heavy and she went to the bottom with the engine. In spite of the sinking, some intrepid salvagers set out later to locate the wreck and attach lines to the motor and haul it up. I never heard whether in fact they were successful.

Many years earlier during World War II, a barge had run ashore off Baker's Brook and it was carrying a great deal of valuable equipment and supplies. Of course, in no time it was cleaned out and the wreck Commissioner who came to report on the matter had to advise the police of what had happened. For days the police made an effort to go around instructing people to put back the things that had been taken. However, it was peculiar how people suddenly knew nothing about the wreck let alone things that it may have been contained. I doubt very much if anything was ever recovered.

Given the long history of sea faring in the region, it is not surprising that all types of sea tales abounded on the West Coast. Legends about pirates always fascinate people. On the Great Northern Peninsula, there are a number of stories concerning St. John's Island which lies off Port aux Choix in St. John's Bay. As previously noted, many ships plied the northern circle route and so used the Straits of Belle Isle. It is not difficult to imagine that from the early days in the eighteenth century to about the late nineteenth century ships under sail passed through and became an easy target for pirate ships stationed in this area. St. John's Bay, with its many islands, must have made a good haven for the pirates to hide in and St. John's Island has one of the most magnificent landlocked harbours I've ever been in. At one time on a visit to the Island a storm sprang up and we were marooned there for two days, but perfectly comfortable and safe in this completely land-locked harbour. It also gave us a chance to explore the Island and to confirm some of the things we had been told about it.

One of the greatest proponents of pirate treasures being buried on St. John's Island was Captain John Shears who sailed the coast in his own vessel for many years. His story was quite simple and it revolved around one essential fact, that somewhere on the island was a rock with a cross marked in it. He always assured me that he knew the formula as to where to go from this point of origination. According to Captain Shears, having located the rock with the cross in it, one then made a certain number of paces in a certain direction and then in another direction and so on until one arrived at a point where all you had to do was dig and there was the treasure in great boxes. He told a delightful story full of tension and excitement and which may well be true. It concerned a man who was sure he had the formula to find the treasure but needed assistance in finding the mark in the rock. This was supplied by another man so that together they formed a team. However, when the man who knew the location of the mark in the rock pointed out where it was he was felled by a stroke which took away his power of speech and paralysed him. The other man was so terrified that he took his friend from the Island and never returned nor ever spoke about going back again. The man who suffered the stroke never recovered and died with his secret, nor did his friend ever divulge what if anything he had seen.

John Shears was convinced that he could find the treasure if someone could find the mark on the rock. For two days while we were on the Island we enjoyed keeping our eyes opened and looking for the cross on the rock but never did see it. However, we did discover that the Island is largely a lava-type, hollow-sounding island, and at one point we located a blow hole into which, when one dropped a log, nothing could be seen but it was several seconds before the splash could be heard as the log hit water. Several hours later the log would appear floating in the harbour. We found this quite fascinating and also the possibilities that someone could have buried treasures in this hollow type island seemed quite real.

It is a beautiful island. It is uninhabited now, but it contains the remains of several business firms and fish stores and also a cemetery with graves belonging to Frenchmen. The graveyard we found greatly interesting and pursued this later to find out more information about why so many French were buried there. We had known that the French had fished on this shore for many years and it was inevitable that there would be accidents or illnesses causing deaths. It was common practice to bury the dead in the island cemetery and when the ship returned to France in the fall the losses would be reported by the captains. The following spring, when the ships came out, they would bring with them the gravestones suitably inscribed, which would then be placed in position. If only the men who were buried in that cemetery could tell their stories what wonderful stories they would be and how they would add to our history.

Pirates were also mentioned in relation to Brig Bay, Flower's Cove, Port Saunders, and Hawke's Bay, which no doubt were the type of places where they could hide away or sit out to prey on passing ships. Portland Creek, however, is a specific place which has been associated with pirates in many a story. It is told that a treasure was buried there in the marsh by a pirate captain. The marsh was in fact a camp used by the pirates. I have been told of the finding of a grave containing a skeleton of a man approximately seven foot tall and lying beside him a great cutlass, which is supposed to be in the possession of one of the local residents now. I don't believe anybody really knows where the treasure is buried. Perhaps it has been found and naturally no one would admit to having a source of wealth which he would well want to keep for himself.

Another story concerns a woman at Daniel's Harbour who went out looking for her cow which had wandered into the woods. In the course of looking for it, she stumbled and fell across a wooden trap door which, when she opened it, revealed a chest of treasures lying underneath. As it was getting dark and since her errand was to find her cow, she pursued this and when she went back later, perhaps the next day or some days later, she was never able to locate the treasure again. Stories like these are not too common, but nearly every settlement has a few and I found it fascinating to listen to and wonder whether or not in fact they had some truth. Somewhere in the distant ages possibly an actual event got them started in the first place.

Many Newfoundlanders are highly superstitious and, in common with most people, have a great fear of the unknown. There are stories in nearly every part of Newfoundland about ghosts, or strange noises, or strange lights or other unexplained happenings which might be labelled supernatural. Not too many people talk to me about ghosts or unexplained happenings but certainly I heard many stories of lights coming into bays or passing along the coast when in fact there was nothing there, of lights crossing the marshes as ghosts sought in vain for their families or friends. I was never able to pin any of these down. However, one event that happened many years ago always stuck in my mind and I can never be sure that it was just coincidence.

One man in Bonne Bay was getting on in years and had a reputation for being able to foresee the future. Most people are either skeptical of this or fear pursuing the matter in case they learn something which will not be in the best interest of their peace of mind. Several examples were given me over the years of this man's incredible ability to tell people where things were that had been lost or to predict certain things that would happen and in fact did.

Eventually one day he suffered a stroke, was paralysed, and in a few days died. I was called to the house to see him when it was discovered that he'd had his stroke and I arranged to admit him to hospital where we would do what we could for him. I was amazed at how clean and neat he was. His nails were cut, he was well-washed, his hair was cut, and in all ways he was a model of cleanliness.

Following his death his family told me that the night prior to his stroke he had been up all night and they had heard him busy in his room. It sounded as if he was taking a bath and cutting his nails and generally preparing himself. There was no doubt in their minds now that he had a premonition of his death and was anxious that he would go to his maker in the best possible manner. Never had they known him before to take such care with himself and to do all these things at once. Ever since that day I found it difficult to get him out of my mind. He had a reputation for foreseeing the future and it appeared that he had also been able to foresee his own death and prepare accordingly.

Over the years, I had many opportunities as I walked alone at night through the woods on calls or as I travelled in *Tinker Bell*, or by snow mobile, or by horse and sleigh to have seen ghosts or manifestations, but I never did. The only thing I can remember seeing very clearly at night were the Northern Lights playing through the skies and providing a variety of glorious changing sights such as man would find hard to equal. It was never my good fortune to see mysterious lights or ghost ships or to find pirate's booty, although I often wondered whether I might.

Chapter 28

NEVER A DULL MOMENT

In the practice of medicine one never knows what will happen next or how a case will present. One has to be prepared at all times for anything. On my first visit to Port Saunders in 1945, the first evening that I was there, and while I was sitting and talking to the nurse in the nursing station, the bell rang and a message was received requesting that the doctor go at once to a house where a man had been stricken with a heart attack. I grabbed my bag and led by the messenger hurried to the house. When I arrived at the house I found the place blocked with people all come to share in the excitement of the sudden illness. With some difficulty, I forced my way in. When I was recognized I was taken quickly to the patient who was now in bed. I found a man who appeared to be having a great deal of pain and, in the course of examining him and getting the story, I discovered that the attack had happened approximately an hour previously. I asked, since everybody knew I was in the settlement, why I hadn't been called earlier. I was told that before they could call the doctor they had to call the priest to find out whether it was the proper thing to call the doctor. I couldn't understand this but I had no time to pursue the matter further and I left it as an unanaswered question in the back of my mind while I got on with my work.

It turned out that in fact the man had suffered a severe and acute attack of indigestion and, fortunately, was not having a heart attack. The matter was brought under control fairly quickly and the patient was given relief with medicine and reassurance following my examination. Later I dropped by the Priest's house to talk to him. In the course of talking, I brought up the question of the patient whom I had been called to see and presumably who had been seen by him earlier.

Father Nixon, the Parish priest, had been there about a year and had followed in the footsteps of a priest who had spent a lifetime serving parishes in the outports and who incidentally was a registered nurse in his own right. He had been a wonderful help in those places where the Parish priest had served where there was no doctor. However, when this priest had been posted to the parish there had been a doctor in residence who had very definite ideas that religion and medicine did not mix. There was an immediate conflict between doctor and priest. The priest was critical of the doctor's ability and his treatments and suggested quite firmly and definitely to the parishioners that they would be very wise after seeing the doctor to check with the priest as to the medications that had been prescribed and as to whether it would be safe and proper to take this treatment. It had reached the point that before sending for the doctor, the people checked every case with the Parish priest.

When this priest and the doctor had both left the district, Father Nixon took over. There was no resident doctor. Father Nixon did what he could to assist the nurse but never interfered in any way. The coincidence of my arrival and the occurrence of this case had brought out the old training in the people. They had sent for the priest first to look at the patient and tell them whether they could and should send for the doctor.

Father Nixon was somewhat bewildered by what had happened. He made it quite plain that he did not intend to follow the procedure laid down by his predecessor. Father Nixon and I got on well together. I had the greatest admiration for this priest, who was in those days so isolated and far removed, and faced many difficulties. Times were not easy on the Coast, the parishioners had little money, and very often they could only support their Parish priest by bringing in food when there was none in his larder. He never complained but went about his work through great hardships, poverty, isolation, and loneliness. Truly only a man with a great vocation could have managed to survive under the circumstances.

One year when I was on the coast I stopped in at Daniel's Harbour. When I arrived there was a great strike of cod fish and all the men were busy. All the boats were loaded to the gunwales. As I sat in Nurse Bennett's kitchen at the end of the day after we had finished the work, she asked me what I would like for supper. Knowing there was such a great quantity of cod around I wondered if there were any cod tongues available. She promptly dispatched a young boy with a basin to the beach with instructions to have the men cut out some cod tongues and send them up. Shortly thereafter the boy returned with the basin flowing over with fresh and large cod tongues and my mouth began to water as soon as I saw them. She started to fry the cod tongues and I started to eat them. The kitchen, as usual, was filled up with curious visitors who came to see what was going on and just sat quietly on the benches which she had supplied. This room also served as the waiting room for the clinic. I suppose I ate solidly for about half an hour enjoying the conversation and the good natured banter that was going on backwards and forwards, and I can't ever remember enjoying a meal of cod tongues more. Finally, I could eat no more and, after the hard day's work, I was satisfied and now well fed. I sat back in my chair and enjoyed the scene around me.

Suddenly the door opened and a man entered carrying a boy of about ten who obviously had an injured arm. Although I was sitting there in full view, he ignored me and addressed his remarks to Mrs. Bennett. He told her that the boy had had an accident and he wondered if she could do anything to help him. Mrs. Bennett ignored me and went about her work of taking the child into the examining room and examining the child and then she came to me and told me that she believed the boy had a fractured elbow and asked if I would see him.

I moved into the examining room and found, just as she had suspected, that he had sustained a severe fracture just above the elbow. Already it was beginning to swell, it was out of position, and it was causing a great deal of pain. The obvious procedure was to reduce the fracture, which means putting the arm in its correct position, and this would have to be done using anaeshetic. I asked her if she had any ether, for I had none with me, and she replied that she had none but had a small amount of Chloroform.

We moved the boy into the dining room and I enlisted Martin Bugden's aid and prepared to set about fixing the boy's arm. I started the anaesthetic, which was an open Chloroform and when I had the boy asleep gave the bottle to Mrs. Bennett to continue giving it under my directions. With Martin holding the boy's upper arm, I reduced the fracture and we then set it in wooden splints, since we had no plaster cast. I then bandaged it in such a way that it would retain its position.

The procedure did not take too long. When it was over and the boy had recovered consciousness, I suggested to his father that he should take the boy to the hospital in the morning, where the arm would be x-rayed. If it was in good position it could then be placed in a plaster cast for the healing process to take place. In the morning, I left at first light for I was on my way back to Norris Point from my tour of the coast and we were followed shortly thereafter by the boy accompanied by his father in their motor boat. When they arrived at the hospital I immediately x-rayed the boy's arm and found to my delight that it was now in perfect position and that all I had to do was to place it in the plaster cast and send him home to return later for further checks when the arm had healed and for eventual removal of the plaster. Many years later I met this boy, and although I didn't recognize him, he hastened to remind me that he was the boy on whom I had worked in Mrs. Bennett's dining room so many years earlier. He had a perfectly normal elbow with complete function.

On another occasion I received a message from Trout River advising me that a man had broken his hip and requesting that I go immediately to fix it. It was quite obvious that I would be able to do nothing by going to the settlement beyond rendering first aid. I decided to arrange his transfer to hospital where he would require x-ray and treatment. I advised them by telegraph that it would be much wiser to bring him to hospital for x-ray and treatment, as there was really nothing I could do under those circumstances by going to visit the patient. In fact, a visit would be delaying the treatment which would eventually have to be done in the hospital anyway.

They refused to accept this response on my part, which was necessitated not only by my common sense, but also by the fact that I was responsible for a large number of patients who were coming to the hospital all the time. I couldn't leave the hospital unnecessarily. To back up their determination to have me visit they wired the Minister of Health who in turn wired me for full details. I was glad to reply and give him the story as I knew it, which resulted in his sending a telegram supporting my stand and suggesting that they proceed as I had recommended. They were quite adamant that the patient would not be moved until I had seen him. I realized it was futile to continue in this way and that they would not move, so I arranged that the next available day when I could safely leave the hospital I would go to Trout River and see the patient.

Within a few days I arranged to make the trip. I arrived at the house and saw the patient who had, as they suspected, fractured the neck of his femur. The patient was in his seventies and refused to be moved to the hospital on my recommendation after I examined him. I realized now that it wasn't so much the relatives who had been adamant but the patient himself. I did everything I could to explain to the man the impossibility of doing any more than setting his leg in the bed with the use of pillows, bandages, and splints but that it would be impossible to nurse him properly and retain the position of the broken bone without proper equipment and care in the hospital. There was no way he would change his mind. I could only do what I could to make him comfortable, set the leg in position, and explain to the relatives how to deal with the situation. Since they had no nurse resident at that time, I suggested that if and when their efforts failed we would have a bed waiting at any time. I was disheartened when I left the house that I had failed to get the patient to see the wisdom of coming to the hospital for proper treatment, but he was determined and so he stayed home.

The difficulties of nursing him and the inability to move him much eventually resulted in him developing complications. He succumbed later that year. There always have been and I suppose will be patients who know better than the doctor. Some people refuse the proper treatment, which is always offered in their own interest, and one has to accept the fact and continue the fight to bring education and assistance wherever one can.

One night in wintertime I received an urgent call to go to a settlement some distance away from Norris Point to see a man who had had a stroke. It appeared from the message that he had been stricken suddenly, was unable to speak, and was unable to move. I made my way as fast as I could to the house. This trip took about two hours and I entered to find him lying on a day bed in the kitchen, with the room full of curious onlookers and relatives as was usual.

He was an elderly, heavily built man, and he was breathing noisily. His breathing fitted my first impression as I entered the room of a man who probably had a stroke and who in his present condition had noisy breathing known as "Stertorous Breathing." I took off my coat and settled down on a chair beside him to examine him and automatically my hand sought his pulse. As I began taking it, his eyes opened and he looked at me. His pulse appeared quite normal-regular, rhythmic, and strong. There was a peculiar odor to his breath which I didn't recognize immediately. I took out my stethoscope and checked his heart and lungs and all appeared normal. With my flashlight I checked his pupils which appeared to react normally. I ventured my first question, "How are you feeling?" I asked. "I'm feeling a bit better now," he replied. "Can you move your hands?" I asked. He replied by gripping my hands. This was a good sign. "Now, move your legs," I told him. He moved his legs by bending them up and down. This is excellent, I thought, for apparently he is not paralyzed, he appears to be thinking alright, and he can talk. "Tell me what happened," I told him. "Well," he said, "I wasn't feeling too good today and I've been a bit bound up for some days so I decided to take some medicine. I took down the bottle of castor oil from the shelf in the corner and I took two good swigs." I looked in the direction in which he pointed and saw a shelf in the corner with a number of bottles on it, one of them clearly marked castor oil. "Then what happened?" I asked him. "That's when it struck me," he said. He pointed to a bottle on the table beside him and I picked it up. It was marked "Camphorated Oil." Now I recognized the smell on his breath and I realized what had happened and he confirmed it. Wanting to take some castor oil he reached up to get the bottle which was turned slightly away from him and he saw only the word "Oil." He took it for granted that this was the castor oil and without looking at the label fully took off the cap, put the bottle to his mouth, and took two good, big swigs. No wonder he was unable to talk or move. The camphorated oil had just about made him paralytic!

He appeared to have recovered fully by now and I looked at him and said, "You must be very careful when you take any medicine to read the label and make sure of what you are taking." "You're right my son," he replied, "that's the second time I've done that self-same thing."

On occasion some situation would develop where the doctor and the Ranger would find themselves on the same case. Usually it would be a case where the law was involved and in some way there was a medical aspect. The most obvious type of case would be an accident which was under investigation or an unexplained death which had to be investigated.

One such case occurred one year just before Christmas when I was notified that a man's body had been found at the foot of a cliff at Cow Head, and I was asked if I would proceed to the settlement to investigate the cause of death. At the same time, the Ranger was instructed to make an investigation, and we hired a boat and went together. It was a flat, calm day, fortunately, and although our progress was slightly slower in the cold sluggish water we arrived at Cow Head around about mid-day.

We went immediately to the house where the body was and while I set about examining the body, the Ranger interrogated the people who had found the body and relatives and friends of the dead man. The Ranger joined me in a short while and advised me that it appeared that the man had been out to a party and on his way home had missed his way and fallen over the cliff. I assured him that from my examination of the body it was quite evident that the man had sustained a fractured skull with severe damage and hemorrhage into the brain and that this was the cause of his death. We were both sat-isfied that it had been an accident and the cause of death was quite clear. There only remained the question of the Ranger instructing the family to go ahead and make arrangements for the burial.

In half an hour the Ranger was back and was obviously extreme-ly angry. He told me that he had talked to the man's son who told him that since his father had died accidentally, and because the gov-ernment had been brought in to investigate the cause of death, then it would be up to the government to bury the body. The Ranger pointed out to the man that we were there to ascertain the cause of death to make sure that it was quite accidental. With no evidence of foul play, it would then be like any other death in the family and the family would assume the responsibility of the burial. The man positively refused and as if to make his point even more certain he advised the Ranger that he himself was on welfare and there was no way he could take care of the burial.

The Ranger was livid at the fact that a son could be so callous about his own father. It was normal procedure in every settlement that the families looked after their own and in the event of someone being without friends or family then usually the Welfare Department would arrange the necessary details. However, since this was not the case and the son was standing in the street outside the house where his father's body lay, it was quite reasonable that he would be expected to look after his father's burial. He continued to refuse. Even though the men in the settlement were willing to help him, it was still his responsibility to see to the matter. After two hours of arguing the Ranger had got nowhere and felt he couldn't just walk away without making sure that the necessary arrangements were made. He made a firm decision and twenty minutes later came to me and said we were now ready to go home.

We boarded the boat and set off for home. I ventured to ask him if the matter was settled. The Ranger's face was grim but determined as he told me that he had instructed the men of the settlement to take care of the burial and that he himself would see that the bill was paid by the man's son. It was the only case I can remember where such a situation ever arose and I doubt that it would ever occur again.

Another case where the Ranger was involved was several years later when an American plane crash-landed at Rocky Harbour. The first notification I had came about 6 a.m. on a March morning in 1947 when my phone rang and the nurse excitedly told me that a plane had crashed. My training during the war produced an automatic response as I shouted, "Call out the Crash Ambulance–I'll be right there." The amazed voice at the other end reminded me that we didn't have an ambulance. I woke to the reality of the fact that it was two years after the war and that this was the Northwest Coast of Newfoundland. I asked the nurse for details and she said that all they knew was that an American bomber had crashed-landed at Rocky Harbour on the ice in the harbour and that apparently none of the crew were injured. I suggested that what we should do was phone somebody close by and ask that they go and make sure. If there were any injuries I would immediately go to the scene. Shortly afterwards she phoned again with a confirmation of the fact that there were no casualties and in fact no injuries of any kind and that there would be no point in my going to Rocky Harbour. The crew were taken care of and were all in houses awaiting the arrival of personnel from Harmon Air Force Base in Stephenville.

The story when it came out was intriguing. The Americans were flying from Goose Bay to Harmon and had onboard a full load of cases of whiskey and other useful commodities. When they commenced to get into trouble and began to lose elevation, they realized they were getting short on fuel because of head winds. They were instructed to jettison the cargo and it was with heavy hearts that they began throwing out case after case of perfectly good whiskey. Finally when they reached Bonne Bay they had no choice but to put down and, not knowing the area at all, they headed into the wind and landed into Rocky Harbour on the ice. The pilot was not sure of the strength of the ice, so he didn't dare risk wheels-down landing; they landed wheels up with a belly-landing. Had they turned into the main arm of Bonne Bay they could have landed with their wheels down, taxied up to the wharf at Lomond, reloaded the plane with fuel, and taken off at any time that suited them.

However they got down without injury. In a matter of hours a force of M-29 Weasels, amphibious vehicles carrying Air Force personnel from Harmon USAF Base in Stephenville, 100 kilometres to the south, arrived. They went immediately to Rocky Harbour, having come over the hills and bogs from Deer Lake, to take the men and salvage whatever they could from the plane. It was twenty-four hours before they got organized but it was only a matter of minutes after the plane crashed that the men were organized in Rocky Harbour. The crew of the plane and the local Mountie, who was now on the scene, set about putting guards in position to protect the plane. Two guards were stationed on the plane, one in the nose of the aircraft and one in the tail.

The Americans removed the secret air equipment from the plane and whatever else they were able to salvage, which took them several days. As they were leaving, the two salvage officers called to pay their respects and tell me what had happened. They explained that they were salvage officers of many years, including war time, but they had never seen in their lives such a salvage job as had been carried out by the residents of the area. They explained that while they had guards at both ends of the plane, the local residents would be busy enticing one man to one end or the other. While they kept the guards engaged in conversation, others of them would be sawing off wings, removing cables, cutting wires, or taking anything that could be moved. In spite of the guards, the plane had been stripped completely. The salvage officers were quite satisfied they had got the electronic parts they wanted but they had been somewhat concerned as to what the local men would do with the rest of the plane. The officers were now happy, for it was quite obvious there would be nothing left.

I made a trip to Rocky Harbour to view the bomber. It was a big flying fortress-type aircraft lying on its belly on the ice. Before the ice went out in May there was nothing left, but every home had a part or parts of the aircraft. Later these parts made their appearance in use both in the homes or in the boats. Many boats were fitted with cables and pulleys which were the finest aluminum and with electrical cables the like of which boats had never seen before. For many years, bits of this aircraft could be seen protruding from under houses or sticking up in the back of people's gardens or in their boats as they went about their daily work.

When I first went to Bonne Bay I made it my business to find out what epidemics had occurred over the years and I discovered that in the previous fifty years there had been two big epidemics. The first one occurred around 1910 and was an outbreak of smallpox which took a heavy toll on the Coast. The second epidemic occurred at the end of the First World War when the Spanish flu was rampant across the world. The Northwest Coast and Bonne Bay was struck and suffered considerably. Since that time there had been no serious epidemic. I was most concerned about the immunization program and realized that it depended for its effectiveness on our own aggressive approach to the problem which was largely one of education. The medical forces were thin on the Coast, the people did not understand about immunization and were somewhat superstitious anyway, and obviously it was going to take a lot of education and require a great deal of confidence in us if we were to be successful in this field.

During my years of training and previous years of practice I had seen only one case of diphtheria, but I was aware that it was prevalent in Newfoundland and that sooner or later I was going to see cases. The first case I saw occurred in 1946 in Rocky Harbour and was a young boy who went down with this dread disease. There was no planned immunization program in the schools up to that time for it was all I could do to cope with the work in the hospital and the daily response to sick calls in the district. We still operated in Newfoundland upon the system of quarantine. No one could go in to communities where disease had struck nor could the people leave. I had to arrange the provision of guards to carry out the quarantine order, and to arrange for the people to get supplies of food and other items. The Department of Health authorised the guard and for the moment the situation was under control.

My big worry was the spread of the disease through the settlement and then to the district generally. Without wasting any time I set up a clinic in Rocky Harbour and instructed everyone in the settlement to report for their needles which would give them protection. The response was magnificent. The whole settlement turned out, men, women, and children, and in one afternoon we innoculated the whole settlement. There were no further cases in the settlement and I was determined that if I could prevent it, there would never be another case. I was spurred on by this first success. I set up our immunization program so that every year all the schools received their shots and all the pre-school aged children were invited along as well. Using our school district, the Nurses would spread the program right through Bonne Bay and along the Coast.

The next case of diptheria occurred in Trout River shortly afterwards, where an adult was suffering from the condition. Again I immediately went, quarantined the house and family, set up a guard, and carried out an immunization program. This settlement also received its regular program and from that day on I never saw another case of diptheria. I hope that I never will. The immunization program is carried on now, not so much perhaps at the urging of the health authorities as at the demand of the people who recognize it as an almost sure means of protection.

Over the years we also had our epidemics of poliomyelitis, commonly known as polio. Everybody was aware of this condition and in dread of its appearance. The advent of a vaccine was welcomed by one and all, and people were not slow to avail of the vaccine when it was brought to Newfoundland.

However, smallpox had not struck for many years in Newfoundland, probably because of the effective smallpox vaccination carried out in other parts of the world. In Newfoundland there was no obligation or demand for smallpox vaccination and I dreaded the day when one case might occur in Newfoundland, for it could spread like a forest fire through the population. I felt it might be wise to vaccinate the new born children and was surprised at the reluctance of people to allow their children to be vaccinated. I didn't push this program but let it be known that it was there for those who wanted it. Few availed themselves of the offer.

After a few years I was going to fly to England for a holiday and knew that I had to be vaccinated against smallpox to return to Canada. I decided that I would not have my vaccination before I left, but would get it in England. While I was over there, I visited one of my British colleagues and he kindly vaccinated me. A week later my arm was swollen and inflamed to the point that I couldn't use it and had to put it in a sling. It was not only a violent reaction to the vaccination but possibly had slightly infected as well.

When I returned my arm was still in a sling and I was immediately asked what had happened. I knew perfectly well that if I admitted that this was the result of my vaccination, I would never get another patient in the area to agree to a smallpox vaccination and so I simply said that it was the result of an accident and let it go at that. It was never questioned further and it didn't interfere in any way with our growing program of smallpox vaccinations which was beginning to be accepted. Fortunately, I have yet to see my first case of smallpox in Newfoundland, and will be quite happy if I never, never see one.

EPILOGUE

It is now almost fifty years since I left the Bonne Bay Cottage Hospital. The main reason we left was because we felt our daughters were getting to an age when they would benefit from a larger school for their last couple of years of secondary school–and so we moved to Corner Brook

Edna, who had been a superb support at Norris Point, would get back to the many things which she had missed at Bonne Bay, including movies, theatre, Beta Sigma Phi, and the public library. These activities had been such an important part of her life before I brought her back to Newfoundland in 1945. She had settled in quickly at Norris Point and transformed the place by her presence. She put the doctor's house together and made it a home. She helped out at the hospital, taking and developing x-rays, until later an x-ray/lab technician was added to the staff of the Cottage Hospitals. While at Norris Point, she started the Girl Guide Company, a school sports day, and a public library, and helped in many other community efforts. Edna had trained Molly, the St. Bernard dog, who pulled her sled to get the children to school and to get Edna to the stores for supplies. In the summer she loved to take the children, our two and their friends, on picnics and fishing up the Eastern Arm of Bonne Bay.

She put up with me being on call for twenty-four hours every day, and reluctantly left me to return to England to visit her mother and father every couple of years. We only got our first real holiday in 1950 when I went to Halifax, where I knew my old "chief," Mr. Rodney Maingot, was to be the guest speaker at the Dalhousie Medical School. It was a great reunion, and he already knew Edna from our time at Southend General Hospital. He enveigled me to go on to Boston with my family, where he introduced me to the Mayo Clinic. I was greatly honoured. Then we went to New York to visit Dr. Paul Sheldon, the yachtsman, and his wife.

At the beginning of my stay in Bonne Bay in 1945, there was no road on the Coast, I was the only doctor between Deer Lake and St. Anthony, and the Cottage Hospital was the only hospital between Corner Brook and St. Anthony. Today there is a paved road between Deer Lake and St. Anthony. There are four doctors at Norris Point, one at Woody Point, one at Cow Head, and three at Port Saunders. There are new hospitals at Norris Point and at Port Saunders. However, I was given to understand that there is little surgery performed or deliveries accomplished any more–these cases are referred to Corner Brook, the patients often being transported by ambulance–something which did not exist in my time. Perhaps the biggest changes in the past fifty years are the increase in the number of doctors available, the new drugs, and, most importantly, the development of telemedicine. For doctors working in the rural areas it means the ability to talk with specialists, discuss certain cases, and share x-rays, electrocardiograms, and other technical matters. Much of the credit for this giant step forward must go to Dr. Maxwell House, the Lieutenant Governor of Newfoundland and Labrador until his departure from the office in 2002. Diagnosis and treatment can be speeded in many cases. Yes, it is a whole new world of medicine.

In 1999, I was invited to the last annual Garden Party at the Bonne Bay Cottage Hospital, and I was delighted to attend. There was a good crowd in attendance and many former patients and friends came over to say hello to me. Some of the people who had served on the staff of the Cottage Hospital were there to greet me. It was a great reunion and a very pleasant experience. I was told that the original "doctor's house" has changed. It is now a one-story home, making it smaller, but I did not have a chance to visit it.

I did see many changes in both Norris Point and Rocky Harbour. It seems that many young people have left the area to seek work, often on the Mainland. Many of my older friends have passed away and I miss them. I miss my boat, *Tinker Bell*, which I had for twenty years. I sold that great little sea boat, and later she caught fire and sank. I had my Jeep, a durable four-wheel drive vehicle, for twenty years and then sold her. The Bombardier snowmobile, which belonged to the Health Department, was great for winter travel, but has been superseded by the skidoo. Today our winter roads are kept clear by snow ploughs. Time marches on!

So many memories. My days at Norris Point were a wonderful opportunity to use my medical skills and learning to help people. I loved every moment of it and am most grateful to all the people on the Coast for their help and hospitality. I will never forget you.

Edna was a pillar of strength and very dedicated to our welfare. Nobody could have had a more loving and supportive wife and I certainly could not have accomplished what I did without her. As you have seen, I had many exciting adventures and experiences along the Coast, in all seasons and all types of weather, during my years at Norris Point. We had many visitors–family members, friends, politicians, doctors, clergymen, tourists, and others. Most importantly, we were able to get to know the people of Norris Point, Rocky Harbour, Cow Head, Sally's Cove, Daniel's Harbour, Portland Creek, St. Paul's, Port Saunders, and all the small places along the West Coast. Maybe these memoirs have given readers an idea of what it was like in those days and what life on the West Coast of Newfoundland was all about in those years after World War II.